I0576939

THE ROAD HOME

THE ROAD HOME

New Stories from Alberta Writers

Edited by Fred Stenson

Photography by Keith Zukiwski

REIDMORE BOOKS

CREDITS

Financial support provided from the Lottery Fund by the Government of Alberta through the Alberta Multiculturalism Commission.

Typesetting & Design: Pièce de Résistance Ltée, Edmonton, AB

Photography: Keith Zukiwski

Lithography: BK Trade Colour Ltd.

Printing: Quality Color Press Inc., Edmonton, AB

We have made every effort to correctly identify and credit the sources of all information used in this book. Reidmore Books appreciates any further information or corrections; acknowledgment will be given in subsequent editions.

Reidmore Books Inc
#1200 Energy Square
10109 - 106 Street
Edmonton, Alberta
T5J 3L7
(403) 424-4420

Canadian Cataloguing in Publication Data

The Road home

ISBN 1-895073-21-9

1. Canadian literature (English)—Alberta • 2. Canadian literature (English)—20th century • 3. Alberta—Literary collections. I. Stenson, Fred, 1951-
PS8255.A5R6 1992 C810'.8'097123 C92-091575-2 PR9198.2.A52R6 1991

---

printed and bound in Canada

Contents

SANDRA CHA • *EDMONTON, ALBERTA*

Introduction

LET ME TELL YOU A STORY, ONE THAT ASPIRES TO EXPLAIN THE purpose and the hope of this book.

It begins with a group of nation planners. They draw a line enclosing x square kilometres of North American landscape. The sides of the box are straight except for the southern half of the west border. Here the line is ragged and slanting where it rides the trend line of the Rocky Mountains. The year is 1905 and the nation planners call the box Alberta.

Perhaps I have gone out of my way to make the enclosing of this territory seem arbitrary, but there was a certain arbitrary quality about it. The amazing thing is how few decades it has taken for this place, this Alberta, to acquire a character, one different from the other boxes around it.

The age in which the words "Alberta" and "Albertan" have had meaning in the world has more than just begun. In fact, there has already been considerable turnover in the meaning of those words. At one time, Alberta meant boundless wilderness. Then it was an agricultural frontier and a land of opportunity. Later, it would become an oil-rich sedimentary basin and a land of prosperity.

The meaning of "Albertan" changed accordingly. When Alberta became a province in 1905, Albertans were homesteaders. Next, they were farmers or ranchers. Later, they would become oil men. To some, Albertan has also come to mean redneck. I am reminded of *National Lampoon*'s "Redneck Map of North America," showing large red masses of territory in the USA and a little line up into Alberta with a big red spot there as well. It was not particularly fair, this designation, but it illustrated that Alberta and Albertan are words with strong connotations, ones that travel far beyond the borders of this place.

by Fred Stenson

While it may be a good thing for the people of the province to have an identity, the process of acquiring identity brings with it any number of problems. For one thing, perceptions of identity are never all-inclusive. What they represent is an image of who is dominant in a society, numerically or in power terms. When this box called Alberta was newly drawn and named, when Alberta was a land of opportunity and Albertans were homesteaders, these perceptions did not in any way fit the First People, the Native people of Alberta, who were being displaced. The land of promise was lost land to them.

Similarly, the post-Leduc oil boom that recast the image of Alberta into a prosperous oil frontier excluded as many as it included. The descendants of the homesteaders saw their star begin to fade, especially those who did not find work in the rising oil economy.

Identities do exclude and those excluded by the prevailing identity always suffer in some way. They are pushed beyond a psychological boundary that separates the mainstream from the "other." There are countless ways of finding yourself on the wrong side of these tracks.

By their nature, impressions about a society lag behind reality. At worst, they encrust, solidify, become entrenched, and the gap between impression and reality widens to a ridiculous extent. This has happened in Alberta. The current statistic for immigration into Alberta is approximately 12 000 people per year. That is, every year, by immigration alone, a small city could be added to the Alberta landscape. The sources of immigration have changed. For much of its life, Alberta found its new people in Europe. Now, its immigrants come largely from Asian countries. Africa, the West Indies, Central America, and South America are also prominent sources of new population. Alberta also attracts many people from other parts of Canada. Thirteen per cent of the population of Fort McMurray is made up of people from Newfoundland.

Most of these facts are not difficult to observe. Stand at any busy city intersection for ten minutes and you can see that Alberta is, and is visibly, a cosmopolitan society. Now consider what most people still mean when they say "Albertan," when they aspire to finish the sentence, "An Albertan is _____."

An Albertan is white. An Albertan farms, ranches, or works in the oil industry. An Albertan works hard and does well financially. An Albertan is of European ancestry. He is the grandchild of homesteaders. An Albertan may live in a city but he is the first generation of his family to do so. An Albertan speaks English and in most cases only English. An Albertan wants Alberta to stay the same, or if he wants change, he wants a change back to some previous condition. By the way, the choice of the pronoun "he" for this description is not male chauvinism or accident; the Albertan of this stereotype is for some reason always male.

The above stereotype is not meant to ridicule the Albertans it accurately describes. The point is rather that Alberta society has changed and is changing so rapidly that this stereotype is fast excluding far more people than it includes. The compelling question that we must ask, that this book asks, and perhaps might answer, is *how such a stereotype can persist in the face of so much evidence that it is untrue.*

Stereotypes are fossils: mineralized replicas of what was once there. Even that metaphoric definition is suspect in that stereotypes are seldom true even at their creation. At any rate, stereotypes are *like* fossils in that they survive best in a vacuum, safe from the light of knowledge, sealed off from the air of communication. Exposed to light and air, they crumble.

This book has a grand ambition. Twenty-nine authors, Alberta voices drawn from the present-day community of writers, speak out through their art about Alberta. Light and air. It is the ambition of this book to gather and focus these elements of truth in order to create a composite image of Alberta society in the 1990s that is more accurate. The goal is *not* to create a new generalization, a new single-sentence answer to the question, "What is an Albertan?" It is rather to recognize that any such simple answer must be wrong. There may be 2 million equally valid answers to that question as each Albertan exercises his and her right to be unique.

All the races, cultures, and religions of the world can be found in Alberta; Alberta is the world in a nutshell. One might also say "the world in a test tube" because, whether it was intended to be or not, Alberta is a major social experiment with much riding on the outcome. It is one of the world's last opportunities to prove that people can live together in harmony despite racial, religious, political, and cultural differences.

All the strands of Alberta society are not to be found in this book. Even if by some magic of publishing, every race and religion were to have a member here, it still would not guarantee that everyone was truly represented. The writers appearing here were not chosen to be, or asked to be, official representatives of their gene pool or skin colour or religious persuasion. They were simply asked for their honesty and their art.

The range of response from the writers is extraordinary, I think, a strong indication of how varied experience is within Alberta. The strongest common thread is probably the concern the writers bring to their work, concern for this province and its people, now and in the uncertain future.

For many of these writers, the experience of immigration, still fresh in mind, is the theme of choice. The voices speak of comparing the old home to the new, of loyalties forever torn. They speak of watching in pain as mistakes familiar from the old country seem destined to be re-made here. They speak of a growing sense of responsibility and power, of feeling they must and can effect change.

For other writers, the immigration story is family legend or otherwise not part of their immediate lives. For Native writers, it is a legend older than story. It may surprise readers that so many of these voices speak of painful loss. For example, there is a sense that rural Albertans are learning what the Native has always known: what it feels like to be dispossessed and undervalued by society. The new waves of immigration that bring so much energy to the cities often represent a process by which the earlier arrivals feel threatened and less important, feel that their long-held values are becoming the wrong ones.

The old image of Alberta as a land of opportunity lies at the root of several of these writings. We hear of those who find success here and of those who do not. The image of Albertan prosperity can become a terrible scourge on those who believe it, but discover it is not for them: the special quality of pain that comes from being poor in a land of plenty.

Another image that emerges is of the Albertan as traveler. It is often difficult to focus a sense of personal identity when inside your own society. A common experience is to find that sense while away. The traveling Albertan, returned home, often becomes a liberalizing and broadening force in our society.

Perhaps the most prominent theme is the heat produced by the rubbing of cultural and racial atoms in Albertan society: the collision, confusion, and marriage of values. The results are comic or tragic, sometimes both, and often hopeful, as characters, fictional and non-fictional, emerge from their experiences wiser in some way.

There is much more that could be said about this book, but I would rather it be said by its writers and, later, by its readers. It is in that relationship, the one between writer and reader, that the story of this introduction will truly conclude. Meanwhile, I would like to thank the Alberta Multiculturalism Commission for the opportunity to be the managing editor of this book. I would also like to thank the Commission on all our behalfs for their confidence in Alberta's authors as bringers of light and air.

Fred Stenson
1992

LOUISE M. CUNNINGHAM • *GUNN, ALBERTA*

NANCY HOLMES

Nancy Holmes was born in Edmonton, Alberta. She grew up in London, Ontario and Toronto before moving to Calgary in 1979. During her years in Calgary, she published two books of poetry and won a number of writing competitions. Her collections of poetry are: Down to the Golden Chersonese: Victorian Lady Travellers *(Sono Nis, 1991) and* Valancy and the New World *(Kalamalka Press, 1988).* Valancy *won the Kalamalka New Writers Society National Poetry Competition. Ms Holmes' short fiction has appeared in* Saturday Night *and in the NeWest Press anthology* Alberta Bound *(1986). She is a past winner of both the Alberta Culture and the* Calgary Herald *short story competitions. Ms Holmes is currently living in British Columbia.*

An Ambivalent Guide, and a Welcome

(for Ute, a single mother who wants to come to Canada)

Many strangers, both male and female, have found shelter under our roof, and never were we led to regret that we had not turned the houseless wanderer from our door.

—Catharine Parr Traill
The Canadian Settler's Guide, 1855

by Nancy Holmes

Träume

And all was lonely, wild and savage around him.
—Catharine Parr Traill

dear emigrant
I have never seen you
but we have written twenty years
you have charted my decaying German
ich bin, ich gehe
fröliche Weihnachten
and I have watched your English
tangle into longing
"Canada is my dream"

you have a small son
you are alone
your blue letters
wash up on my prairie doorstep
Atlantic tissue
and mine return to you white as snow

I wish I were Catharine Traill
and could give you a cheerful guide:
here is how we make pumpkin pie;
our pancakes taste like honeycomb;
this is how we cultivate a peach
introduced so improperly
among the wild fruits of Canada

but the forests shrink
can you not see how there is less green
in every calendar I send you?

but when you open April
a glacier withdraws

my country is that glacier
rubbling in your heart
churning granite into transformation
to leave a mirror

Canada is my dream,
my trauma,
my blood is full of glacial silt
and no race,
not one,
was born here

you have a small son
you are alone
and dreaming of a bridge
that broke in two
now we and many millions
force a new one made of paper

precarious and most ancient craft

The Right Frame of Mind

Canada is not the land for the idle sensualist.
—Catharine Parr Traill

Oh god let us not be idle
look at Alberta, look at her—
her bare body rolls down sated
after the orgy of mountains
but does she stop then?
No.
her skin springs into wheat and grass
and luscious hair
wild to be combed and scratched
with the breasts and feet of sliding animals
and the giant rake of the machine
that does such things
an ecstasy of liquid willow
rubs in every fold and crevice
and in the huge bald tongue of the sky
the hawk's wing is but
a grain of salt licked off her heaving back
Oh yes.
look at the doe's wet eye,
the hairy crack of crocus,
the flagellant storm,
the veined leg of the elk,
the warm bark of the tree
that strips before the saw
and Catharine, Catharine,
tell me that
again.

The Sensitive Canadian

No wonder that the heart of the emigrant's wife is sometimes sad, and needs to be dealt gently with by her less sensitive partner.
—Catharine Parr Traill

My friend, Canadian women now
have liberal pasts.
Their passports attract men like scent.
All manner of men want to marry them.
They will pull their collections
out of knapsacks
and show you if you want.

The Hungarian architect
she met in Greece
who looked at the boys
on nude beaches.

The Thai officer on a Malaysian bus
who spoke flowery obscenities
in French
and later stole her Sony Walkman.

He still phones her collect
from Brazil
but now she refuses
to accept the charges.

The Ugandan sociology student
who took her out to dinner once
—she paid her own way—
then begged her to come to Kampala
to meet his mother.

All these and more.
So you see, they will understand
that your African lover
left you with a dark-skinned child.
You phone me, the only Canadian you know.
You go to the Canadian embassy.
You try to acquire a desirable trade.
You learn English.
You want a Canadian passport
more than a ring.

All the time
your child plays
quietly among
the white-haired Germans.

Here
the Chinese girl
who married the deaf computer programmer
stares out the window
at the veils and veils
of horizontal snow.

What Canada Offers

Though Australia may offer the temptation of greater wages to female servants. . . . rather bring them to Canada . . . than form connexions with such characters as swarm the streets of Melbourne and Geelong . . .

—Catharine Parr Traill

Ah respectable men.
Do you dream of them too?
The woodsman who opens a white slit in a tree?
The cowboy who straddles his mare in all that leather?
The coureur de bois who paddles and shoves
his way down a bruising sluice of thunder?
But do you see,
the hard ones, the male sweat,
the men who labour on the body
of the land,
are men afraid of real blood?
And how our longing to be the land
and have rough hands deepen
all our hunger
is worse than nothing, but a sham?
Be wild.
Emigrate with dreams, girl,
or why assault the wound?
I say look for the rogues, the rakes,
the unleashed ones, the heart seekers.
The quiet musician in a Melbourne suburb,
the accountant in Geelong.

Opportunity

Among the wild plants of Canada there are many graceful climbers.
—Catharine Parr Traill

My Lebanese neighbours
bend white sheets into a craft,
spill cargoes of wheat
freshly plucked and drowned
onto the cloth
that blows into the lawn
like sails.

The grass flattens itself in ecstasy,
straining excess juice
through cold white cotton.

My neighbours rake the clotted gold
at the edges of my lawn,
rake it into memory
and a deep bowl
my Ukrainian grandmother
mixed with wheat and milk, poppyseed and honey,
between the thin bone of the skull
and the tongue.

Gone now.
The prairie has receded from the city streets.
The harvest is divided from the body.

But if you get here
I will show you, cunning,
the immigrant's way.

Watch my hand launch
my baby forward
through the invisible border
that splits our lawns.

He staggers on bright legs,
trips into the ocean of grain,
falls into food,
food for a year.

Seeds break and die
against his belly,
his eager feet still sling the air.

Immigrant heart,
he knows,
the neighbours laugh and shriek
as he knuckles in the pulp and sweetness
and eats
a golden baptism.

Welcome

I, who had been so timid, grew brave and fearless amid the gloomy forests of Canada.
—Catharine Parr Traill

I will not urge you more than this.
I do not know my own country.

Sometimes it seems to me
the maple leaf holds up its hand
in warning
and the fleur de lys
is splitting into blue barbed tongues.

The snow falls down
in strange collusion with the sun
between the shafts of wheat
and silver buildings.
A mysterious second summer
creeps off the lake
and drowns us in its falseness.

Turn back, turn back,
the red hand flashes in the woods.
My letters burn like snow
in your bitter fingers.

What cautious dreams we make
in these wild, wild nights.
Here, we are no different.
Our hills are ripening weapons
we load with all our children.

And yet to them
the fallen forest floor
flies up in wild colour
as unloosed, exotic, flashing
as gold and satin in our hands.
Each cell in their fresh skins
drinks a lake of sparking ice.
Perhaps when you land here
with all your baggage
you will see
that it is spring,
our melted brittle heart,
that is our most uncertain season.

EVELYN DAVID • *EDMONTON, ALBERTA*

WADE BELL

Wade Bell was born in Edmonton and now lives in Calgary. The life between those two addresses has covered a great deal of territory. His university education was completed in Ontario. He lived in Spain for an extended period, in Barcelona and in a village on the Costa Brava. He has traveled widely in Canada, the USA, Mexico, and the Caribbean; in Ireland, England, and France. He has worked as a journalist, a civil servant, an editor, a taxi driver, an oil field roustabout, and a salesman; he has co-translated children's books from English into Spanish. He has published one book, The North Saskatchewan River Book *(Coach House Press), a mixture of stories, found literature, history, and poetic prose about Edmonton and its famous river. Mr Bell has recently completed a second collection of short fiction.*

From Immigration On

SHE STARED, UNABLE TO BELIEVE HER fiancé was shouting at the immigration officer. She saw the officer's face grow red, then redder, and her heart fell. She was certain that Tom, ranting, pacing the small windowless room, was on his way to the Calgary jail while she would certainly be put on the next flight back to Spain. They may as well have had their suitcases packed with heroin for all the chance she had now of being allowed out of the airport and into Canada, of marrying Tom.

She watched Tom's long, nervous body as he paced the room and gestured with his arms like a Spaniard. He was coming back to his country after a half dozen years living in hers. He was so much a Canadian, she thought, yet he'd picked up something of Spain in his mannerisms, and in his heart. Seeing this in him she felt a momentary rush of tenderness for the hybrid man who was fighting for his right to bring his fiancée home and marry her. Her moist, exhausted eyes implored the immigration officer if not to ignore Tom's outrageous behaviour, which of course she knew would be impossible, then at least, *por dios*, to charitably forgive it.

But the officer paid her no attention and instead explained something to Tom in a loud firm voice. Ana was too tired to translate and, anyway, she had no hope left. She retreated into the memory of how Tom and she first met and wept more openly at the thought that she might never see him again.

They had met in Barcelona on Tom's first day in Spain. He'd stumbled into a demonstration against the dictator who then ruled her country and who was dying, but not quickly enough. The demonstrators shouted slogans while keeping a collective eye on the riot police who were watching from a line of grey Land Rovers. A girl, young, sixteen or seventeen years old, yelled something at the police and two of them jumped out of their Land Rover, grabbed her and flung her hard, face first into the side of their vehicle. Tom, standing near Ana and some of her friends,

by Wade Bell

had charged from the crowd to attack the police. He did not get far before one of Ana's friends tripped him. Ana and two or three others subdued him and dragged him deeper into the crowd. They took him away through the narrow, winding alleys of the city's Gothic Quarter and bought him cognacs in a bar to calm him because he was trembling with indignation at what the police had done. Ana translated what her friends were saying to him because she was the one whose English was best. After the cognacs, the Canadian had grinned at her and told her he was an anarchist. She had not translated that because she knew her politically sophisticated friends would laugh and consider him naive. That night she took him home with her.

This time there was no one to trip him as, shouting, arms dramatically waving, he charged once more into battle, ensuring, Ana thought, that both of them would become victims of his anarchism. Which of them did that make more the fool, she wondered; Tom for his behaviour or her for loving him? Her eyes dry now, she watched Tom hovering over the official who, in a state of contained rage, was scribbling furiously on a form.

Then, suddenly, Tom grabbed her hand and led her out of the room. He was waving the form like a flag stolen from an enemy army. In the hall he put his arms around her and lifted her off the floor. "I did it!" he said. "You're in. All we have to do is get married within three months."

She turned her mouth away from his, broke free and ran to the door marked Women. She stayed inside for twenty minutes crying out her confusion and her fear. When she emerged Tom was sitting on the floor, head against the wall, grinning at her. She waited for him to stand, a smile creeping across her face. She put her arms around his neck and kissed him very hard.

Querida Mama:

As I told you in my first letter, which you probably haven't received yet, the weather has been so cold I've been afraid to go outside alone. I'm trying not to be disheartened but it's difficult, and in more ways than just the weather. It's so different here with Tom going to work and me staying all day in this tiny, empty apartment. (We have no furniture yet and only a double sleeping bag and large pieces of foam to sleep on.) It was much more fun in Barcelona with me working and coming home to him.

Today is Tom's third day at his new job. Last night he spent hours complaining about it. He couldn't think about anything else.

We have a car! It's orange and ugly and old. He wants to take me to the Rocky Mountains in it! Can you imagine being lost in Canada in the midst of an Arctic Vortex in a car that suddenly won't work? Me neither. But don't worry. I'll be fine. (I'll let you know later what an Arctic Vortex is. I don't want to ask Tom. I want to find out for myself.)

Say hello to a palm tree for me!

Besos,

Ana

She had seen no one on the street all morning. She thought perhaps no one went out walking when it was so cold. Yet boredom and a growing sense of claustrophobia were making her irritable and she determined to go out and mail the letter, to prove she wasn't a prisoner of the weather. She put on two of Tom's t-shirts and her heaviest sweater. She put on the tuque Tom bought for her yesterday on their way to a restaurant. She had on her leather boots and a scarf, and she pulled on the woollen gloves she wore in Barcelona on those days in January when the temperature wasn't so much above freezing.

Her cloth coat was fine for a Spanish winter but she knew as she slipped it on that it would be like a flimsy rag out there. She looked in the bathroom mirror and laughed. She was in a good mood now. She felt like someone in a Russian fairy tale. She thought of her excursion as an exotic adventure.

A car went by as she opened the building's front door, its exhaust visible. *Visible*, for God's sake, she thought. As visible as her breath suddenly was. She choked on the thin cold air, gasped, then coughed. Her eyes ran and her eyelashes became coated in rime. For a moment she panicked, thinking she would not be able to open her eyes, then settled down when she wiped them and the rime came off on her gloves.

She began to walk. Then her foot slid and she almost fell. She coughed again, then inhaled deeply. It was like inhaling a razor blade. She walked on, looking down, her heart pounding. She decided not to turn corners so as not to get lost. If she got lost she knew she'd die.

She thought she saw a post box at the next corner. She walked and tried to forget about her burning ears, her toes that might already be frozen.

It wasn't a post box. It was a newspaper box. She realized she didn't know what a post box looked like in this country.

A short way ahead she saw a woman at a bus stop. When she got to her, Ana asked about a post box and the woman directed her. "Three blocks this way then a block that way, then a block that way," she said, gesturing, and Ana thought she might as well walk to the mountains as five blocks today.

"I'd never imagined cold like this," she said, torn between the need to keep moving and the desire to communicate with someone, anyone.

"It's not cold," the woman said sharply, defensively, as if Ana had insulted her personally. She asked where Ana was from and then proceeded to list all the things that made Canada the best place in the world to live.

Ana was amused, thinking the woman was joking. When she realized she wasn't, she laughed and asked, teasingly, "Do you really believe that? Just because you have no scorpions or volcanoes or earthquakes or floods or bull fights? Do you think freezing to death while waiting for a bus isn't a natural disaster?" But the woman seemed not to understand, or not to want to.

And then, because she had a sudden urge for a steaming bowl of *café con leche* to warm her stomach, she asked the woman if there was a bar close by. The woman stared straight ahead into the empty street and refused to answer.

Querida Mama:

I do not know for sure what Tom is jealous of, but jealous he is, I'm sure of it. Yesterday I walked out to mail your letter and because it was so dreadfully cold I stopped at a grocery store to get warm. Last night in the sleeping bag I told Tom about it and he was upset but he wouldn't tell me why. I told him I found it amusing and stimulating to conquer the elements and meet strange people. I told him he should know how I felt because he'd done the same in Spain but all he said was, "Please don't remind me of Spain." I suppose he'd rather I have my adventures with him than by myself. But he had most of his adventures in Spain without me.

Anyway, there was only one person in the store when I walked in, utterly frozen and desperate for a refuge. He was the owner, a young Chinese man who told me he came from Brunei, which, he explained, was on the same island as Borneo. I thought of jungle and impossible heat, and couldn't imagine any place more different than Canada or anyone more exotic, until a second man appeared. This one was wearing a turban and had a black beard and dark, sharp eyes. He was a Sikh, a people I had only heard of before. He joined our conversation and turned out to be a pleasant man. He was a taxi driver and apparently often stopped at that store. The store owner offered me a cup of coffee which I drank to have something hot inside me, even though it was café americano, weak and foul tasting.

When I told Tom that the Sikh man gave me a ride to the post box and then back here, for free, and that he invited me to have tea one day with his wife and that I was going to, and even that I would like to draw the Sikh man's portrait (because, Mama, I even feel like drawing again, something I haven't done since university), then his eyes grew cold and he turned his back on me. Even when I told him that the Sikh man, whose name I could not spell even if I could remember it, was an intellectual and was writing a dissertation for his doctorate at a university back home on the psychological effect of alcoholically-drugged passengers on an Indo-Pakistani taxi driver in a Canadian city, he did not relent and we went to sleep without saying good night.

Pues, another letter soon. I wonder if you've replied to my first one yet?

Besos,

Ana

They sat on the floor before plates of spaghetti and Ana's homemade sauce. She was dressed in an outfit that had always, in Spain, drawn Tom's interest. Yet tonight, even with the bottle of Rioja half gone, he was silent, even morose. When he did speak it was to say things like, "I hate this job. I'm not a salesman. It's going to kill me."

"I know you're not a salesman," Ana said, shifting her leg so that a little more flesh became visible in the shadows inside the dress, "and I hate to see you working as one since you dislike it so. But after all, it's only been a few days. You'll find something else soon, I know."

"No job here will be good for me," he said. "I'm not at home here. I don't like it here."

"But we're going to get married here, *amor*," Ana said. "We have to be here. You couldn't find a job in Spain and you didn't want to live on my income any longer. We came here because you said that only here could you find a job that could support us when we were married. Are you forgetting so soon?"

"Damn it, I know. But I hate it here."

"Because of the job."

"Because it isn't Spain."

"But you couldn't live in Spain any longer. Don't you remember? You were broke and getting depressed."

"I wasn't depressed," he said testily, lying on his back on the floor and closing his eyes. He went on, lifting his head and pouring out the last of the wine, "Whatever stupidity made me think I could be a salesman?"

As she watched him toss back the wine she tried to contain her growing anger. It occurred to her that he might say next, "If it wasn't for you — ." If he said that she knew she'd lose control, walk out into the weather, call her taxi friend from the grocery store and tomorrow buy a plane ticket home.

She tried another tactic to bring him out of his mood. Coming around behind him she lifted his head from the floor and massaged his neck. He sat up, then leaned back into her hands. She kissed his neck but he leaned forward, shaking his head as if to free himself of the touch of her lips. He got to his feet and she watched him walk to the window where he stood and stared at the windy darkness. She thought of the Arctic Vortex and imagined it as a whirlwind that would suck him away, out through the window and into the night.

"I wish we were back in Spain," he said and suddenly she understood what was behind his words and her heart sank just as it had in the immigration officer's interrogation room. Tom was telling her what he had probably not even articulated for himself yet. He was saying he was afraid the job would change him, that he would no longer be the free and gentle anarchist, the man she had loved in Spain. He was telling her he was afraid of that and at that moment she was afraid of it too. His world was getting hold of him and his world was a very conventional one. She knew that once it had him it wouldn't let him go.

She wondered what other changes might occur in him. She tried not to let herself imagine him among Canadian women.

Then he turned from the window and came back and sat beside her and told her he was sorry, but because they were unable to go beyond the worry and the sadness, they only held each other tightly without kisses or whispers or caresses to surrender to in the barren room while the wind bit at the windows and walls.

She had tea with the Sikh couple and wrote to her mother that the wife was charming, as were their two small sons. "Their house is decorated as I imagine it would be in India," she said. She wrote that she arrived home from the visit before Tom and had his supper waiting. She said everything was going as well as could be expected and knew when her mother read *that* she would wonder what was going wrong.

The car was warming up. Ana stood inside the back door of the building looking into the parking lot, holding a knapsack that contained sandwiches, a thermos of strong coffee, and her camera. She was happy, excited, feeling adventurous. Tom had been happy last night; they'd gone out for dinner at a Thai restaurant and he'd talked for a long time about Banff and the Rockies and how much they had meant to him as a child, how they somehow seemed to belong to each person individually, though no one owned them and never could. He was as happy as on the good days in Spain. Back in the apartment he'd been in the best of moods. He said that tomorrow, Saturday, was going to be a special day. She'd made a note to tell her mother in the next letter that she was sure he was very much in love with her.

She opened the door and stepped into weather that was blindingly sunny and very much warmer than it had been. Her confident smile seemed to say that the Rocky Mountains, visible today as peaks of white against the azure of the distant sky, were out there only to be tamed by her. Tom took the knapsack, put it in the back seat, and they got in the car. He put the car in gear and revved the motor. The wheels spun. Ana waited. Tom revved the motor again and again, and again and again, yet they went nowhere.

"You drive," Tom said cheerfully. "I'll push."

Ana laughed. "Why not? I've driven motorcycles since I was ten. Why not a car?"

As Tom pushed from the front Ana revved the car's motor. The tires whined. Tom strained. The tires whined some more. He pushed and relaxed, letting the car rock back and forth, but it wouldn't come free of the ice it was resting on. He pushed so hard Ana was afraid he would hurt himself; she called to him to stop. He pushed once more and Ana put the gas pedal to the floor.

She never imagined a wreck like that could go so fast backing up. The motor roared. She whipped the steering wheel around to avoid a car parked behind her. She heard Tom yell "Whoa!" and she swung her head to look at him and tried to understand what he was saying. "Whoa!" he yelled again and again, running after her, his arms flying.

After the car went through the fence on the other side of the alley and got stuck in the snow in someone's back yard, Ana turned off the ignition, congratulating herself for having the presence of mind to do so, and only then allowed herself to be furious.

"Whoa?" she screamed, getting out. "Whoa? Just what is whoa exactly, Tom? I am sitting in a moving bomb going backwards faster than I've ever gone backwards in my life and you are yelling whoa, a word I've never heard before? What did you expect the word would make me do? I'll tell you what it made me do. It made me wonder what the word meant. That's what it made me do. And in the meantime, if it hadn't been for the fence and the snow, I might have gone to the mountains without you, and backwards at that!"

"It means stop," she heard him murmur as she marched toward their building. "It's what you say to a horse to make him stop."

She stopped and shook her fist. "A horse? A *horse?* Just let me buy spurs and I'll show your ass how we make a horse *start!*"

Later, feeling less humiliated, she looked through the bedroom window and saw that Tom had found a couple of men to help push the car out of the neighbour's yard. When they were done she called Tom to come in and eat sandwiches from the knapsack. After lunch, he borrowed tools from the building's caretaker and, Ana with him, went to try to repair the fence. The owner of the fence came out of his house to help and surprised Ana by not being angry. After a while, his wife called for them to come in and warm up with coffee and cake. The wife was a nice older woman. When the men went back outside, she and Ana talked. They arranged to go downtown together next week to shop and explore. The woman said she hadn't been in the city centre for two years, so it would be an adventure for her as well.

That night, in the double sleeping bag on the foam mattress, Ana caressed Tom's back and asked if he minded that she was going downtown with the neighbour.

"No," he said. "Why should I?"

"Even though you and I haven't been downtown together yet?"

"No."

"I thought you might," she said. "I thought you might want to show me downtown yourself."

"This isn't that kind of a city," he said. "There aren't the secret places to look for and discover. This isn't a city of many surprises. It's a North American city."

"Perhaps you say that because you don't know. You've been away a long time. Have you looked at the city yet?"

"How could I?" he said. "I've been working."

"Perhaps you'd be surprised," she said, feeling adventurous still, her fingers wandering across his body.

"Would I?"

"I've seen things that have surprised me. And delighted me."

"What do you mean?"

"The river, for example. It's frozen into those savage shapes, like hard little icebergs fused together. It's the first time I've ever seen a river frozen. When I saw it I didn't even know it *was* a river. I don't know what I thought it was."

"Oh," he said.

Becoming still more adventurous she told him there was a Metro bridge across the river downtown that she liked very much. "It's beautiful. Postmodern. Haven't you seen it?"

"Yes, of course," he said. Then he asked what she knew he would ask. "When did you see it?"

"Yesterday." Her fingers stopped moving and rested on him.

"How did you get there?"

"The taxi driver and his wife and I went sightseeing." His body stiffened. She took her hand away.

"They live in a duplex," she went on, "and their neighbour is a French Canadian woman whom I met the day I was there for tea. She's very interesting, an artist like me, or like I used to be. She went sightseeing with us. She said that when summer comes we'll sketch together."

He said, "I want to go to sleep now. Pushing the car and rebuilding the fence have exhausted me. And all week at that job — ."

"That bad job. You'll have to get another one. You can't stay the way you are now, so unhappy."

"What can I do?" he said gruffly, turning his back to her.

"Get another one. Be happy again."

"When we're married," he responded. "I won't look for a job until after we're married. We have to do that pretty soon, you know."

"Yes," she said, but her tone was guarded and she knew he sensed it. At that moment she was wishing they had six months instead of three.

He said, "If there was anything to sleep on out there I'd go into the living room."

"Why?" she asked, startled.

"Because I don't think you want to marry me now."

"If you went into the living room," she said, "I'd go back to Spain tomorrow."

"Why would you do that?"

"Because maybe it's you who doesn't want to marry me."

"Shit," he said.

"I know."

"I do want to marry you." He turned toward her and embraced her. "Of course I do. You know I do."

"I know you did."

"I do," he said, nuzzling her neck.

"How are we going to see the Rockies?" she asked, feeling it was time to change the subject.

"I don't know," he answered. "I'll figure out a way. I'll buy a new car. I'll do something. I'll get you there one way or another."

She thought about telling him they could go next weekend with the taxi driver and his wife and her friend Marie in the taxi driver's car, because they'd talked about that when they went sightseeing downtown, but she thought she'd better not. Banff should be left to him. After all, he felt the mountains were his. In showing them to her through his eyes, perhaps he'd feel that she was his too.

"I know you will," she whispered, drawing him on top of her. "I can't wait, Tom. I want to see the mountains where that wild river comes from. We'll go there every weekend. You'll be the old Tom again, no matter what job you have. I know you will, *querido.* I feel it. Yes, I do. Yes, yes, I do."

Afterward, her head nestled on Tom's shoulder and her mind on the verge of sleep, she wondered what there would be to tell her mother in her next letter home. Something about her friends, she supposed. Certainly more about the renaissance of her art, which was exciting her greatly. And a lot about a wedding.

She fell asleep holding hands with Tom across a frozen river that was narrow and very close to its source in the mountains. In the dream, Tom leaped across the ice. He had a ring and he slipped it gently onto her finger. He picked her up and she wrapped her arms eagerly around his neck and her legs around his waist. He shouted like an avenging angel into the dark mountains, laughed and shouted.

They were married in a dimly lit, wood paneled rec room-cum-storage area in the house of a Justice of the Peace. Only twice did Tom interrupt the ceremony, once to comment to Ana, in Spanish, about how degrading it was to hold such a ceremony in a sordid suburban basement, and the second to announce, when asked to produce it, that he hadn't bought the ring yet.

When the man said Tom could kiss her, he tried, but at the last minute Ana's face swerved away and he managed just to brush her ear.

The Justice of the Peace took their picture with a Polaroid camera. The JP's wife served cookies and tea and, after asking where Ana was from, talked about Disneyland.

JOHN BOYCHUK • *CANMORE, ALBERTA*

NIGEL DARBASIE

Nigel Darbasie was born in San Juan, Trinidad, arising from roots which he describes as "Africa and India, with a trace of China." A former student at Queen's Royal College, Mr Darbasie entered the University of Alberta after immigrating to Canada in 1969. Through those early years he held a variety of jobs: as a construction and forestry labourer, laundry worker, an assembler of stained glass lampshades, and as an assistant to a contact lens manufacturer. After graduating with a BSc, he worked as a laboratory technician, then switched fields to become a community development officer with the Company of Young Canadians. This was followed by a career as a writer and researcher on projects with social services agencies and government departments, and later as a public affairs officer with the provincial government. Mr Darbasie also worked as a musician, mostly on weekends and occasionally full-time. For the past ten years he has been running a desk-top publishing and writing business in Edmonton. Mr Darbasie's poetry collection, Last Crossing *(NCI), was published in 1988.*

The Home Front

Take it from me
you real lucky to be in Canada.
Is drugs, corruption
and high cost of living down here.
To make it worse
plenty thiefin an shootin going on
seem like everybody have a gun.
The place change, is a real mess.

By now you must be hear the news
the attempt to overthrow the government.
Well it nearly succeed.
A whole set of people get kill
buildings burn down and everything.
All that death and destruction, for what?

Imagine in this society
where Negro and Indian almost equal
plus Chinese, White, a cosmopolitan mix-up
with Catholic, Protestant, Hindu
Moslem, Jew, and Buddhist
they have politicians and so-call revolutionaries
preaching race and fundamentalist religion
thinking they could build a country on that.

No wonder why people rushin to Canada
they just want to live a decent life
without all this violence and fear.
See them lining up at the embassy
with their few sweet memories
ready to go in the north and reminisce.
And if they want a real Carnival
I hear it have a big one in Toronto
fete and mas just like home.

So I tryin to get up there by you fast
before they close the gate.
I know it cold too bad
and it have some discrimination
but that is no problem at all
when every day in this place
is serious life and death.

by Nigel Darbasie

Writing Home

So you want to come up to Canada?
Well the place hot, hot, hot, yes.
All this thing bout culture and religion
have people feeling threaten too bad.
Let me tell you what goin on out here.

A woman see a picture
of a East Indian RCMP fella wearing a turban.
She figure he breakin Canadian tradition
so she start a protest. Thousands of people agree
and rush to sign petition—how the RCMP uniform
is like majority Canadian culture
and ethnic groups mustn't change that.

Now some ethnic boys say
if they allow turban, they want skullcap.
A next man want braids and headdress.
We own Rasta say he want dreadlocks.
Of course all of them right: that is them religion.
Well the RCMP ask the government for a ruling
have politicians thinkin bout the ethnic vote
and the White backlash.

They make a Canadian compromise
tell the boys they could wear turban
skullcap, braids, and dreadlocks
but in RCMP colours: red, blue, and gold.
A few boys have to dye their hair.
But you know what?
The Rasta say he don't like the colours
it don't have green in it.

One day the fellas dress up in uniform.
Hit the Legion Hall for a little refreshment.
The doorman tell them they have to stay out
because all their headgear violating Legion dress code.
Then he say he would let them in
if they come back at Halloween.

At the same time this going on
a White fella, a new immigrant from Europe,
make a pin that have a East Indian, a Oriental
and Black man with a bone in his nose, carrying a spear.
They surroundin a White man, like they threatening him.
The pin say: "Who's the minority in Canada?"
Well it start selling like crazy.

Things gettin hotter still.
The city council decide to mark places by the road
where people dead in accidents
to remind everybody to be more careful.
So they come up with a sign, a cross over a coffin.
Right after they do that, big article in the newspapers:
"Cross symbol dropped after ethnic protest."

Some groups say the cross is a Christian symbol
the city shouldn't use it because other religions here.
To tell you the truth, I didn't see no religion in it.
But I could see a next pin comin up:
A White fella with a big stick
chasin all them ethnic minority
and the caption sayin, "Haul your ass."
Boy, Canada hot, hot, hot, yes.

Lineage

My maternal grandparents
enjoined the blood of Africa and India.
From my paternal great-grandfather came China
a single long plait falling from a brimless cap.
In these austere portraits a trinity of streams
passed on in the union of my parents
whose sanguine lines make me
some would say, a fine mongrel
arising from the confluence of slaves
and indentured labourers
outcasts of ancient worlds.

Play Mas

What wrong with you at all?
Now you in Canada you don't like to dance.
It don't look respectable
when the sweet rhythm take in your body
an carry you down the road feelin nice?

This place need a mas too bad
the real carnival, Caribbean style
is ancient thing, really
a moving meditation to the drum.

That kind of behaviour is not for you?
Don't be playin sophisticated.
Man, come an dance, come an play mas
let the sweet rhythm bring back your spirit
and turn you human again.

The Question

Let me tell you something
it have black folks with roots in Canada.
Slaves in Quebec since the seventeenth century.
Loyalists in the Maritimes and Ontario from 1783.
Settlers in British Columbia going back to 1858
and on the prairies from the 1900s.
I meself here since 1969.

Well I know a few descendants of these people
and man, they does get so vex
when somebody make the mistake
and ask them if they from the islands.
I have to cool them down, laugh an thing.
What you could do about it? I say.
Is in the skin.

Now I don't mind the question
but there should be a time limit
especially when you settle in the place
sowing seed and cross-fertilizing.
But what does get me
is how some white folks like to approach you
pretendin that they here for generations
when they still have luggage on the boat.

I could just imagine
being in this country for ninety-five years.
Have a long grey beard, write a whole set of book
supposed to be a famous Canadian
talkin like one an everything.
And a fart old like meself creak up beside me
screw up he face and ask: "Where are you from?"

Nappy-1

I ran into Nap in the parking lot
outside the West Indian Food Store.
He had a big smile, face lit up proud
as he stood by his new Mercedes
licensed Nappy-1.
For a little more money
he could have bought a house.

We went for a drive downtown
sunroof open, luxuriating in traffic
to some calypso, reggae
Afro-beat, and jazz.
What a ride! Never before
had I been skewered
by so many eyes
from occupants of passing vehicles
pedestrians on sidewalks and intersections.

Nap said he didn't give a shit
about hard looks.
They just made him more resolute
in going after the high life
he had come here for.
But when I saw him a few months later
he had tinted the windows of his car
encasing himself in dark glass.
And from the rearview mirror dangled
a small medicine bag from home
insurance against maledictions and blight.

Trust Walk

It's Friday afternoon
and I'm at the supermarket
at the end of a checkout line
that has a half-dozen shopping carts.
From out of the crowded aisles
comes a tall white man, semi-retired.
He looks into my trolley and asks:
"Want to split a coupon
fifteen dollars off on a hundred?"

Is he trying to set me up
expecting to find compassion
or gullibility in a dark face?
Maybe when we get to the cashier
he won't be able to pay
so he'll ask me to help buy his groceries.
Or using a well-practised sleight of hand
he'll walk off with some of mine.

"No thanks, that's all right," I tell him.
He moves to another checkout to try his luck.
"I know you've got about fifty dollars worth,"
he says, pushing his way back.
"The cashier can keep our stuff separate.
I've done this before.
You'll get a receipt
there won't be a mix-up."

The woman ahead of me loads the conveyor belt
then positions a space bar at the end of her items.
Other shoppers join the line
wedging the coupon man behind me.
I take another look at his cart
and I'm as certain as he is:
between us we'll spend
a hundred dollars.
"Let's try it," I say.

He leans over to the cashier
tells her we're together
but want our orders kept separate
with a sub-total for both.
When the tallying is almost over
he draws his wallet and I notice
several twenty-dollar bills.
Relieved, I throw in some coupons of my own.

As we pack our groceries he asks where I'm from.
Says he's done a lot of traveling
and has a daughter who has been teaching in Africa.
There's little time for conversation
as other people's items start coming down the conveyor.
"It's really been a pleasure meeting you," I say
wanting to thank him
not for saving me some money
but for the trust walk.

KAREN LUMSDEN • *BARRHEAD, ALBERTA*

REG SILVESTER

Reg Silvester was born in Moose Jaw, Saskatchewan in 1945. His family settled in North Battleford, Saskatchewan in 1953 and he lived there from the age of eight to the age of nineteen. The next six years were spent in Ottawa where he acquired his training as a professional journalist. After beginning his writing career in Regina, he moved to Edmonton in 1976. Edmonton has been his home from that time to this. Mr Silvester has worked both as a reporter for the daily newspapers and as a freelance journalist. He founded the Edmonton Bullet *in 1983 and has recently returned to that publication as editor. Two collections of his short fiction have been published by Coteau Books of Regina:* Fish-Hooks *in 1984 and* Wishbone *in 1990. After serving the Writers Guild of Alberta as treasurer and vice-president, Mr Silvester was elected president of the organization in 1991. "I believe in the value of community," he says, "and the strength we gain from knowing our similarities and tolerating our differences."*

People of the Siwash and Boh:

ALBERTA'S ULTIMATE INVISIBLE MINORITY

TO OBSERVE THE SASKATCHEWANIAN IN Alberta you have to be alert for subtle clues. You overhear someone mentioning their Aunt Jane in Melfort and you've probably found one. People going to Waskesiu for their holidays could only be Saskatchewanians returning for a breath of the air they were born breathing. (The only Albertans who go to Saskatchewan for a vacation are Saskatchewanians; the others go to the mountains, BC, or Vegas.) Watch for people in Cowachin sweaters, the ones hand-knit in BC—in the fifties and sixties they were part of the national costume of Saskatchewan and to wear one still gives you away.

The best time to spot a Saskatchewanian in Alberta is that week in May when the time zone changes from standard to daylight saving time. Watch for the person with the dazed look, with bags under his eyes, yawning in mid-afternoon, asleep on the bus home after work. While Saskatchewan has a reputation for being ahead of the pack in development of social policy and potash mining, the most advanced thing the province ever did was to adopt daylight saving time year-round. The time change is hell for the transplanted Sasklander. Even if we go to bed the hour earlier, we toss and turn all through it, and it takes a week of adjustment before we get to work in the morning remembering having driven there. It's dangerous, and it's enough to make you forget prosperity, oil, art, or whatever it was that brought you to Alberta. You long to go back to where the provincial flag is as green-green as the grass of home.

You keep threatening to leave. But you never carry through.

Quiet! People will think the best way to spot a Saskatchewanian is to look for someone having a conversation with himself.

by Reg Silvester

You'll never leave.

There's something about Alberta.

We'd watch with awe, back when we were kids, as the big, red, white, and blue Greyhound Bus would roll in and out of town. There was something exotic about that lean, leaping hound on its side, an animal unfamiliar to us in coyote country. We'd watch the people climbing aboard, knowing they were going to Alberta, Edmonton probably, home of Barry Allan and the Expressions who had a hit song called "Arm Full of Teddy Bears" on the radio. If we ever took a bus we'd more likely ride the cream and rust-coloured STC (that's Saskatchewan Transportation Company, state-owned transit) to Saskatoon or Regina. But if you were really going somewhere, you took the Greyhound.

We were just kids, of course, so we had no idea of the significance of the STC. Years earlier, our government had kicked Greyhound out of the province, except for transcontinental buses. It set up its own company to provide bus service to every town and hamlet within the borders, not just to those lucky enough to be on the route from Winnipeg to Edmonton or Calgary. We hadn't been away yet, so most of us had no idea what a challenge it can be in the rest of Canada to keep a piece of the action in local hands when the multinational organizations are so pervasive and so hungry.

We hadn't been away yet, but we'd all be going—sometime, somewhere. Children in Saskatchewan are raised to migrate. Usually on the Greyhound. Sure, the politicians and our parents would moan about wanting to create more opportunities for their children at home, and we'd talk about it at high school ourselves sometimes. But then there'd be this river of cars pouring in at Thanksgiving or Christmas, just bristling with the black and yellow Alberta licence plates of those days, and the parents would count them proudly, and we'd give them a kind of wistful gaze . . .

A lot of Saskatchewanians came to Alberta in the seventies and eighties. We've tried, in our little ways, to make this place more like home. In the meantime, the people we left behind have tried to turn Saskatchewan into Alberta without doing themselves any good. It really doesn't matter what stripe of government you elect in Saskatchewan, the province won't hold more than a million people. And so the excess population continues to spill over the invisible border and more of our folk keep arriving here to study, to get jobs, to find a life in the theatre, to discover more oil.

We are a large and invisible immigrant group. Even the Americans are more obvious to the average Albertan. You hear someone say "hause" for "house" and you know you've nabbed someone from over the southern border. But the Saskatchewanian rarely gives himself away with language and quickly learns to hide quirks of speech. As a group, Saskatchewanians have little in common. They don't get together for feasts of their heritage food, nor to dance their traditional dances, nor to relax into animated conversations in their native tongue. The only time you'll see Saskatchewanians together in great number is when the Saskatchewan Roughriders come to town to play the local Canadian Football League heroes. They'll don their green sweaters, round up their poor deprived Alberta-born kids, and head off to the game.

Oh, come out of hiding, Reg. Speak for yourself. It's you who does that, isn't it?

Okay. So I took my kid to a game in Edmonton's Commonwealth Stadium a couple of seasons ago. The Roughriders, after years and years of losses and losses had, for once, started off winning, while the arch-rival Esks were slow on the uptake. It was a good chance for the boy to see his father's team on a winning streak.

Sadly, my son, whose preferences and prejudices I'd worked so hard to mold, was an instant Eskimos fan. He cheered every gain by the green and gold. He laughed when the Saskatchewan quarterback got sacked. And when I cheered a Rider pass reception, he gave me the raspberry. "Take it easy, boy, or you won't get a ride home," I warned. And then the middle-aged guy next to him said, "Don't worry, bud, I'll give you a ride." What can you do when you're all alone? I could only assume that the other Albertan Saskatchewanians I saw scattered through the crowd were also suffering rejection by the second generation and smarting from the solidarity among Eskimo fans.

You could tell which Rider fans lived here and which ones had chartered in from the homeland by their relative sobriety. Most of the visitors, with slogans and decorations in green all over their faces and torsos, were showing the effects of drinking too many Bohs on the bus.

A pair of them cruised our section chanting: "Who's 4-and-0? Riders! Riders! Who's 1-and-3? Homos! Homos!"

My boy asked, "What's a homo, Dad?" And I had to explain that Saskatchewan may be the home of all kinds of advanced political thought and social programs but that some of the people there are still Paleolithic in their understanding of human rights. I tried to tell him quietly, but there was no way to avoid those eavesdropping, grinning Edmonton Eskimo fans all around me. I'm trying to teach my Alberta-born child that Saskatchewanians are, bluntly, better than Albertans—humbler, more cooperative, kinder and more tolerant—and this is the proof? And then on the way home from the game, my eight-year-old tries to pick a fight with one of the visiting Saskatchewanians in the parking lot. I'm embarrassed. Kids in Saskatchewan wouldn't behave this aggressively. And what does our green-bedecked visitor say? "Way to go, man! You're raising your son real good." Then he climbed aboard a chartered STC bus for the long ride home.

And the game? Eskimos is a stupid name for a football team. There are no Eskimos on the Eskimos, never have been. And Native northerners prefer to be called Inuit anyway. Did you know that reporters for the *Edmonton Journal*, of which I used to be one, are not allowed to refer to Inuit as Eskimos. Only football players are called Eskimos in the *Journal*. It said in the paper the next morning that the Eskimos had won the game.

The truth hurts. Let's try fiction. Old reliable lies and exaggeration based on a little event that might actually have happened.

A kid, maybe seventeen, with a fresh face and an unassuming manner, sits in a booth at the Ambassador Hotel Coffee Shop (he says "café") on 106th Street in Edmonton. He's wearing the Cowachin (he says "siwash") knit sweater he inherited from his dad.

"Maybe I'll have a Vico?" he tells the waitress, hesitant because he hasn't found it on the menu, which he has folded over limply.

"You'll have a what?" she asks.

"You know, a Vico," he replies, holding out his hand as though it's resting on top of a glass of rich brown fluid.

"A what!"

"You know, Vico. Chocolate milk."

"Anything else?"

"Some chips, I guess."

"French fries, you mean. You want chocolate milk and French fries."

"Yeah."

"Is that all?"

"You know, gravy?"

"I know gravy," she nods.

"Gravy on the chips."

The waitress leaves with his order, smirking. He hangs his head, still a little jet-lagged from his ride on the Greyhound. Poor kid just wanted to get his feet on a piece of the prairie that had oil under it. He didn't know they wouldn't speak his language when he got here. Didn't expect things to be much different at all. The country looks to him pretty much the same as it does around Cut Knife. Edmonton's a lot like Saskatoon, he figures, but bigger.

He finishes his Vico and wanders the four blocks back to the bachelor suite he's rented in the El Mirador, an old-fashioned apartment block that makes him think of Saskatoon. He sits down to phone his mother back home, to let her know he's doing okay, that he's found an apartment where his green provincial flag is just the right size for a curtain, where his Roughrider jersey hangs on the wall, where he's got a gas fireplace with a mantelpiece that now displays his family pictures and his orange and crystal-white souvenir chunk of potash.

"Mom, they've never heard of Vico here," he says. "We have to call it chocolate milk."

Who was that comedian who told the Saskatchewan jokes?

About how Regina had the strangest burial customs? They sat their dead up in nightclubs and asked you to entertain them.

Yeah, that guy. The one who told about the dog.

Saskatchewan is the only place you can sit on your front porch and watch your dog disappear—for three days.

That's the guy. What's his name?

I don't remember. He's probably an Albertan.

Just looking around, you don't see that much difference between Saskatchewan and Alberta. So why does the newcomer from Saskatchewan become immediately fascinated with that puzzling, minuscule, intangible difference?

The similarities are the most obvious, starting with geography. The two provinces are almost identical if you ignore the mountains, which is easy to do if you share the Saskatchewanian attitude that all they do is spoil the view. Other than the jobs in the petroleum industry, of which there are clearly more in Alberta, the people in both provinces make their living in identical ways on and off the land. You start wondering what makes Albertans so smug and uppity. There are great stretches of prairie in both places, so why do Albertans call us flatlanders? The harvest leaves behind identical stubble on farmland in both provinces, so why do they call us stubblejumpers? And there's no shortage of gophers in either province, so why are we the prairie gophers?

There are historical similarities. Both became provinces of Canada in 1905, political twins in a way. Both, in the midst of their grievous suffering during the Depression of the thirties, elected church-oriented parties to deliver them from the dust bowl.

Well then, what are the differences? You can start with the name-calling. Saskatchewanians don't call Albertans belittling names. Second, there are important political differences. In Saskatchewan, medicare was developed within a tradition that included the first universal hospital insurance and auto insurance plans, not to mention the STC. In Alberta, the Heritage Trust Fund was developed within a tradition that included Social Credit Funny Money, low prices at the gas pumps, and no sales tax. You can't say Alberta wasn't trying, but you wonder about the priorities.

When I was just a fresh-faced newcomer to Alberta, I made frequent trips back to Saskatchewan. Reality checks, perhaps. On one trip to Regina for a conference, I was able to put my question about the origin of the differences between the two provinces to a leading historian. Well, he said, it's relatively simple. Alberta absorbed large waves of immigrants across the American border while Saskatchewan's newcomers were Canadians from the east.

Aha! So it's a microcosm of the old empire versus the new empire, Brit versus Yank, SK versus AB. So it's a matter of hurrah words. I say "freedom" and you say "liberty." I say "one for all and all for one" and you say "all for me." I say "I might disagree with what you say but I'll defend your right to say it," and you say "shut up."

You might just find the essential difference between Saskatchewanians and Albertans on four-lane highways. The Saskatchewan Department of Highways puts up signs that say "stay right except to pass"; Alberta Transportation puts up signs that say "slow traffic stay right." And so, contrary to the political traditions of the different provinces, every Saskatchewanian drives on the right and every Albertan drives on the left.

So, what're you gonna do, guy? Who're you gonna be?

The need to have an ethnic background wells up in me each summer as Heritage Days loom on Edmonton's social calendar. Without an ethnicity I am nobody in August. I have three generations of forefathers buried in Canadian soil, but that only makes me Canadian, not ethnic. As for national origin, well, if my forefathers had stayed where they were, I'd have been born as English as Ringo Starr (at least I share his initials). Instead, my people wound up in Saskatchewan, Dad's family after a one-generation stop-over in Ontario and Mom's family straight from the Old Country.

But I never learned to Morris Dance, and dwyle-flonking (that perverse British pub sport) means nothing to me. I can't rally to the Brit pavilion, and I can only dream of the day when my Saskatchewan heritage is something to celebrate. We could wear our siwashes and run videotapes of the Roughrider Grey Cup victories of 1966 and 1989. We could wander around the grounds offering to give people a hand. We could give out brochures for the co-ops and credit unions.

My Saskatchewanianism is my hope for August, and the source of questions I ponder in wasted time throughout the year. For example, you must notice that the Englishman never loses his accent in a long life in Canada. And though his sons speak like real Canadians, they still put vinegar on their chips. So I ask: if we Saskatchewanians spend our long lives in Alberta, never losing our affection for the green and white Roughriders, will our children grow up to be drivers who keep right except to pass? Will Alberta, some day, perhaps next year, grow to have a year-round time zone? Will it adopt mountain-and-a-half time, half-way between daylight and standard time, and bring changes to CBC program notes—"half an hour later in Newfoundland; half an hour earlier in Alberta"?

Will the continuing influx of Saskatchewanians and their children be the political force behind any such changes? Will Alberta and Saskatchewan always be so different? What if the oil dries up? Are the twins really Siamese? If there ever was a merger, would we have to keep using those ugly red and white Alberta plates, or could we choose the graphically superior white and green Saskatchewan plates with those lovely stylized golden heads of wheat in the centre?

You'd better end here or people will think the best way to spot a Saskatchewanian in Alberta is to look for someone who can't stop talking.

Yeah, that's enough of this. Let's go get a Vico.

Vico, shmico, it's time for a Boh!

CATHERINE STRIKES WITH A GUN • *BROCKET, ALBERTA*

LEILA SUJIR

Leila Sujir of Calgary describes her literary and video work as "coming out of my experience of being from two cultures—and that precarious and somewhat dangerous sense of being located in a gap across two cultures." The two cultures of which she speaks are the Albertan culture of her mother's family and the Indian culture of her father's. Ms Sujir herself was born in Hyderabad, India. By the age of eight she had lived in several parts of India, in the Gaspé region of Quebec, and at High River and Granum in Alberta. From age eight onward, she has lived in Calgary. As a writer, video artist, and college instructor, Ms Sujir has involved herself in a broad range of artistic and social issues: issues of race, class, and gender. Her video works include Working Portraits; My Two Grandmothers, Her Great Grandfather, and Me; *and* India Hearts Beat. *The latter is in the collection of both the National Gallery of Canada and the Canada Council Art Bank. Her fiction, essays, interviews, and reviews have appeared in many Canadian periodicals.*

The Dreams of the Night Cleaners

For my father, Raghu Sujir, and his sister, my aunt Manorama, and for all of the night cleaners who helped me with this project

Beginnings: an incident
Several years ago, my brother found a copy of *The High River Times* dated December 19, 1957 in an abandoned house in High River. On the front page was the headline,"Pilot Missing in BC. Believed to Be Roger Sujir." He was shocked to find this trace reminding him of our father's death. It was for both of us a movement of plot we didn't understand: it was as if the article had found him.

Beginnings: a dream
I dream of my mother dreaming. In her dream, she is writing a story at the keyboard of her computer. Behind her, lit in shadows, is a kitchen. It is a warm, summer Calgary night. She paces around and around a small statue of Shiva and a number of household cleansers piled on the floor.

My Mother's Story:

A Story of Maps and Time Lines, Mops and Brooms and Vacuums
A Story of Perseverance
A Story of Visibility and Invisibility
Day and Night, Night and Day (and not the Cole Porter version)
Or the Dreams of the Night Cleaners

by Leila Sujir

Or was it cleansers?
My fingers slipping on the keyboard—is that how to begin?
With those figures who change the world?
Not with Mister Clean, Ajax, Comet—
although they,
the North American household gods, represent power,
the power
to change
and transform.

And one of my household gods, Shiva
the dancing Nataraja encircled in fire beside the sink hears this story
unravel as I pace around and
around
the kitchen
mop in hand
thinking and cleaning cleaning and thinking

this kitchen the place where the future reveals itself.

Shiva, not yet named a cleanser
although he's known as
the "destroyer"
the one who changes the nature of matter,
what matters.

Shiva, who dances a new world in
with a beat to his drum.
His dance
my husband's call,
to death.

Years ago now
a cold mountain. It was close to
the longest night of the year.
Late December.

His death by
cultural displacement.

His death
a call in the night, a call which keeps ringing,
calling us to answer, to join him:
a call we cannot, must not
answer

yet.

Summer Solstice: Refusing to Answer That Call For a Journey Into Death And Me, Cleaning, Trying to Change the Story

This June night
shortest night of the year
daylight illuminating the almost night sky

and me hoping to unravel not only the coils of this vacuum tangled up in the kitchen cupboard behind me, but also to untangle this narrative,
this mystery, or
is it a ghost story?

A haunting coming out of terror:
lost on another continent, another culture.
Lost out of home.
That loss a bellow, my mother-in-law's sorrow for her son
lost in Canada: the pilot, Raghu—known to the family as Lalloo.

Her gift (the diamond necklace)
to the temple in India
undone by her husband who didn't believe in
such magic, such
protection. Two years later, and
two sons gone—both dead—her husband—gone. Dead.
All the dead.

Suddenly, a crack of thunder in this summer night in Canada.
This crack of thunder
a call for my daughter.
This call
a story with diaphanous folds which
move and shudder,
roar,
echoing the vacuum.

The folds of the story beginning to
hide the bones of the dead,
the long dead,
the almost dead in a history

stretching back, and which

threatens now to reach forward,
engulf us in its folds of time.

And in Canada, me,
trapped here in my kitchen with these

indelible stains:
death
on the fabric
of our lives,
a death I can't wash out but only watch it spreading

A movement of plot
accumulating
bursting
most dangerous around this cycle
of seasons,
the solstices, with their noticeable marking of time:

the longest day
the longest night.

Rewriting the Story, or Delaying the Inevitable, and Thus Forestalling the Possibly Tragic Outcome

So on this shortest night of the year in the late twentieth century, before this summer night ends

I must go back,
then forward
clip the threads of that cycle
of death

then back
again to begin to
explain and to
uncover how this strange, and until now,
secret story with ghosts,
and haunting nightmares came about, making us
strangers,
even to ourselves.

A family of
strangers.
A community of the lost,
disconnected, maybe because we're
lost on this continent,
lost out of history.

This mystery a circle
of stories,
another beginning,
a cycling again last December when my daughter phoned, that time from the airport,
telling me about this person she'd met,
a night cleaner at the office,
telling me this story before she flew off to her training course,
her telling me this on the longest
night of the year because of her fear of
flight,
this time to a meeting in Toronto, then Ottawa.

And then she phoned again when she arrived.
And then phoned again,
her phone calls a trail marking her passage across space and time,
memory
her fear of disappearing (another flight into
death).

It was close to the end of her contract, she explained—she had to be there, finish up some schedules, when Devika, the night cleaner, arrived along with a family of women, to clean.

This telling now a conglomerate,
an amalgamation of phone
calls across distance and
time.

My Daughter's Story:

Another Winter Solstice:
Not Mountains, But Office.
Not Endings, But New Beginnings:
The Meeting,
The Secret Sharing

Two AM in not even the middle of this long night which extends until late morning working late on the schedules for the flight crews: working out how a captain and crew might fly, say, from Tokyo to Vancouver, then across to Toronto, making sure to include sleeping time along with flying time. Invading their lives, the crews', with our schedules hurling them back and forth across the night and day skies of the planet, the globe beneath, and people sleeping, with, we assume or hope, ordinary lives, on-going, uninterrupted. Without the continuum of fear, or a fear of stopping.

And now, even in this nighttime sky, the stars are faint—the blizzard of snow lighting up the night. I thought at first this woman windexing the Canon copier machine, she, a night cleaner, had if not financial security, at least a routine. Her life a link to a reality which will keep on going, some kind of certainty in the midst of so much—not knowing. Her face a reminder for me of where I'd come from, India, but what I don't look like, because I'm only half, Indian that is. And so half, located neither here nor there. And she, seeing me, would hardly imagine me as "sister," even countrywoman, even if I did look like I came from that place, because of this position, at the desk, not in front of it, with a vacuum. She perhaps wonders if I'm more—lucky. In terms of the economy. But this luck is just a day-to-day juggling with the uncertainty of the part-time. No way to know when it, or I, will disappear.

But her story of uncertainty, she explained that night to me, when I apologized not only for my crying, but for the disdain and suspicion of the daytime workers, the ones who leave pennies under the desk, testing the night workers, making sure: "Are they *really* cleaning?" Or George, who leaves trails of staples around his desk. Why bother cleaning up? he figures. They'll do it—that's what they're paid for. Or Alicia who left a half-folded package of matches tucked in the garbage can. A test? How many tests? How much disbelief? Or the inquiry from the previous day, when one of the bosses found his files rumpled. "The cleaners," he growled, "are unreliable. A security risk." And my apologies don't help much, in the workplace, which can suddenly make her disappear even though she feels largely invisible now, in the night. Invisible, yet highly visible, because of the colour of her skin, her job: these demands on her and the other workers growing steadily every day. And her longing, she tells me, for home: lost between two countries. Two homes. The absence of home. Home now not place, but memory.

"This story," she explains, becoming now, for a moment, a lecturer, coming out of the studies she started at the University of Bombay, "can be found in the library in statistics, and in the reports, say on the `globalization of capital,'" the economic story given in these three, seemingly small, but official words that catch in her throat and make it impossible for her to speak through the tears of all of our impending uncertainty. She gasps, finally having had it. Enough of this endless work which never is completed: this vacuuming, this mopping, this dusting, and the disdain which accompanies it. And the eyes always watching, willing to tell. Am I one of these? Eyes or ears or mouth? with a story? I wonder, looking across at her.

And she tells me about her friend who cleans at the Palliser, who taught her the rounds, who warned her about the need to keep smiling, to keep making friends, because "the hotel has eyes." And they don't like what they see. "Maybe it's the colour. They don't like another colour—of skin. Or maybe it's the job. Cleaning. Because you clean, they say you're dirty. Not clean." He explains after they've finished their rounds of cleaning, sitting now in the lounge having a drink. A coke. It's almost five AM, and there is, for her, a feeling she exists in a highly unlikely moment, as if she's no longer subject to gravity, floating up from the surface of the chair: just the two of them in the almost darkness, talking, sipping their drinks in the lounge of the Palliser Hotel. The big high-ceilinged room empty except for them. The dusting cloth, the vacuum, and mop leaning against the bar.

And here, too, in the Canadian Airlines office, again in the middle of the night, she plays a part, pulling out the flip-chart, pointing to our maps. She now the authority, the subject of her story speaking. And having spoken, come this far in the journey that is her story, that beginning an outpouring, she goes on with: "Another three words," she tells me, "perhaps part, perhaps worse than `the globalization of capital.' Three words floating out of the hallways, the building speaking when I left the Canada side of the Toronto airport, went through customs, going to visit my cousin, Vasanti. Meeting first the harsh gestures of the officials which accompany me on my entrance into the United States, then those three words come out from the walls, the `military-industrial complex.' The reaction of the officials to me: was it my colour? The same response as at work? Those eyes.

"Not yours," she adds. "Those ears waiting for slip-ups. A shady story? Or the fact that I'm a cleaner? Without a `suitable' word to fill in the blank for `occupation?' Almost disintegrating in front of the official. Crying. Explaining how fast we have to go, cleaning. Explaining how I cried for the first two years I was here. But I didn't. Can't cry ever again. Pretend indifference. Stifle the anger. Tuck in the disdain. Walk now in the line-up in a movement across another border."

It's so difficult to keep going, living our lives. Our routines disrupted. The familiar gone. Knowing these forces—economic, military—are impervious to us all, we who are small characters in a story taking place, in Alberta, in a place that they, those officials, have barely even heard of. Maybe they know of Lake Louise, because of the movie with a singing mountie, what was it—*Rose Marie*? Or maybe they've heard of Calgary, now that we've had the Olympics, had the sites televised, placed now in the media geography, briefly, back in 1988.

But the geography, the landscape of our lives, she explained to me—that doesn't exist. We're not reflected, not even present in that media dream. Her geography a continuous journey, she says, almost continually west except for a few movements southeast, then north, she explained, when she left that village in the Gujarat State, she part of the rural migration to the city, the industrial complex of Bombay, because there she could at least make 49 Rs. ($7 Cdn. in 1983) for a day's work, *that* before the strike at the cotton mill. And then another beginning, because of some family savings, all gone now, into another life, at the University of Bombay, a study of her story—her village, her country, the world—through economics. A story which kept her moving, she explained, now to the Western world, not exactly in Columbus' steps, not trying to find the treasures of the East in the movement West, because they're all owned, now, by the West, or at least centrally, that "globalization of capital" taking all the treasure away, where? But for her, in the West, there is just enough treasure to survive, say to the next day, to keep on. Living. Even though her grandfather warned that once she left the soil, that place, India, she could no longer call herself Indian.

And so she found herself, she said, "not Indian anymore." At least not in her grandfather's eyes, moving through immigration, where certainly she seemed to them, East Indian. And did they, like Mackenzie King, think that East Indians are unsuited to this climate when she arrived at the Toronto Airport, and then finally began cleaning airports, and then moving west, one airport to the next: west with a family of friends, a cluster, points of light in the starry, starry night, carrying "home" with them? "Home" now not place, but smell: smells caught in the scent of oil in her hair. "Home" caught in the *pani-puris* she and I go out for, say at the Skylark, a small restaurant in Forest Lawn. And moving finally to the office where we meet. At Canadian Airlines. Two of us, East Indian Canadians.

Immigration, a series of movements that make us, along with the first peoples here, in North America, unplaced. Immigration, a journey across one culture into another, making us cycle back to an other place, an other time. A series of overlays. Overlapping, as if we're seeing double. One place inside another: a pocket of India here in Canada. Separate. Like a lot of us. I go with you later, to your brother-in-law's fabric store—that too in Forest Lawn, beside the Skylark restaurant. Amazed by the vibrant oranges, pinks, yellows of the silks draping over the raised platform of the display, I am surprised when he asks me about the prices in the "Canadian" stores. You say, protesting that this location, here in Calgary, is Canadian. He too, Canadian. Ten years later he can call this place home too. This story, Canadian. Not a pocket, India, within a Canadian landscape. Protected, maybe, or if he likes, two homes, two places, in a cycling between that other place and here when he can: save enough money, the trip. Home. Homes.

And you to Gujarat State. And me, further south, to another village, Mangalore, its sounds, enclosing that fruit that returns me, its smell to childhood and to India. India, now of the memory, the one I can't find when I go back.

And the difficulty, now because you and I are the same but different: mapping now not the journeys, the crews' schedules, but our differences. Even though I look the part, Canadian, people still ask me, "Where are you from? No, really," when I say I'm from Calgary. A trace of foreignness and longing, so we don't feel home in either place. Perpetual motion a cycle, so as to delay the ending, keep us from crashing. Splintering into pieces. "Nothing. Nowhere. That's where I fit," you said. Uncertainly. Uncertainty.

And what I am bound up in: mapping the geography of our lives. Exhausting because the two of us are both lost, strangers to ourselves. I whisper to you, whisper because it's night and I'm afraid someone might hear me. That fear rising up from the stomach keeps me on guard perpetually.

And we,
the night cleaners now
    not only of buildings
    but stories, you explain aren't interested in that
    perversion called "purity," that—
    not clean, but defiling. What they,
    the night cleaners, and now, you and I are doing is
    dreaming of cleaning the nightmares,
    that collective history which is haunting and hurting and killing

    dreaming a new story, a story which puts the world back together again,
    a new order perhaps, call it
    healing.

G. STEVEN GROSSICK • *EDMONTON, ALBERTA*

EVA BREWSTER

Eva Brewster lives in Coutts, a small town on the Alberta-Montana border. As a civic leader, journalist and radio and television personality, Ms Brewster has had an important impact on Alberta society. In recognition of her work, she was named a Ms Chatelaine in 1976, "Woman of the Year" by the YWCA in 1977, and received an Honourary Doctor of Laws Degree from the University of Lethbridge in 1986. Ms Brewster was born in Berlin, Germany, into a "liberal Jewish family whose roots in the Berlin area traced back to the thirteenth century." She attended the Cecilien Lycee in Berlin until 1938 when she was expelled under Nazi racial laws. She was arrested in 1943 and confined to the Nazi concentration camp at Auschwitz until her escape in January, 1945. These war experiences are told in Ms Brewster's 1984 book Vanished in Darkness—An Auschwitz Memoir (NeWest)*, which won an honourary mention in the 1985 Alberta Culture Non-Fiction Award. After the war, Ms Brewster lived in England, Scotland, Nigeria, and Cameroon. She and her family moved to Alberta in 1969. In the 1970s, Ms Brewster promoted sponsorship of Chinese-Vietnamese refugees in southern Alberta. Asked why she felt so strongly about the plight of these "boat people," Ms Brewster explained that her sister once fled Nazi Germany on the* St. Louis*, a ship that no country, including Canada, would permit to land. Most of the Jewish people on that boat were forced to return to Germany, to their deaths. Only her sister's reputation as an Olympic-calibre athlete saved her and allowed her to find refuge in Argentina.*

Culture Shock is Mutual and Good for Us

"TIRED? HUNGRY? HOT? COLD? HAPPY? Homesick?" The answers from the newly arrived Chinese-Vietnamese refugees the day in 1979 my daughter and I met them at the Lethbridge Airport were quizzical smiles accompanied with a "yes" to everything. We took the four young people to a Chinese restaurant so that our Cantonese interpreter could explain a few basic things and ask questions.

One of the first things I told them was that our house in Coutts was almost opposite their new home. If they needed help or just parental advice, they'd only have to cross the street. They bowed deeply over their soup bowls and said, "Thank you, Mother." One added, "But where is our Papa?" So young and childlike were they that it seemed quite natural for me to reply, "Your father is working. You'll meet him later."

Then, at my request, the older girl wrote down their story in an English I found easy to understand although everything was written backwards by our rules of grammar. Their experiences were all the more devastating because she put them down without frills or comments:

> *Vietnam—Songbe—4 June, left on small boat. Sinking 6 June. Saved by USSR ship. Back to Vietnam. Stay one week. 26 June back to boat. Two days after to Malaysia, refused to let us land. Then pulled (out) to sea—drifted to Indonesia, Berakit refugee camp 7 July. 10 August, moved to TivukDalan, then to TanJung Ungget camps. Five brothers still in Thailand camps.*

There were sisters left behind too, the youngest (of the sisters) was still in Vietnam with her mother and grandparents, the others in refugee camps. We've learned since then that "sisterhood" is somewhat loosely defined. The oldest of the Chinese-Vietnamese sisters, for example, was a cousin to the other three. Also, just as they adopted me as their "mother," my daughter became their sister. To this day, they call her and treat her as their sister.

by Eva Brewster

On the way from Lethbridge to Coutts, the English-speaking girl kept pointing at the vast prairie and farm lands, saying over and over, "But there is nothing there! Where are the people?" Months later she heard that their friends, who had been taken to another rural town, had put their heads on their arms and cried when they saw only cows and horses. They associated country life and isolated homesteads with the deportation of vanquished South-Vietnamese city people to "new economic zones."

In Coutts, their sponsors had put the finishing touches on the small house we had rented for the young refugees. The members of our three main churches had coordinated their efforts and provided everything the kids could possibly need. Shown into their new home, they seemed to accept most things with equanimity; but it was interesting to see that the two brothers were immediately and without argument allotted the much larger and better of two bedrooms. The boys were definitely male chauvinists from our point of view, yet kept falling over each other to honour me with the best chair, the best of everything they found in their house.

They instinctively considered it a sin to waste electricity. No sooner did I switch on a light or an appliance, to show them where the switches were, than they switched them off again.

Their questions were endless: "Brush? Floor mop? What is hot water tap? If hot water comes from wall, why boil cold water for tea? Why waste fuel? Will you teach us English? Can we work in air (plane or airport)? In an office? In a supermarket? Can I be a merchant? Can we visit Pincher Creek on Sunday?" (Six of their friends had arrived at the same time and were taken to Pincher Creek.) "Can we have a telephone? Can you phone America? Can you take us to visit to US? What is blanket?"

They never used blankets in Vietnam and went to sleep on top of the beautiful quilts the ladies of the Mormon Church had made for them—to wake up cold and shivering in the morning. They wouldn't turn up their thermostat either. "Too much fuel!"

Cooking with electricity was a mystery to them and they were therefore our guests for meals for a few days. During those meals, I began to wonder who suffered the greater culture shock, the Vietnamese teenagers or their Canadian hosts. Nobody in our village had come across such exquisite politeness. To pull out a chair and help us into our coats came naturally to these young people, as did clearing the table and helping to serve a meal.

We brought an interpreter from Lethbridge to explain the health tests and vaccinations the teenagers needed to have, and to explain the school system and the hours they would share with children in our local elementary and junior high school. The Chinese-Vietnamese students would remain in these lower grades until they spoke and understood enough English to progress to higher education. The interpreter was also needed to introduce them to some of the technology involved in day-to-day living.

But there was nothing we could teach them about good manners. Basking in their veneration of, and trust in, our "wisdom," which they attributed to our age, it soon dawned on parents and grandparents in the community how much our own children could learn from the Vietnamese teenagers.

Just about the whole community got involved in helping the four young Chinese-Vietnamese to adjust and in trying to make them feel at home. We began to realize how little we knew about their lives and culture.

Given how well the refugees fit into the community after a while, it became hard to believe what a struggle there had been over their coming in the first place. Although it would be easy to gloss over it or to omit it from this account, there was a great deal of hate and cruelty expressed when it was first suggested that our community should sponsor Asian refugees. Although I was only one of many who were active in seeking to sponsor "boat people" in the Lethbridge area, I received more than my share of abuse, I suppose because I was a well-known writer, broadcaster, and television commentator at the time. After the refugees arrived, the problems continued for a time.

Because the refugees wouldn't or couldn't give us their exact birth dates, for instance, a particularly nasty letter to the editor of the *Lethbridge Herald* suggested that they were all "inveterate liars, gold-diggers, and probably criminals" in their own country, and that "Mrs Brewster should go back to where she came from and take the unwanted immigrants with her!" The truth was that some Asians were uncertain of their ages since, in the Chinese culture, birthdays are celebrated on New Year's Day, which goes by the moon calendar and changes from year to year. The reluctance of some to specify their birth dates came from their experiences in Vietnam. There, and in some refugee camps, data such as a birth date could be used to identify an individual, to deport the person, or to draft him into the army. It took the refugees a long time to believe that Canada was a free country and that they themselves were free. Nor did they easily accept my word that they would not be beaten up for mistakes or misunderstandings.

Gradually, we got a few details of their recent past. The kids looked at magazines and, for a few months, saw pictures of boat people in overcrowded boats. The girls, who seldom cried, would have tears rolling down their cheeks as they told me about the time Malaysian soldiers pulled their miserable little boat out to sea again after stealing most of what they had. The soldiers had taken everything from earrings to Vietnamese-English dictionaries. They then commanded the younger of the two brothers to pull in the ropes. He didn't understand what they wanted and was cruelly beaten, while his sisters, knives at their throats, were forced to watch. But there were reasons other than fear of a beating for their reluctance to admit what they thought and felt. They would suffer agonies rather than offend us in any way.

So many things were new to them. Because they could tell time on clocks or the inexpensive watches we had given them, it was puzzling to see them either too late for school or much too early for classes or appointments. We eventually discovered that they didn't know that their watches had to be wound once a day. They also didn't realize that when their electric radio and kitchen clocks stopped, they would no longer tell the right time. This happened regularly because they unplugged them for hours "to save fuel." Later, after they had learned to correct these problems, they would still get up at five in the morning to make sure they got to school at nine sharp.

Their teachers said they were a pure joy, so keen were they to learn and so grateful for everything offered to them, whether they understood it or not. After only a few days of English lessons, one of the girls read fluently from some book she had picked up, "Beauty is in the eyes of the beholder." "Hallelujah," gloated one of her sponsors, "she is word-perfect already." "Yes," she said with a shy smile, "I am, but what does it mean?" Refusing payment for cleaning all our windows one weekend, the younger brother wrote laboriously on a small pad, "Dear Mother and Father! I help Mother, no money. But where (what) is `clean'?"

Physical tenderness of the kind we are used to in our culture was foreign to them. They showed us love in a very practical way. To this day, whenever they visit us, they wash and put away even just a few dishes left by the sink before they take time to hang up their coats. Once, to thank the girls for their willing and unsolicited help, I kissed one on the cheek and embarrassed her terribly. But she must have understood my gesture because she folded her hands, bowed, and said gently, "I thank you, my mother!"

The refugees were welcomed with open arms and soon adored by the much younger children in our community school whose classes they joined. Their friendship and care for our own kids, and the love they received in return, must have been humbling to some of the people who had expressed a lot of hate for the Asian immigrants and their sponsors alike. But there were still a few of those who had been against bringing boat people to Alberta refusing to cooperate with our efforts. They continued to use every little problem or misunderstanding we had with the young people as ammunition against sponsorship.

Because there was a recession looming, and particularly because we soon found jobs for the refugees we sponsored, there were accusations that we were taking jobs away from Canadians.

The young immigrants were accused of having come from the ranks of the "educated rich" in Vietnam and, raised in a city, they would "have to be taught how to hold a shovel." But, by now, the unpleasant criticism was coming from outsiders, people not resident in our district. My community surprised me again: the same people who, twenty years earlier, had resented any newcomers whatever the colour of their skin, and had not exactly welcomed my family when we moved down from Edmonton, were now up in arms in defence of the four young refugees.

I will always remember a public meeting we had where the forces for and against the immigrants squared off in an honest debate. Frequent criticisms were that the refugees would bring infectious diseases into the community and that they would exploit our free health care system. At the meeting, the public health nurse met this criticism head on.

"To put your minds at rest," she said, "the four refugees were checked for all infectious diseases on arrival in Canada and again by the Public Health Department in our county, and were pronounced healthy. What's more, never having received free medical treatment in Saigon, the older boy insisted we keep his first pay cheque to recompense the doctor and nurses in our local hospital for tests and medicines after he was treated for a bug he'd caught from us. The refugees pose no threat to public health and, if you don't believe me, go visit them and see for yourself. Young as they are, they keep themselves and their house so clean that they would put many of us to shame."

That night, one after another, people spoke up in defence of the refugees, people I had never known to attend public meetings, and people I had never known to be talkative. One of their teachers got up and said, "The `educated rich in Vietnam?' If you accusers consider nine years of elementary schooling in their war-torn country the acme of education and their grandparents' vegetable stand in a Saigon market `enviable wealth,' you may be right. Their parents even owned a small black-and-white television set, although they were not quite well enough off to have a telephone, an electric cooker, or a clock radio."

Then, a farmer who had employed the younger Vietnamese boy rose to speak. "To the letter-writer's advice that we `must teach the kids how a shovel operates,' we did teach the young man and he learned the art a lot quicker than our own city-born youngsters. Indeed, nobody in this community has ever seen any teenager shovel manure with as much diligence and enjoyment as did that eighteen-year-old refugee. No, he didn't take that lucrative job away from an unemployed Canadian. There were no other applicants."

That night, parents and teacher alike told the assembly how much their school-age children enjoyed, and benefited from, having the refugees as classmates—not just because of their ability to relate to and understand each other (there never seems to be a language barrier between children)—but also because it bolstered the much younger kids' confidence and self-esteem to be able to explain elementary problems in a language the refugees seemed to comprehend.

There was one problem brought up at that public meeting that could not be so simply argued away. It had to do with the role of the older brother in the family and with the amount of work he did compared to the others. At the time, we believed it was a problem and I was given the unenviable task of dealing with it. The older brother, in the absence of the father, had become the self-appointed "head of the family." In Vietnam, this role could only be taken by a male and that male demanded the total subservience of the rest of the family. By this time, the refugees had fairly well-paying work cleaning the school after school hours and looking after the school grounds. The supervisor, who happened to be a woman, complained that she always found the older brother sitting down on the job and delegating his duties to his younger siblings. He wouldn't obey the supervisor's instructions although the other three, she told us, worked very hard and did an excellent job. Yet, on payday, the older brother came to collect all their wages. When questioned, all four insisted that the "Head of the Family" worked hard supervising and inspecting their completed tasks and should never have to take orders from a woman.

I should have acknowledged that the kids were only acting out the culture they had received from their parents, but my own life-long commitment to fighting for women's rights prompted a somewhat angry reaction. After I made it clear to the young man that, in this country, women bosses had the same right to demand respect as did men and that, if he didn't do his share of the job, he would no longer be paid, he did change his ways. However, I don't think he ever forgave me for interfering.

Shortly after this episode, the town opened up a new sub-division and the two boys were employed in the construction of sewer lines where, under a male boss, both worked equally hard and well.

Many years have passed. The refugee teenagers whom we regarded as "kids" then are quite grown up now; some have kids of their own.

By the time they had adjusted to Canadian customs and had learned enough English to stand on their own feet, they had to move on to other centres for more advanced education and for job training our small town could not provide. The older girl had started work for the federal government at the border as an office cleaner and was later posted to Calgary where she graduated from university and college courses as an accountant and computer operator. She still works for the federal government in that capacity, is married, and has a son.

The other three moved to Lethbridge to stay closer to "home." All enrolled in second-language courses and took every job they could get, often working three shifts in different establishments, mostly at jobs in hotels and restaurants, that Canadians don't seem to want.

From the start, they saved and pooled their incomes until, a few years later, they had enough to prove that they could support and sponsor their widowed mother and younger siblings without help from government or private sources.

The youngest of the refugees is also married. All her sponsors, past and present employers, co-workers and friends were invited to and attended her almost fairy-tale wedding. She now has a three-year-old daughter and a baby boy who, like their mother, capture all hearts.

All in all, these one-time boat people, now well-established Albertans and Canadian citizens, have become an asset to our society. They have never been a liability. They have repaid us a hundredfold with their loyalty, friendship, and gratitude for everything we have tried to do for them. I, for one, am proud of their achievements, as I was of my community's efforts to help them get over ordeals they had in getting here, and their initial difficulties of adjusting. They taught my small, closely-knit border town many lessons, not the least of which was that culture shock could be mutual and good for us.

MURU KHAMISI ABDITAM • *EDMONTON, ALBERTA*

CHRISTOPHER WISEMAN

Calgary, Alberta has been home to Christopher Wiseman for over twenty years. He has lived in Calgary longer than he has lived anywhere, including his early homes in the north of England, where he was born. He is the author of six books of poetry, including Missing Persons *(Sono Nis Press, 1989),* Postcards Home: Poems New and Selected *(Sono Nis, 1988), and* An Ocean of Whispers *(Sono Nis, 1982). He is a winner of the Writers Guild of Alberta Poetry Award, and has twice won the Alberta Poetry Prize. His poetry has been broadcast on both the CBC and BBC radio networks. Chris Wiseman has taught at the university level for over thirty years. He is presently Professor of English and Creative Writing at the University of Calgary, where he was founder of the creative writing programme. Mr Wiseman is also a past president of the Writers Guild of Alberta, a past member of the Board of the Alberta Foundation for the Literary Arts, and past president of the Calgary branch of the Humanities Association.*

Every Immigrant is a Pioneer:

A MEDITATION WITH PORTRAITS

IMMIGRANT. THIS NAMING STARTED twenty-three years ago and I haven't been able to change it. Being an immigrant tears a life, a heart, in two. By searching, moving, committing, you must spend your time comparing, always trying to knit two geographies, two histories, two frames of references together. And they don't ever fit exactly. Not the grain of a life. The texture.

There are 15 million refugees on the planet, looking for home in cities like Toronto, Vancouver, Calgary. In planes, in leaky ships, in old cars streaming smoke, clinging to sides and roofs of trains, crossing rivers and deserts, those who need home, a place, shelter, a future, acceptance are a-move. Listen to the voices. One by one they come forward. My name is. And I'm an immigrant. Help me. My children are mocked at school. There is no room in classes to teach me English. I left my parents and grandparents behind. I try to be happy. My house is big and warm. Like a palace. Mountains ring this white world with beauty. It's all for the children. Always. Such hope from so many. Yet such fear from those already here. Listen again. Talk, all the time, of the country's problems. Quebec. The CBC. The train. Rural post offices. Things older Canadians relied on for stability, identity. It hurts to see the dead farms, the Americanization of culture, sport, media, economy.

We all know that no policy, no politician, no simple dollar-throwing, can make people live together mildly, with respect. Even in Alberta, so empty, so full of newcomers. Beautiful beyond belief, this land. Eyes should be scanning the future, bright with hope. Visions of future generations. We have reached an important junction on the map of Canada's history and culture. The wrong roads are inviting. We must avoid them. That sort of exploration has been done. A new sort is much harder. The right road is long and rough. The new clean sheet has margins. But many have made it with pride and sacrifice. Look for a moment at one. Look at King Loo, my neighbour in Calgary for sixteen years. Canadian. Albertan. Immigrant. What roads he traveled.

by Christopher Wiseman

KING LOO'S POEM

Black cars on the white street. Slowly,
slowly out of our life. Passive Chinese
faces. Going to bury the old man in the hard
Alberta ground. All Chinese.

Think of the life. The tearing. Think.
Came here in the 1920s. Worked. Worked.
Finally bought the corner store. Went back
in 1963 for his wife and daughter—1963.
Forty years apart! Just two short visits back.
His wife never left the house here. Not once.
Died in 1970. His daughter spoke no English.
Never tried. Just "Hi." Smiled and bobbed at us
over the fence for 16 years saying "hi."
Walked one step behind him down the street,
always. Her husband in Vancouver. Daughter,
then grandchildren. Working in Vancouver. Always
work, work, work. In the long whiteness
or the rain. Work. His family. Eyes failing
in his last years. Every Christmas he'd be
in our house with boxes of chocolates for the kids.

Other Chinese moved into the street.
His contempt. Gentle old man, cigarette
always dangling from his lips. "New China boys.
Hong Kong China boys. Not real China boys."

Behind him. Always one step. The old man.
The torn life in the whiteness. How he made
Christmas rich. The cars glide away,
one behind the other. Even that day
his store stays open. Work. Work. How could
a man rip his life like that? His great-
grandchildren flourish, real Albertans.
This was a huge life. The black cars.
My neighbour. I go and cry for him.
The heart's grain. The heart's weather.
One step behind.

Faced with such lives, what do we do today? Statistics are irrelevant to hearses. Canada will admit a quarter of a million immigrants each year until 1995. Most from non-European backgrounds. Can we "de-ethnicise," to use the ugly word? Get rid of "hyphenated Canadians?" Should we? What do the newcomers want in this cold white world, torn from their past by hoping? How do we stop them being cold and lonely? Keep hope alive? The jump into newness is a high frightening one. The old life and the new tear each other. I stand in my classroom at the university trying to teach freshmen Jane Austen. A Cambodian student comes to talk to me. *Pride and Prejudice*—hard not to smile at the title in this context. Doesn't follow it, but has looked up all the words in the dictionary. The poetry, as Frost knew, lost in the translation.

No poem for him, for his portrait. He can't, how can he, SEE a coach arriving at an English mansion house in 1800. He can't see the landscape, hear the ironies, the tartnesses, the sharp wit which make Jane Austen what she is. What can I do? I try. But he can never FEEL this book. What book could I use instead? In his essay he writes, "In the 14th. sentry Jane Austen new that men and ladies liked big balls." He has a straight A average in his science and math courses. He works. Works like King Loo did. I must try not to have to fail him. What are his hopes? Memories? Cambodia. The killing fields. White skulls stacked up in huge piles. Is he angry with me? He smiles. I like him. Could I ever know him?

Albertans are tolerant and decent. The handful who aren't are seen to be pathetic—burning crosses, distorting history, calling radio talk-shows, selling lapel-pins. There is fear, yes. But we are not on the road that leads to the Beast. The racists can't read Jane Austen either. They are mean, small people, untouched by love. They don't understand the problems or solutions. My name is. And I'm an immigrant.

"Sexy" and "unsexy" immigrant groups. Brits particularly "unsexy" now. The new Canada has to reject the old colonial power. English-accented Canadians go to elocution classes to lose their accents so they'll be accepted. Others go to BC or Ontario. Some go back to Britain. I swing between past and present. It don't mean a thing if it ain't got that swing? Mid-Atlantic man, accepted fully by neither side. The ache of memory modifying the present. This is turning into my portrait. I'm not allowed in, to be an Albertan. Not fully. A person or writer. White heterosexual male with an English accent these days? Forget it! Stereotype. Colonizer. The word "Canada," they tell me, means "home" or "place of welcome." Imagine a tv commercial on CBC mocking the accents of, say, East Indians or Chinese, making them seem ridiculous and incomprehensible. Or any racial group. No. Not in the new politically correct Canada. But there IS one, mocking the English. Selling tea. It's open season on Brits. Bio-note for a recently published poem of mine: "Wiseman is a native of England and . . . recalls a trip home several years ago." This after twenty-three years. How long must I make my home here before it's my home? It hurts. And how much worse for the non-white, the non-English speaking? For Native Canadians, still immigrants on their own lands? People tell me I'm not a *real* immigrant because I'm English by background. My friends, I *am* a real immigrant. And it's not easy. It hurts in subtle ways and it has affected my life, my writing career. Irony. I'm accepted as an Albertan writer when I read and talk in *British* schools and universities.

I'd be more Canadian if I were allowed to be. Central Canada is far more snobbish about western "red-neck" culture than the Brits. I look at the preserved (for how long?) Lancaster bombers in Calgary and Nanton, and wonder what they mean to 90 per cent of Canadians. The Cambodian student won't find it in his dictionary, yet the Lancaster is a deep part of my childhood, and of many older Canadians' experience. So many exclusions. What is Albertan, Canadian, anyway? Would I be one if I changed my accent? Only wrote about Alberta people and places? I have it easy. The uniformed crazies don't, I think, want to shoot me, or send me back where I came from. And those good folks who order a "white driver please" when calling for a cab don't say "a white driver without an English accent." Look south, not east, I want to shout. Britain won't hurt you any more. My children flourish here. Always the hope. But where do *I* belong? I swing, roots far away, branches here, memory pricking like a thorn. How can I recapture the feeling of the first poem I wrote here, two days after I arrived, which concludes

> impatient
> I unpack my life
> from trunks?

If I changed to suit the anti-Brit, anti-"Eurocentric" bandwagon, I'd be rewriting my own story. I cannot and will not do that. Twenty-three years so far. Longer than Brian Moore or Malcolm Lowry. There are other writers here who aren't known to people. Cut-off writers we never hear about. Joe was a fine writer of classical Chinese poetry before he fled to Calgary. A lawyer. Now he's the janitor at an elementary school, close to retirement, entangled, caught, by his lack of language. The English language. The weight and weather of the heart is not well served by discontinuities.

JOE'S POEM

A caretaker takes care
of children, of teachers, of buildings.
Of language, each evening, just to keep
my hand in. Would they remember me
now, there? I used to write so much
in the old styles, schooled myself,
became a learner, then a teacher.

Long nights here in the white country,
which is good for writing my poems.
Refining them. And if they're just for me
then that's the way it was meant.
I miss the law. I can no longer argue,
read the subtleties. No words. No words.
But I take care of children, of teachers,
of buildings. Each day. The work. The work.
Up and down the halls. The children's
eyes float like white petals on the stream
of my night words. My mind grows,
my broom a rhythmic pen.

His name is Joe. He's an immigrant. May his words shine! And for more than just himself. Alberta is its people—the cliché to end them all. Joe, King Loo, the Cambodian student, the Brit with the funny accent. Harjit Brar, the East Indian who threw her children and then herself into the Bow and became a terrible symbol, to immigrant and non-immigrant alike, her tragedy raising our awareness, cutting complacency like a dull knife. No room here for her poem. Her heart's weather. The handful of skinhead racists in their uniforms. The warm, hospitable ones. Hate. Love. The sort of changes Alberta is experiencing can't happen without pain and fear. But let's look beyond.

So much depends on how we see. And we must look. And, looking, how could anyone not respond to Alberta? Stop by Bow Lake, out of season, alone. Hear the silence. Stare into green glaciers. Drive from Calgary to Edmonton in late September. See the colours, poignant with coming cold, more subtle than any painter's palate. Walk around the Banff Centre and see the artistic talent there. Stop in some small-town café and talk to the old-timers in their checked shirts and baseball hats. Stroll through the magnificent enormity of the Banff Springs Hotel. A meditation with portraits. I can't finish with mere postcards. But stand by Moraine Lake, and see how pathetic human history is when earthed in this place's size. People come and go. Arrive here at airports, bus depots, bewildered or confident; poor, rich; every colour, every background. Come and go. Not many talk of Michelangelo. Not all will be happy, accepted. But where else for them? A world with fifteen million refugees. Take a plane to Europe or Asia. Talk to parents of new immigrants, going home after visiting Alberta for the first time. Listen to them. They're stunned by the place. Proud of their children for coming here to bring and build the future. They are right to be, though they'll never know the immigrant's pain, the loss of roots. People have barely touched the surface of this place. The past is tiny. The future immense. It's frightening. For everyone. We need more courage than we sometimes have. If we are true to the best of the past and open to what might be coming round the next corner, then even shaking, battered, bankrupt, changing Canada, and Alberta, will survive and grow. This huge banquet of land, laid out for all of us, assiduously prepared and tended in the past century, yet still so new, can give massive sustenance. Can be home, and privileged home, to all who want to sit here. Let us not be smaller than we need be. Let us grow to meet mountains.

OTTMAR H. SETZER • *CANMORE, ALBERTA*

SARAH MURPHY

Sarah Murphy was born in New York City. When she was six, her father, a staff writer for The New Yorker, died on assignment in South Africa. Her stepfather, a Native American from the Choctaw nation, a seaman, became a central figure in her life. He gave her an awareness of Native culture and history, of the tragic story of dispossession of Native culture and lands. It was one of the beginnings of a life-long commitment to civil rights and social activism. At the age of fourteen, Ms Murphy joined The Students for a Democratic Society and was active in both the American civil rights and anti-war movements. At twenty-one, she moved to Mexico and, six years later, she moved again, this time to Toronto. In all three countries, she attended university, studying both fine arts and literature. Though Ms Murphy's original training was as a visual artist, her career has shifted increasingly toward writing since she moved to Calgary in 1979. Her short fiction has appeared in journals across Canada. Her first novel, The Measure of Miranda, *was published in 1987 by NeWest Press. This was followed by the short fiction collection* Comic Book Heroine *in 1990, also from NeWest. A second collection of short fiction,* The Deconstruction of Wesley Smithson, *was published by Mercury Press in 1992. Her careers outside literature include teaching Spanish and English as a Second Language, translating and interpreting for the Courts and for Immigration Canada, and serving on the national board of directors of Oxfam Canada.*

Aca Nada:

A REFUGEE'S STORY

*F*OR A LONG TIME I WOULD IMAGINE YOUR *story that way, I can't help it or stop it, how I see you leaning against the doorjamb perfectly framed in the rectangular dark of the door, just as your story was perfectly framed within the pages of your journal, one of those personal response journals English as a Second Language students are always asked to write, and to which we as teachers always respond, sometimes more personally than others, the tears always springing to the eyes for the little horror stories tucked between the recipes and the trips to the Calgary Tower and the first time in Lake Louise. So that yours was no more surprising than many others, though it always is like a bomb going off, the plain simple sentences (you had learned to put in periods by then to discipline the endless commas of Spanish sentence structure) until it was too simple really, but I was hardly going to argue.*

I will never forget the day I came home. I stood in the door. My mother was crying. My father told me that men had come for Cuca and Luis. She was my sister. He was my boyfriend. They were led away. I knew they were dead. That's why I left my country. That's why I'm here.

With those few brief but terrifying sentences right before the cheerful, if sarcastic, story of how Canada got its name. An anecdote a friend who has lived out east assures me is commonly told among the Portuguese community of the Kensington market, so that I still have no idea how widespread it is, though I am sure you must have heard it here, rather than in Guatemala before you came. Because you were not only sure it was a Spanish explorer, but that he was moving up the BC coast,

by Sarah Murphy

not Portuguese at all that man, and surely not moving down the St. Lawrence, as one of his sailors turned toward him, and spoke those words of naming.

Something so much more pleasant to think about than your previous story that I quickly rushed that from my mind, thinking no more of its few words than to register the horror, and the sorrow. And imagining its events resolved, I wrote some brief note with an exclamation point about how brave you must be, to come here and to start again, thinking that you had grieved for them, and ended it, and could now go on, smiling and content, settled and working, building yourself a new life. Probably exactly what you had expected me to believe, the way you had expected the immigration officials to believe the same, when you spoke the story to them, honed and polished, the one for public consumption, that claimed your status as a refugee.

So that I never imagined how the words spoken to that Spanish explorer could have any more significance for you than they did for me, another good joke on the emptiness of the frozen north, how they might have echoed in your mind. Even then, as you persuaded those officials you were just the person they most wanted you to be, you must have felt so much like him, or like the sailor who turned to him, except that you did not imagine you had anyone to turn to, not really, not even to us. As your mind would replay his words again and again, hearing them in your language, as you looked out the windows of the Tower, or across the park behind the school at the skaters, or down from Sulphur Mountain into the scarcely inhabited bush. The sailor speaking, Spanish or Portuguese, it wouldn't matter which. After all, he could have just as easily been Portuguese on a Spanish ship, or the other way around, and they would certainly understand each other, that captain and his underling, as they would look out at the endless trees, and turning, the sailor would look hard at his captain.

Ca Nada, he would say, in Portuguese, or maybe it was *Aca Nada*, spoken in rapid Spanish, the first syllable not so terribly important, almost swallowed, as he would repeat it again. "Here, nothing," "Nothing here," the *CaNada* that all those Hispanic immigrants giggle about, quite sure it is the secret of the country's name: here nothing, nothing here, *Ca Nada*, *Aca Nada*.

The same CaNada you had held out as a promise to yourself for the longest time, looking at pictures in travel brochures or books, after all it had been so hard to listen to the details of their disappearance. The ones that never appeared in your journal, but that your father would tell you again and again, from the moment you had moved out of the doorway and were doubled over in the living room, or later when you would bring him his drink or hold his hand. How their thumbs were wired behind them as neighbours and family stood by helplessly, looking upon the work of "*hombres vestidos de civil*," "men dressed as civilians," the typical phrase, because everyone would always know that civilian dress was a costume for those men, and that it did not become them.

With your plans for coming to Canada arising only later when you could not stand it anymore, the stillness of that tableau, as the grief would not let up, and more than the grief: your helplessness. That you must think each night of them dying, dying now, dying before, dying this instant, dying terribly, and know there was nothing you could do, nothing at all. To help them or to assuage your mother's pain as she swayed back and forth in her chair in the kitchen, repeating: *M'hijita, m'hijita*, what did she ever do, my daughter my daughter, as she would reach out her hand as if wiping the tears from the face of a child not yet turned three: *m'hijita, m'hijita*, my daughter, my little daughter, over and over, what did she ever do, what did she do, she only talked, she never did do anyone harm, not ever, not anyone.

While your father would sit in the living room, sometimes with that drink you brought, sometimes empty-handed, but always with one hand splayed out on the chair in the living room where the old tv was. I'm sure you said that he would sit in front of the tv, talking as if they were still there, then closing his eyes to repeat his own monologue: I told them, I told them, I kept telling them, it's not worth it, I said, they're too strong, the military's too strong, you may all think it's a game down at the University I said, but it's not I said, a lot of stupid young people like you have already died I said, you may not think it means anything to do what you're doing, you may think it's all right to read those books you read and admire the guerrillas, but it's dangerous, dangerous, you have no idea how dangerous this is.

And then he would get up, and call one friend or another, someone who knew someone somewhere, your oldest brother who worked in the Economics Ministry, a cousin with the army, but the answer was always the same: that there was nothing to be done, nothing at all. No one knew anything. Except to leave it. They were dead. You all must accept that they were dead. Your father and mother, and for that matter Luis' parents, should take pride in the family they had left to them.

And protect them better.

As your father would put down the receiver, and then repeat it all again, not the pride he had once felt at how smart Cuca was, and how brave, what a wonderful *novio* you had picked. Back then, he had liked how they could talk with him, a man who could repeat almost the entire history of Guatemala, hour after hour, from the burning of the Maya codices to the coup of '54, sharing the opinions he had not dared voice since. Because he had fallen into silence from the moment the Americans, the Americans and the *Unay*, he would still call it, the United Fruit Company, had toppled Jacobo Arbenz, the great reformer. While Luis and Cuca would laugh and agree, and tell him how it would be different this time, this time there would be a real revolution. Real change. Real agrarian reform. The popular movements would see to that.

Only what he had found instead was further silence. With only enough voice left for a terrible self-blame: I never should have talked to them, I never should have led them on, I'm the one who should have known, I've been through it, I knew where it was going, I'm the one the soldiers should have taken it's all my fault for opening my big mouth, Oh God, oh God, and for a moment he would sound like your mother, choruses of oh God, oh God, *Dios Mio, Dios Mio*, combining with the *m'hijita, m'hijita* coming from the other room. Until that was all he would say: *Dios Mio Dios Mio*, it was my fault, mine.

While you would just look from one to the other, not at all sure whose part to take, whether to scream and cry at the unfairness of it, or to blame yourself. After all, you had believed them even less than your father had, you had just smiled at Cuca and Luis and made the food, nodding every once in a while as you patted out the tortillas, even if you never quite believed anything they ever said, all their *patria o muerte*, "homeland or death," their *Venceremos*, "we shall overcome," repeated from one to another, or painted onto walls, chanted in demonstrations, their hands raised in the V, while you just shook your head and loved the enthusiasm in them, the belief in themselves, the belief in the future, the wonderful subtle intelligence you thought you would never have, but that made you help them a little sometimes, typing things they wanted typed. Even if it meant little more to you than it did at work, except for the sense of danger in it, that even then gave you nightmares or made you cry out to them: you must be careful, oh so careful, while they would just smile in answer and talk about bravery and sacrifice, and even the martyrs of the revolution. Until the nightmares came true and it was just that terrible grief and to work and back, actions repeated with even less meaning, without enthusiasm or belief, even if it was their belief not yours, tortillas made now without flavour or joy, calculations done without dedication or reward, even your pay cheque, a large part of it destined once to be put aside for your imagined home with Luis, saved now without meaning or future. But all of these, all of these, just different ways to make time pass.

Just the way the encounters with new suitors that were thrown onto your work schedule, your boss leaning over your desk, or an old friend from high school calling you up, colleagues or men who worked in the same building looking you over, your older brother trying to fix you up with men from the Economics Ministry, seemed much the same. Because you always did attract them through your unusual looks and your radiant smile, a quietness that even among the other English students could easily and often make you the centre of attention. With your straight copper hair, the same colour as your copper skin and copper eyes, one of a piece you sometimes describe yourself, picking out clothes of the same colour, subtle oranges and earths, your high cheekbones and the richness of your skin tone the only clue to the Amerindian ancestry most Guatemalans in some proportion share, and that many, at least those of your class, and urban background, curse. The way your suitors might, talking of programs to *mejorar la raza*, "better the race," the way they do in Bolivia, blaming Guatemalan poverty and lack of industrial development on some sort of missing entrepreneurial gene rather than on centuries of exploitation near slavery. Though your father had taught you not to do that, he admired the Maya civilization, one of the greatest in the world he would say, and if the Native people occupied that pinnacle no longer, well, they hadn't fallen, they'd been pushed, a slightly patronizing attitude perhaps, but one that taught love for both sides of the *mestizo* mix that formed you—even if you would consider yourself a typical urban Guatemalan, hardly Indian at all. While for us, through the prism of white Canada's racial stereotypes, we might decide that your silence was an Indian silence, a warm southern small delicate Indian silence. Instead of a very personal inscrutability built of the quiet resolution you tried to project, and the terror and pain and numb emptiness you so successfully hid for the longest time, even from yourself.

So that it's easy to understand how, as you would turn away from the typewriter, and look up, one of your co-workers would be there. Or maybe your boss. And he would say: what is a beautiful young woman like you doing without a boyfriend? And the knot of pain would come back, and rise up to the base of your neck, to your throat, and you would try to pull it out and wave it away, with a hand moving from your throat to out beside your face in an idle gesture. As you would smile to protect yourself from the tears so near to rising into your eyes, as they always would, at even the whisper of that very simple word, boyfriend, even as you accepted the invitation that always came next. Because you should, you knew you should, get out more, if for no other reason than to please your mother, who, behind her crying, still wished for one of her daughters to make a good match.

And besides, you could hardly say: I don't have a boyfriend because the last one disappeared after going on student protests with the rest of the people in the Law School. And my sister too. Those were the unmentionable facts of a life designed precisely to pretend that nothing ever happened, just as the newspapers did. Which means you would find yourself instead out for an ice cream in some American-style restaurant, and taking in a movie. Surrounded by people just like you, men in suits and youngish women in skirts and blouses, all American- or European-made, or made in Guatemala to look like those American- or European-made, with maybe a couple of those wool suits with the piping Guatemala City is famous for throwing in, and all of them making the same idle conversation as you, the women speaking in their high sing-song middle class Guatemala City accents of where they had gotten their clothes or who had gotten them for them on a buying trip to the States, while the men would speak of their jobs and their prospects. As you would all the time look around and wonder, always wonder, how many of them carried the same secret wound as you, how many of those secret wounds there were, and how those people felt, really felt, about it all.

Not just the predictable opinions about the communists stirring up the poor and the students and worst of all the Indians, all those too stupid or too young or too uneducated to know better, the ones who didn't have the judgment to figure out what the rebels' agenda really was, the old argument about outside agitators, from Mississippi to Kahnawake to Soweto to the Sierra Quiche, our Natives or our niggers just wouldn't do that if someone wasn't putting them up to it, with the slaughter of those same people then becoming a kind of suicide through stupidity as far as the comfortable are concerned, while the refusal to kill on the part of the forces of order is seen as a noble restraint. As you would just want to scream: but what do you really think, how do you feel, have you seen any bodies, what about the disappeared you know about the disappeared my sister my boyfriend they disappeared you know what happens to the disappeared they tortured my sister until she died I know they did do you think my boyfriend is one of those headless bodies by the side of the road where there are human parts floating in the river?

As instead you would look away. Or smile. As you would watch how the light brown ladyfinger leaning on your ice cream dish had grown a fingernail and a knuckle joint and was turned to flesh, while that gouged out eye floated up through the whipped cream on your sundae, and you would want to scream again, wondering how many of them had ever seen anything like that, had experienced anything like what you had experienced, if there was a secret code to unite you, if you could only figure out its signals, because you were starting to see the wounds everywhere. In open gashes on people's faces, bullet wounds in their new wool suits, screams of pain in their parrot-like chatter. Until you just couldn't stand it anymore, and you started, without telling anyone, to make your plans. To get your future back.

Not on a buying trip to the States, or the requisite upper middle class family trip to Disneyland, but that other one. The permanent wetback adventure that was mentioned often enough since every family seemed to have at least one wetback cousin and maybe even one who had gotten legalized, and either way sending money home. So that you learned quickly enough that any number of travel agencies would arrange it, a kind of long distance rent-a-coyote, all the details taken care of for you from the first legal plane ride into Mexico, to the overcrowded van or false-bottom pickup to take you across the American desert to past the US Immigration check-stop five miles in. And always then the bus depots, and the bathrooms, and the restaurants, and the second-class hotels with their cockroaches, and a final destination in California, as far as the agency would take you.

No one was going as far as the Canada you had settled on from the beginning. So that after California you had to figure it out yourself, who knows how you had settled on Alberta but you had, maybe it was the pictures of the mountains, or even of the Stampede, or just that it seemed the easiest border crossing. Into a land you had long ago learned was cleaner and more peaceful than the States, you could see that just from the pictures, and then all your friends who had met its representatives in Guatemala's tourist spots always spoke of Canadians as kinder and more low-key, their bright maple leaves and mostly European features, advertising, whether they spoke English or French never seemed to matter, that they were Yankees without the Imperialism.

Something Cuca or Luis might have giggled about, to make you feel that at least you were not betraying their ideals, running off to Uncle Sam. So that your mind started to hum that tune in all those restaurants as you would listen to the tales of *"el norte,"* and in the government offices as you would deal with getting the necessary papers, *a Canada, a Canada,* the chorus went in your mind, until the bus wheels picked it up, *a Canada, a Canada*. "To Canada" they sang, as you sat and looked out the window, and you put your story together in your mind, you knew by then that refugee status was much easier to attain up here, with the Canadian government actually believing that something terribly repressive and wrong was going on in Guatemala and El Salvador, which meant that all you would have to do was prove that part of that repression had befallen you, to tell your story well, to make them believe what was so obviously true: that there was a great deal for you to flee from. That any one part of your story—the disappearance of your boyfriend and your sister, your father who had once favoured the regime that had ended in the coup, much less than your leaving and then being sent back on a cloudy day when the colonel in charge of the nearest garrison had a headache—any one of those reasons could have brought down the full weight of the repressive apparatus. Onto your head.

So that your story was easy to get into its proper proportions, you wrote it in Spanish the first time, then organized it with a lawyer, planning out exactly how to express it. Only you didn't plan on what would happen next, when they asked you that question you had been told to expect, the formal opening of a refugee hearing, when they informed you of the nature of refugee status according to the UN convention on refugees, asking if you felt you had a well-founded fear of persecution for reasons of race, nationality, religion, social group, or political opinion. Well as you knew the answer you found you wanted to laugh. To giggle hysterically or to shout, to tell them you had no such fear. What you feared wasn't the military, it wasn't death, it was people who were mortally wounded who didn't know it, streets that ran with blood that nobody could see, prisoners who screamed in an agony nobody could hear, rotting flesh that nobody could smell, missing body parts nobody could feel. No. No. No. You weren't afraid of the military, you weren't afraid of the death squads, you weren't afraid of anything. After all, how could they hurt you any more than they already had? Taking away Cuca and Luis?

And maybe then, as instead you smoothed your skirt and smiled, just the way you had at your suitors in the restaurants, maybe then, you knew it wasn't over. Maybe you even heard that chorus, *A Canada, A Canada* turning to *Ca Nada, Aca Nada* in your mind. Just one change in syllabic stress, moving from the second syllable in the phrase to the third, one small mental slip, and you had gone from "to Canada, to Canada," to "here nothing, nothing here." Nothing for you here. Nothing you could feel. Neither homeland nor death, but a frozen waiting. Even as you said so very forcefully exactly what you came to that hearing to say. I have come here for peace, you said. For peace and for freedom. Freedom from persecution. I know I will find it.

Only you hadn't. And as for the syllables in that small chorus, they must have gotten so much louder that day as the bus carried you toward my class. The morning after you had learned exactly how much could still be done to you. How much remained to you, that could still be taken away. How much you must still fear persecution, the persecution of that dreadful, hidden, enlarging wound: the wound of your country. Even as you walked into my class, and there I was chirruping like a little chickadee, a Monday morning, as I introduced the new members of the class (we had just done a new intake) to those I already knew.

Because those introductions are always a wonderful opportunity to teach polite questions if you're at an intermediate level, speaking of how you never ask a question you think might embarrass the person you are speaking with, and how we even answer the question: How are you? with: I'm fine. Whether we're fine or sick or suicidal, just not to have to explain ourselves, or bore our audience. Because that's the cultural bottom line: never ask a question if you think the answer will be something you just don't want to know, or to deal with. And never give more information than you think the questioner really wants.

And then there's how you always introduce yourself first, giving your name before you ask for the other person's, people feel safer when you are willing to tell about yourself instead of just asking about them—after all, if you just go up to someone and start asking questions, what's your name, and where are you from, and how long have you been here and what do you do and what are you doing, every ESL teacher's favourites to teach tense as well as content, then the person is bound to think you're with the secret police. A line that always gets subdued giggles from around the room.

Only by then I was up to the question about your immediate family. How many people are there in your immediate family? The most neutral question I've ever come up with to ask for family information, you can't just go up to someone on a park bench and ask: are you married? or even: how many children do you have? So that I go over how *immediate*, in this case, will usually refer to the people who live under the same roof with you, and may include your grandparents, though never your cousins or your in-laws. And turning to you, as you moved in from the door, unusually late but I hardly noticed, you were such a good person to ask this question of, I was sure I was safe because I already had the answer, there could be no cross-cultural faux pas here, as I said: well, Marta, how many people are there in your immediate family?

And you answered: eight.

Then thinking I had a perfect example, to show what we might mean by immediate, and thinking you had made a mistake, that perhaps you had forgotten your grandfather, I said: why, Marta, I thought you told me there were nine.

And you burst into tears.

At the same time as you met my eyes. To silence me, I think. The way the perfection of your story had always silenced us all. To stop me from even moving. From going on. From doing anything at all until you could speak.

They called me, you said. They called me. From Guatemala City. Last week I had three brothers. This week I have two. They took away one of my brothers this week. My sister disappeared before I came here. And my boyfriend too. Maybe they will take away my whole family. One by one. Soon, teacher, soon. Maybe when you ask again. I will have no immediate family at all.

Because I am sure my sister and my boyfriend are dead. Soon my brother will be dead too.

And you looked at me. The way you must have looked at the immigration officials as they took your testimony. From so far away. Holding them at a distance with your eyes. Only this was too immediate, and I was flustered by my mistake, and before I knew it, or thought about it, whether it was a good idea, culturally or pedagogically correct, I had rushed forward.

And short-circuited everything by taking your hand.

Oh Martita, I said: don't say that. Maybe, just maybe, it's not true. And then I told you that sometimes, in these cases, at least my friends told me that, the people I knew who worked with Amnesty, or with the Red Cross, said that international protest would sometimes help, that sometimes it got people returned, if not unharmed, at least alive.

And then I told you how sorry I was. And turned to the rest of the class, some of whom were refugees too, and asked them what they thought you could do. With the rest of the time spent on that. Figuring out who to call, and making the first calls. That would later spread to become calls to MPs and to Immigration and to churches, with telegrams and calls to Guatemala City, until two weeks later your brother was returned.

And there was a party in the class, and we giggled over my mistake. And someone suggested that sometimes, making a mistake was not the worst thing you could do. Even as I said that it is very important, when you get information you are not prepared for, to recognize that you are responsible for asking, and for what asking then asks you to do. Though I did not go on to say, because I did not know it yet, that the small gesture I made—I still do not know why, if I thought we really could do something, or just that it would keep you busy—had shown you the beginning of a new community, an *Aca* that was not *Nada*, that did not consign you to living and reliving the past, but in which you could go on and build a new homeland. Just as you told the immigration officials you intended, but one from which you could witness your past and thereby build your future, working so that what happened to Cuca and Luis and to your brother, one day will never happen again.

Work that you still do. Because that small beginning mobilized you. To do what all of us said, even after we saw your brother returned, could not be done. To sponsor all of your family, and not your immediate family of nine either, but your extended family of twenty-five, into Canada, as refugees. So that I got to hear your father tell his stories of the ancient Maya astronomy and of the coup. While your mother still spoke of your sister, but only of how beautiful she was, almost as beautiful as you, as she showed me pictures of the picnics you used to organize, with you smiling, between Cuca and Luis. While I smiled too. And I listened. And I held the hands offered me, and tried not to be too afraid of my awkward questions, whether they were culturally, or pedagogically, correct.

And then when it was over, you went back to the same work. Not for your family now. But for others. And not just bringing refugees here, but working with them, and for human rights, in Guatemala. So that I see you at meetings sometimes still. After all, you started me into a more serious consideration of the issues my students face, and I watch as you enter the room. For that brief moment when you stop in the door, and lean briefly against it, when you must remember it all. But I see also now, not how your eyes then stop and go blank, and your gaze flees quickly out the window, or down toward where your hands twist your skirt, but how your head then raises up, and your eyes look out over the room, alighting briefly on each face. And you smile. At the faces of your Canada. Much more than nothing, after all.

In tribute to Hilda, in memory of Luis

SHENAZ JIWA • *EDMONTON, ALBERTA*

RUDY WIEBE

Rudy Wiebe was born into a Mennonite community in northern Saskatchewan. From 1947 to 1953, his junior and senior high school years, he lived in Coaldale, Alberta. An educator and leader in the Mennonite community in Coaldale urged Mr Wiebe to go to university. He did so and it was during these years of study that he chose the writing of fiction as his principal career. His first novel was Peace Shall Destroy Many *(McClelland and Stewart, 1962). Of the many novels that have followed perhaps the best known is* The Temptations of Big Bear *(McClelland and Stewart, 1973), a fictional account of the life of the Cree Chief Big Bear which won the Governor General's Award. His latest book is* Playing Dead, A Contemplation Concerning the Arctic *(NeWest, 1989). For many years, Mr Wiebe taught creative writing and English at the University of Alberta. He is a past chairman of The Writers' Union of Canada and a past president of the Writers Guild of Alberta.*

The Beautiful Sewers of Paris, Alberta

The sewer is the conscience of the city. All things converge into it and are confronted with one another. In this lurid place there is darkness, but there are not secrets.

—Victor Hugo, *Les Misérables*, 1862

One August day in 1952, a few weeks before I entered my last year of high school, I bought Victor Hugo's massive novel Les Misérables. *The English edition, 1222 pages long and published in 1931 by The Modern Library of the World's Best Books, the Giant Series, translated by Charles E. Wilbour. That same summer I worked on the construction crew that was laying the first water and sewer mains under the streets of Coaldale, Alberta. I was seventeen.*

Coaldale, population 800, had no bookstore. Neither did nearby Lethbridge (population 22 000), but some time earlier I had discovered that the stationary store on Seventh Street South in Lethbridge did offer a back corner with a few "world classics"—none of which had been written in Canada, of course. In December 1951, I had bought my first book there—*The Pickwick Papers* by Charles Dickens—and I spent all of Christmas Day (except the compulsory morning church service) lying on the living room couch laughing myself into fits until my mother, whose gift to me the book was, decided she had made a mistake in letting me choose it. She had had no choice: I wanted a book and she could not read English, but to waste an entire serious holiday laughing? Fortunately I was a fast reader, though enjoyment and coughing fits slowed me down on this one.

by Rudy Wiebe

But *Les Misérables* is no novel of laughter and forgetting, not even in a brilliant, windy southern Alberta summer Sunday of the early fifties. Nor can the present world-touring musical version of the story make it that. As Hugo states in his 1862 preface, the book deals with "the degradation of man by poverty, the ruin of woman by starvation, and the dwarfing of childhood by physical and spiritual night."

Now the fact is that most modern Canadians like myself are immeasurably fortunate; not one of those conditions has ever really applied to us. Nevertheless, in July 1991, when I walk along the beautiful streets of Coaldale, I remember the deep trenches that piled up the earth here in pyramidal rows thirty-nine years ago, the sewers that surely still lie where I helped place them. And I also think of the hero of *Les Misérables*, Jean Valjean, carrying his unconscious enemy with such ineffable honour through the immense, leviathan sewers of 1830 Paris.

To descend into the sewer is to enter the grave.

Anyone in their right mind knows that no prairie town is a Paris, France. Such knowledge is particularly obvious to those who year after year live in such a town. The main irrigation ditch which still marks the southern boundary of Coaldale, the ditch which then watered all the gardens and small strawberry patches and corn and beanfields, which filled every cistern (or the common open reservoir where you could go, like Cosette, with a pail), filled each cistern under and beside every tiny wooden house through an intricate web of overgrown ditches supposedly kept clear of weeds and wading, widdling children by the one hired town worker who was all at the same time constable, volunteer fire chief, dogcatcher, wooden sidewalk repairman, and waterman—that ditch of reversed tributaries was certainly no Seine River.

The glazed clay or much larger concrete sewer pipes which the workers of Bennett and White Ltd., Edmonton, nested in sand, fitted together and buried beneath the streets in 1952 under contract with Mayor Russell Davis and the Coaldale Town Council, were nothing at all like the legendary architectured Paris sewers begun sometime in the Middle Ages which became both a grave and an asylum for crime, intelligence, social protest, liberty of conscience, and every conceivable human debauchery, day and night. I know that most of the Coaldale sewers were too small even for a child to crawl into; not a single one was (then) large enough for a big man to walk in erect, leave alone carry another draped over his shoulder.

And I, at seventeen, was certainly no Bruneseau, who in 1805 would be the one man in all of Napoleon's empire brave enough to enter the Paris sewers, and then spend seven years expanding their network. In fact, though I was hired on the first day of the project, in less than two months, before it was completed, I was fired.

Like everyone else Bennett and White hired in Coaldale, I was a labourer—a "grunt." Our work was mostly lifting and carrying things, digging them up or burying them in the places designated by the foreman and various bosses, who all came from somewhere else. A nice brainless business, being a grunt: you just do everything anyone orders because you're right down there with the sewer pipe, as low as you'll get without more digging. I, however, was a shade less grunty than most; for some reason (because I could read and write? I cannot remember having to demonstrate that ability to anyone) on the very first day the project engineer pointed at me and the foreman said:

"You, go with him."

So there I was, frequently without a shovel, riding about town in the engineer's brown Model A Ford—a curiosity even then—the "rod and chain" man. While my fellow grunts heaved sand and gravel and cement into the grinding maw of a mixer, or backfilled around pipe deep in the trench, or muscled clay joints and concrete manhole sections off the trucks, I held a graduated stick motionless, or anchored what I at first supposed was an endless measuring tape—"Hold it right there, don't move it!"—but soon discovered was a "chain." A steel chain certainly but nothing at all like the one riveted around Jean Valjean's neck to march him to the prison galleys of Toulon.

If my life were a massive romance like *Les Misérables*, where everyone (especially the villains) always and continuously returns until all are either dead or married, I would by now have met that engineer again: perhaps five years older than I, a third year Civil Engineering student at the University of Alberta on his summer job, his blond, tough and compact body shorter than mine, his slightly lopsided grin with a tooth missing on the right side. But I cannot remember his name, nor will he remember the gangly kid he left to lounge in the shade of his Model A while the other grunts sweated and gasped in the burning sun and he argued with the foreman.

I didn't lounge often, for within two days I had learned a grunt's basic survival rules: 1) *never* sit down; 2) *never* stand with your hands in your pockets. But often the engineer did not need me and then I worked with the rest; that was when the others, who were never told to sit in the Model A, got their small revenges on me: the heavy ends of the pipes, the extra shovelling where there was room for only one to work, the deepest mud after a rain where the huge planks supporting the trench walls oozed, bulged ominously between their horizontal braces.

> *He was wading in the hideous muck of the city . . . All dripping with slime, his soul filled with a strange light.*

The best trench workers quickly proved to be the older immigrant men who had somehow survived the war and had managed, with what was left of their families, to get into Canada. Those who were refugees—Displaced Persons, or DPs as they were called derisively, or "schmoes" after the sub-human critters in the very popular Li'l Abner comic strip—worked at anything without question. Their lack of English saved them from the precise details of racism, but it certainly did not save them from its pervasive, abusive tone.

The racism bothered me; mostly, to be honest about it now, for myself. After all, though born in Canada, I was of refugee parents myself; at home we had never spoken anything but an obscure German dialect, a language I used to explain the foreman's peremptory orders to my fellow Mennonite labourers. But tired muscles and common sweat soon push such attitudes in a workgang aside: work hard enough together and you get to deride a man not for his race but for his evasions, his laziness. It seems to me now, thinking back to 1952, that male concepts about women are much harder to change than concepts about race.

O, the summer girls walking by with their brief blouses knotted under their breasts, their white shorts, their arms and legs week by week turning a deeper, more limpid golden brown under that libidinous sun.

Psychologists inform us that boys of fifteen to seventeen may well be the most sex-dominated creatures on Earth. If I was that, I wanted to keep it strictly private. My horniness—I could not, then, have expressed it that way—was a burden I carried in absolute silence, an ogre to be wrestled with, and occasionally indulged somehow, loathed or loved, and fought with again, fought into and through guilt and then inevitably back into guilt again with remorse and inner rage.

Given that, to hear such tangled privacies brayed about the streets by the other young grunts in our workgang every time a beautiful girl—they were *all* beautiful, always!—became visible, embarrassed and humiliated me. Wolf whistles, cries of "Hubba Hubba!" howls, obscene offers, brutal and violent gestures: the older immigrant men worked on, oblivious. After surviving both Stalin and Hitler, they must have found these endlessly repeated performances merely childish, banal. But I listened, I couldn't stop myself, though I mostly pretended to ignore them, as I tried to ignore the bragging about weekend conquests. And so I came to prefer the depths of the trench. From below, at least they sounded indistinct, merely animals yowling.

The young engineer spoke very little; he never said a word when a woman passed us. Sometimes he would smile, but he kept on working. One of his main jobs was to make certain the sewer was laid absolutely on gradient, and that's where his arguments with the foreman started. Time and again, to prove his point about the violation of benchmarks he had set, I'd have to slide down into the cool, sweet earth and work my extended measuring rod, as directed, from one joint to another along those interlaced pipes. And then he'd be expostulating again:

"You put in a `little bump,' like you say, when you lay the pipe and you cut capacity—look, almost a third!"

Diagrams, formulas, circled numbers racing left-handed across his spiral notebook from that ever-sharp, precise draftsman's pen.

A sewer is a cynic. It tells all.

The longest, biggest line cut down Main Street, which was also Alberta Number 3 Highway between Medicine Hat and Lethbridge—just recently paved, of course, so we really sliced it up, wide and mountainous along the north side and a smaller branch at right angles into every house or business. After carving up the residential streets with feeder lines, we had begun very deep (eighteen feet?) on east Main, and as August lengthened and the huge trencher steadily chewed us up toward the town hotel near the western end of the business section, the arguments got louder.

"You do that, you've got to lay twice the diameter! It's supposed to handle *all* this town's shit!"

Throughout the summer I had wondered how whoever-it-was had decided on the various pipe sizes anyway. Had they interviewed every homeowner and business about length of residence and then gone into each outhouse and measured it for hole capacity and percentage filled?

"Besides all the other crap that always gets shoved down sewers," the engineer muttered grimly to me, who could have no opinion but at dislocated moments might provide an ear. Shit, apparently, was the least of it.

Why in this sewer summer of 1952 (at 82 cents an hour it was the most I'd ever earned) did I begin with Hugo rather than with any of the other Modern Library Giants ($2.95 each)—Cervantes, Dos Passos, Pushkin, Joyce, Tolstoy—I bought later? Perhaps because of its giant intestine, the "cloaca" which, as Hugo explains, "has been the disease of Paris" throughout history. In Part Five of *Les Misérables* he describes it for fifteen pages, and then devotes another twenty-three pages to getting Jean Valjean, with Marius on his shoulder, out of it. Well, why?

Perhaps, to be blunt about it, I was wondering how one dealt with shit. Clearly the world, including me, was full of it, and here on the apparently open prairie there were neither enough bushes nor even spaces—as it seemed to me there had always been in homestead Saskatchewan where I lived the first twelve years of my life—for it to be voided properly unseen, and thereafter to be permitted the privacy of its individual disintegration. In sunny southern Alberta it seemed necessary to rip up the landscape and yell about it in the streets.

Holding this great novel in my hand, in 1991, I am suddenly certain that I bought it originally because of the sewer. For I had read the story much earlier, in Saskatchewan when I was twelve: a simplified version by Solomon Cleaver that, from somewhere, contained a few pictures. In that one-room Speedwell School I am reading *Jean Val Jean*, leaning against the warm galvanized guard of the heater which is two gas barrels welded together; on the temporary stage across one end of the room five girls are practising "Good King Wenceslas" for the Christmas concert. The black and white picture, when I turn the page, is captioned: "Jean carries the wounded Marius to safety through the filthy sewers of Paris." Jean is a lank-haired old man, face contorted, over his waist in what seems to be molten lead. Behind him the gleaming maw of the sewer twists away into darkness.

"Carried to safety." When I go to find *Jean Val Jean* in the university library, I discover it in the Canadian Literature section. It seems Solomon Cleaver was "a young minister in Winnipeg [who] decided to tell the story in his own words . . . he repeated it more than 800 times to over 100 000 people, and was obliged to reject one invitation in every four which crowded upon him." So, the Publishers' Foreword continues, he was "prevailed upon to have it published:" first in 1935 and then, after ten reprintings, Clarke Irwin of Toronto brought it out as a true *Canadian Classic.*

And the pictures: fourteen in all from an early thirties French movie. Cosette leaning over a dying Jean looks like Greta Garbo in golden ringlets.

And the sewer? Surely every young lover deserves to be carried from the fallen barricades of His Revolution to safety through a filthy sewer.

How could Solomon Cleaver squeeze Victor Hugo's gigantic story onto 119 small pages? Jean Valjean's passage through the sewers shrinks from 39 pages to 627 words; the final two chapters become a verse from a Scottish Covenanters' hymn. How truly classic Canadian.

Well, Paris, France is a place, but Coaldale, Alberta is most certainly a place also. In late August 1952, the trench had reached the western end of town, and my fellow grunt and I were hand-tunnelling a small branch of it under the sidewalk in front of the hotel, directly beneath the "Ladies and Escorts" sign. We took turns, one lying on his back, loosening and pulling back a short spadeful of earth while the other used a long-handled shovel to throw it up onto street level. At the moment of crisis I could see at my feet only his head, sprinkled with red clay and talking, talking Low German as he had all afternoon, me intense with listening.

"Holy ssshit, you buggersh! How'll we ever get this fuckin' job done at that speed!"

The foreman, his bulging red face tilted down at us, maybe about to topple in, but I am somewhere far away, in 1944 watching refugees push their carts through the frozen mud of Stalin's oppression, surrounded by the German army's disastrous retreat across the endless, devastating vistas of the Ukrainian steppes.

"Shit yourself," I yelled up. "You workin' so hard in the hotel every day, gettin' drunk!"

After that we had nothing to do but drop our shovels right there, get out of that ditch and hoof it to the office portable and pick up our last cheque. The foreman drove his pickup there to tell the bookkeeper, but he sure as hell wasn't givin' no smartass bastards a lift. So we walked east the length of Main Street all cut up with bumpy trenches, and I felt very stupid because my big mouth had gotten Pete fired. He just laughed; he was two years older than I, but his father had vanished long ago in Stalin's Siberia and he and his mother and younger siblings were true refugees, working at anything to make a living. He laughed and said school started in a week anyway; he was going to school and learn to be a good Canadian. Like me.

A prairie town, uniquely its own place in the dazzling summer sun. Spread across the wide land, dark trees and roofs surrounded by the white spray of sprinklers moving steadily across, around fields. No more men in gumboots leaning on shovels over openings in little ditches—"Welcome to Coaldale, Gem of the West, Population 5280." Here and there among the bungalows the small, old, houses sit back well below street level; the green rushes grow in the seepage along the Main Ditch, the giant cottonwoods still lean over its surprisingly clear water. Pouring over falls between the same old timbers that might, just might, still record the scars of my boyhood knife. Beautiful, pastoral, the air shining to the line of the Rockies and the drift of snow on Big Chief, that always distant, holy, mountain. No revolutionary barricades ever anywhere in these streets, so it is perhaps unnecessary to seek that strange light in the treacherous, filthy, safety of sewers.

> *At present the sewer almost realizes the ideal of what is understood in England by the word "respectable." . . . The filth comports itself decently.*

MATTHEW HOVE • *BARRHEAD, ALBERTA*

SHIRLEY SCOTT-BRUISED HEAD

Shirley Scott-Bruised Head was born on the Peigan Reserve in southwest Alberta. She lived there to the age of fourteen, then moved to the Blackfoot Reserve for three years and on to the Blood Reserve, again for three years. For the past decade she has been living in Coaldale, Alberta. Her short story "Afternoon in Bright Sunlight" was originally published in Canadian Fiction Magazine, *in 1981. It has since been reprinted in two anthologies,* The Last Map is the Heart *(Thistledown Press, 1990) and* All My Relations: An Anthology of Contemporary Canadian Native Fiction *(McClelland and Stewart, 1990). Her work has also appeared in the periodical,* Fireweed. *She wishes to acknowledge the support and encouragement she received for her writing from two authors: the Native American author Thomas King and the Alberta poet Martin Oordt, both of whom she met and worked with at the University of Lethbridge.*

From Scott's Coulee

The old shack has turned to dust
the log house, farm house,
barns and corrals
gone
Isstssimaátsisa
(Joe Scott)
and
Awákaasáakii
(Irene Soloway)
gone
the coulee that bears
only his priestly name
spreads out west and east
turns north gradually loses itself
in the
Old Man River basin.

Of the children
first-born Helen
tempestuous and proud
ignores age
lives in a world of her own making
pretends indifference
flies over waves and says
The sea on a calm day
reminds me of prairie grass
waving in the wind.

by Shirley Scott-Bruised Head

Margaret lives miles to the southeast
beyond Split-ridge Coulee
tethered to the land
she greets each new life
looks for Isstssimaátsisa's eyes
smiles, laughs the laugh
heard through generations
He has Scott eyes, she says.

Young Mr Scott
Wesley
eldest of the sons
tries to find an image of himself
as he saws, hammers, planes,
blueprints show the way
he becomes
hazy and confused
as he sees only wood
Oh well, he says softly
with a resigned smile his eyes dim
he shrugs his shoulders and
saws, hammers, planes.

Jessie wanders far
eyes searching
valleys, mountains, flatlands,
walled off
he returns home
Time to check the old ranch, he says
his laugh echoes words
eyes search
eagle calls

Echoes Charlie's lament
as he paces from room to room
stops, listens to the rain
water spills down steep sides
seclusion of the coulee calls
he runs
wanders aimless in alcoholic haze
telephone rings, disembodied voice
Collect call from Charlie.
Will you accept the call?
Come and get me
echoes through the line.

Kerry lives on flat land
close to the Porcupine Hills
his dream of home and family fulfilled
busy with daily chores

his mind wanders down mystic paths
searching for spiritual guidance
he braces himself for a long journey
It's something I have to do.
His smile softens, his eyes see far
he remembers
Isstssimaátsisa.

Although he knew them
but for a little time
Isstssimaátsisa and Awákaasáakii
live in their youngest child
Casey
now a man
his eyes blaze at the pain
he sees in children
His spirit soars in verbal flights
His heart aches as his mind travels
into the past as he looks to the future
and sees images of these children
Things will change, he says.

As far as my mirror image
Barbara lives up to the name
Isstssimaátsisa
she picks up her first-born grandchild
and marvels at her beauty
as the sun warms the house on
Crow Flats,
through the window
she sees her twin boys
exploring the coulees
their shrill voices float on air
Soon you'll be out there,
she says to the child in her arms
and holds her close
and rocks her.

As for me
I'm the younger mirror image
my eyes see beyond the glass, concrete
and steel
My ears hear the words and wisdom
spoken long ago
I search for ways to give life
to the people
whose stories have gone before
and
I remember
My Coulees.

ALBERT TOMLINSON • *EDMONTON, ALBERTA*

RUTH SCHROEDER KRAHN

Ruth Schroeder Krahn grew up in Tofield, Alberta. Her Mennonite grandparents emigrated from Russia to Alberta in the 1920s. She lived in several parts of Canada before settling in Edmonton, where she is currently working on a novel. Her short stories, often richly detailed looks into rural childhood, have appeared in two NeWest collections of Alberta short stories, Alberta Bound *and* Alberta ReBound. *As well, her work has been published in many literary quarterlies (*Grain, Prairie Fire, Prism International, *and* Fiddlehead, *to name some).*

The Fall Turkey Supper

ON THE NIGHT OF THE SUPPER IT IS snowing softly. There is no wind and the snow is coming straight down. Main Street is almost empty of traffic, except in the block where the Tofield Community Hall is situated, between the Bank of Montreal at one end and the doctor's office at the other. Dozens of cars and pickup trucks are parked here, some with their engines still running. At the four-way stop half a block from the hall, I can see a small hand-printed sign, set up in the middle of the intersection.

TURKEY SUPPER TONIGHT 5:00-7:30 PM

It is the middle of November and, at 4:45 in the afternoon, already dark outside. Two more cars drive up and park illegally. People get out wearing oven mitts, clutching huge Dutch ovens. They hurry into the hall. Walking up to the door I find myself checking the billboard—automatically, as I would have done twenty-five years ago when I lived here—to see what movie is playing this week. My parents would never have allowed me, as a teenager, to so much as set foot in this strange, dark, somehow threatening place. But on this night the smell of home cooking, the soft lights, and the dozens of mainly older people sitting, talking, waiting patiently at the luminously white paper-covered tables create an atmosphere of virtuous calm; it feels like a church basement social more than anything. Now people are forming a line that quickly extends from the lobby right up to the kitchen, where members of the Mennonite Young Women's Association, better known as the *Ladies' Aid*, are working frantically. The Ladies' Aid was formed in the fifties by Mennonite women in the Tofield area, many with young children at the time, who wanted to get together and do something useful. Twenty-five or thirty women began meeting regularly in each other's homes, preparing clothes, blankets, quilts, and baby layettes to send overseas to the poor and needy. Later, they branched out into auction sales and, eventually, the more lucrative catering business.

by Ruth Schroeder Krahn

Most of these women are in their sixties now. Mennonite *Young* Women? They laugh. What about the Senior Ladies' Aid? they remind anyone who wants to know. The senior group still has six members, so there!

How many in *their* group, in the *young* group? Only fourteen, and that's counting Helena, who's a "silent" member. That's why it was so hard this year. Almost everyone had to cook a turkey on top of all the other work—the gravy, the dressing, the vegetables all cooked at home. (Health regulations allow them to cook everything at home and bring it to the hall.)

"That's why I got out," says the woman with whom I wait in line. "You had to do everything from scratch, just ask your mom."

I can see my mother in the kitchen, looking harassed and desperate. I know what she had to bring:

One turkey and stuffing (three loaves of bread minimum) plus two quarts of gravy (all to be cooked at home, ready to go), one canner of potatoes, one large pot carrots, one jar pickles, one quart jar of cream, one Christmas decoration, five pies.

"But that's why we get such a crowd," says the woman standing behind us. "People know they're getting the real thing."

The crowd at this early stage of the evening is older than it will be later on; most of the people in line now are white-haired, the women with short curly permed hairdoes, wearing dresses and snow boots, and the men in dress pants and checkered shirts, some wearing cowboy boots. There is a steady growing hum of conversation. Everyone keeps an eye on the two long tables beside the kitchen, where dishes of pickles and cranberry sauce are set out. There's my Uncle David joining the queue.

In the bright fluorescent-lit kitchen, Katie and Ann mix quart jars of gravy brought by each person. Liz and Helen carry huge tubs of mashed potatoes to the tables. Someone else follows with dressing. Here comes the meat, huge trays of it. Carrots, turnips, the gravy—they're about ready to start. What are they forgetting?

Back in the fifties it was baby layettes—that's what the two women in line remember. Once a week they left the kids with their husbands, hoping nothing too terrible happened while they were away, and drove like demons to get to meetings on time. They didn't care how hard they had to work, it didn't feel like work. They even had a president and a secretary-treasurer. They took minutes at the meetings. They bought a loose leaf folder for the minutes, which the present Ladies' Aid group still uses!

"Liz was telling me they've been asked to cater for the Trappers' Association banquet in two weeks," says one of the women. "Two breakfasts, two suppers, about three hundred people a meal. That should remind us why we quit."

"I'm surprised they're going with our Ladies' Aid when we have a `no drinking' policy."

"I guess they know a good deal when they see one. Anyway, they just have to wait until the girls clear out—until the caterers leave, that's the rule—and then they haul out their booze."

I hear chairs scraping, a low rumbling sound, as if a signal has been given. People have been watching closely and know, when the gravy comes out, that it is time. There is a sudden mass convergence on the two tables full of steaming food. The Ladies' Aid women hurry back and forth.

In the kitchen, Mary and Katie are laughing. Mary, squirting dollops of whipped cream on to each pie, missed and got a huge blob on the floor. Katie, behind her slicing the pies into pieces—six per pie, they decided—slipped in the cream and almost wiped out on the floor.

The trouble with the kitchen is that it is poorly set up. They are allowed to cook the food at home but the cupboards are still a problem. For years the women's catering groups which use the place—United, Catholic, Mennonite, Anglican, Lutheran—have complained that they needed more cupboards. Finally someone built cupboards. Who built them? Nobody seems to know, but they agree that whoever it was never spent more than five minutes in a kitchen. It is as if he said, *You want cupboards I'll give you cupboards*, getting so carried away he forgot to put in counters! So now the original problem is magnified. There is no place to set anything down. If you put boxes of food on the floor you can't open the cupboard doors. The Mennonite women shake their heads. They discussed it with women from the United Church, with the Anglicans, the Lutherans, everyone! They've all agreed, *something has to be done*. There's a new work-island in the middle of the kitchen which helps—that's where they've put the turkeys—but they need more than that.

I sit at a table with Elaine, whom I haven't seen in years. I often see her parents, but not her. We used to ride on the same school bus. Our brothers used to get into the odd bit of trouble; they were boys "to watch out for" at certain times of the year, say around the end of October. They drove some interesting vehicles over the years, had some narrow escapes, wrecked a truck or two. A miracle, we agree, that they're still alive.

The man sitting across from me says that he and his wife come for supper every year, making the fifty-mile drive from Sherwood Park. They wouldn't miss it. I automatically think of the only thing I really know about him, that, as an airline pilot, he once had to land a burning plane, thereby sustaining severe burns to himself, but saving the lives of the other passengers. He became an instant hero in this town.

Far away I see my Uncle David getting up from a table.

I talk to someone whose father just had a triple bypass. He's "doing good," will be home by Friday. The man on my right had a triple bypass in May. He says he's "doing fine" but has to rest a lot. Did I know so-and-so had a heart attack last week? Someone else "just up and collapsed" over in front of Tilley's after an asthma attack. Tilley's? But then I remember that it's a restaurant. So-and-so's Alzheimer's is getting worse. She only knows the daughter now. The daughter brings her husband home and the mother says, who is that man with you?

There's the local businessman who asks my mother every year—months ahead of time!—when's that supper of yours? I went to school with his daughter; she got to go to CGIT (Canadian Girls in Training) once a week after school. They lived in one of the bungalows I admired as a child, a place that probably had carpeting in the living room, not linoleum. He had a car dealership on Main Street—the Ford dealership? My brothers, or almost anyone in this hall, would be able to tell me.

A group of men sit at the next table, talking. They have already finished eating and are drinking coffee. In one glance, I see an uncle, a cousin, and a man my age whose parents used to be our neighbours on the farm.

I am approached by a man who asks if I know who he is. Of course I know. He is a former farming neighbour and member of a barbershop quartet my father began some twenty-five or thirty years ago. I used to play the piano for their practices. He looks the same as he did then, his dark hair greying slightly.

Two more people approach my Uncle David. People are constantly seeking him out. I see a hand on his shoulder. They listen attentively when he speaks. I have not yet spoken to him.

Children are running up and down the steps leading to the stage. A local real estate agent walks purposefully up to the children and yells in a mildly loud voice, loud enough for everyone sitting at that end of the hall to hear.

"Hey! Cut that out! No more running, do you hear?"

Everyone laughs. *That Hank*. They all know him, know he's just kidding around. The children, including his own, must know it too because they ignore him. That's my brother, my brother Henry. When did he become Hank? And how did he learn to do this, play this role?

Two members of the Ladies' Aid are hurriedly making up plates at one end of the work island. It's a nuisance, having to stop working, they complain good-naturedly.

"So fiddly. We went and bought tin-foil plates this year. That helps a little."

"But it's for people like Mary, at home in her wheelchair, so it's worth it."

"And the girls working at the hospital who don't get off until 8:00."

By 6:30 they are sold out. The women are frantically making instant mashed potatoes at the single stove. They are not pleased. How did it happen? Never, *never* have they run out of food. Well, cranberry sauce maybe, but not potatoes. How could they run out of potatoes? The bad news: they have run out of dressing as well. Unheard of.

A man arrives at 6:40, wants to buy a ticket, is told that there is no dressing and the potatoes are instant. No problem, he says, tossing down a ten. In he goes.

But the women have their pride. Next year they will have a strict policy: stop charging the second they are out of anything, even if it's pickles. Who let that man pay anyway?

I finally meet up with my Uncle David as we are both getting coffee. He went in for his first chemotherapy treatment today. He must have told this story a dozen times tonight but he tells it to me too. He will suffer visibly in this community, surrounded by all the people who know what is happening to him. Everyone knows how long he had to wait to see a specialist, the details of his surgery, his prognosis. Many of them have encouraging stories for him. They know someone in BC or a relative who recovered from exactly his type of cancer.

It must stop you in your tracks, to be given this news. The doctors have told him (he tells me) that he can expect to feel weak and nauseous shortly, perhaps as early as tomorrow. In a few weeks his hair will start falling out.

A woman from the United Church joins us near the coffee-makers. She asks about my uncle's health immediately, directly, and he faces her squarely and begins again. I can hear him talking about his ordeal as I wander off, thinking how fortunate he is to have this huge network of friends and relatives in whom to confide. Imperfect, caring, *nieschearijch* (Low German for nosy), they will talk about him, to him, listen to him, phone him, phone his wife Mary. Some of them will pray for him. They will be there when his hair falls out, week by week, as he returns from the city every Friday afternoon after his treatments. They will shake his hand on the street, ask how it went, maybe offer assistance. Pale and weak, he will still go for coffee on Main Street with other seniors. He will go to church on Sunday mornings, to suppers like this.

By 7:30 the hall has emptied; maybe seventy-five people are left sitting around the empty tables, talking. Some people smoke, everyone has coffee or tea. Several groups of people are in the lobby on their way out, coats and hats on, still talking. In the kitchen three women wash dishes at the three sinks. Others dry, put cutlery back into the drawers.

"My back's killing me," says a young woman at the sinks.

"The sinks are too low, that's why," says another woman, washing. "Whoever designed this kitchen never had to do any dishes."

"You got that right."

"A person gets tired just reaching down into the water."

"She's from town council," murmurs my mother. "Town secretary. No, not town secretary. I forget. She has a position of some kind."

"It's even harder if you're tall," says a tall woman. "You have to bend further."

Everyone laughs.

"How long have we been standing here?"

"You don't want to know."

"Hey, girls! Guess what!" call several women from the other end of the kitchen. "There was *one* piece of pie left over. One piece. What do you think we should do with it?"

"Just think, we had pie for 500 people."

"Now we can go home and start on our own kitchens. Yeah, I just left the whole works and walked out the door at a quarter to five. I don't know if I even locked my door."

"Imagine, we used to charge a dollar-fifty a plate when we first started. Hard to believe, isn't it?"

"Seven-fifty a plate is hard to believe too," says Liz, up to her elbows in dishwater. "We couldn't do it without Ann, could we?"

There is a chorus of approval.

"Next year we absolutely have to stop charging as soon as we run out of anything—anything! Even if it's cranberry sauce."

Men are starting to wander into the kitchen, to carry boxes to the car. The Ladies' Aid asked for help this year "from the pulpit" because there are so few members left and because the proceeds this year are going to the church-building fund, not to Third World relief. They announced that they could use a clean-up crew to stack chairs and fold up tables after the supper. Now, at 8:30, there is a veritable army of people dragging and stacking chairs—men, women, children, also many "town" people. I see a shopkeeper, a former elementary school teacher, a minister, all trying to figure out how to fold table legs. Someone gathers up all the paper tablecloths. Someone else picks up Christmas decorations and other odds and ends—a kettle in a wicker basket—and lines them up on the stage where the owners can collect them. Children are wrestling on stage now. Then they are running, a pack, past the deer-in-the-moonlight backdrop, behind the curtains.

One of the women slaps a roll of white cloths over her husband's arm. Tea-towels, she says matter-of-factly, and hurries off to join the brigade of women walking around with garbage bags. Crumpled paper table cloths gradually unravel in a corner.

Any more help needed in the kitchen? Absolutely not, is the answer. It's already chaotic in there.

"Agnes! Agnes!" One of the women comes running out to the lobby. "You forgot your plate!"

She hands over a plain glass pie-plate. How did she know it belonged to Agnes? She shows me the tiny piece of adhesive tape on the bottom. Of course.

As I gather up boxes for my mother I see Aunt Mary, Uncle David's wife, standing at the back exit doors of the hall and looking out into the darkness for a minute. What is she staring at? The snow? There has probably not been much time for her to brood over what is happening to her husband. All the women have been working around the clock to get ready for this event.

It is about 11:00 when I leave. The snow on my car is so light I could almost blow it off. As I drive down Main Street I hear the lonely blaring sound of the train as it moves full-speed through town. My grandfather once got the train to stop in Tofield when it no longer stopped here. Outraged when he discovered it was going right through to Edmonton, he gathered up his suitcases and informed the conductor that he would be getting off immediately. I think about the family that was killed at the Creamery Road crossing in the early sixties, as I do every time I cross these tracks. There were six or seven children. Everyone knew someone in the family. We were all in a grade with one of them. I remember that a certain woman was found, more than once, wandering along these tracks near her home, when the train was already in sight. Neighbours led her by the hand toward her house. Sitting at the red flashing light, waiting for the train to pass, I hear a car horn behind me. Margaret comes running up to my window with my camera bag!

"Barb Cooper noticed that you forgot it!"

Barb who? Who is Barb Cooper? And how did she know it was mine?

Margaret hurries back to her car before the train disappears and the cars behind her have to wait. But the person behind her must be someone she knows too because she leans into that car window for a minute.

I'm the first in a row of four cars heading out onto Highway 14. The sky is clear now and I speed up to get rid of the three sets of lights in my rear-view mirror, remembering that this highway is a favourite midnight haunt of the RCMP. But soon all the cars have turned off onto side roads and I am alone on the highway, the vague isolated light of the town behind me glowing mildly in the sky.

KEVIN MCKENZIE • *BLUE RIDGE, ALBERTA*

GORDON PENGILLY

Gordon Pengilly was raised on a farm in the Stirling area, south of Lethbridge, Alberta. After high school he went to Edmonton to study at the University of Alberta where he earned an MFA in Playwriting. He was the first U of A student to earn that degree. A four-time winner of the Alberta Culture Playwriting Award, he was twenty-five years old when his play Hard Hats and Stolen Hearts *was produced in New York City. His many playwriting credits include* Swipe, *first produced by the Toronto Free Theatre in 1981, and Seeds. After four years in Toronto, Mr Pengilly returned to Alberta to take over the position of playwright-in-residence at Theatre Calgary. While living in Calgary, he wrote the CBC radio dramas* The Saga of Tom Three Persons *(1990) and* The Ballad of the Existential Cowboy *(1989). The latter was selected by CBC as one of its* Best of the Decade *radio dramas. Mr Pengilly's paternal grandfather came from Wisconsin to homestead in southern Alberta in 1910. His mother's people came from Florida. They were Mormons who trekked west in the mid-1800s. His is "a farming family on both sides," carrying on to this day.*

"They Don't Call Them Farmers Anymore" is dedicated to Ben and Lee.

They Don't Call Them Farmers Anymore

The sheriffs have already been to call. They took the tractors, the machinery, and the grain in the bins. They even took the kid's pony. The chattels move soon to the auctioneer.

Farm foreclosures are occurring all across the prairies this spring as banks, trust companies, and governments call in their arrears. The farm shake-out taking place will eventually mean fewer farms and a consequent reduction in the number of families working the land independently.

The emotional attachment some Canadians have for small farms is being factored out of the national way of life by economic pressures well beyond any individual's control.

The farm family just thought it could never happen to them.

Southam News April 1991

1. They Don't Call Them Farmers Anymore

The driveway hasn't been shaled. It's potholed and dust-blown. The roof of the barn has started to sink. There are no animals afoot. The gate leading into the yard is falling off its hinges. The caraganas haven't been trimmed. Crab grass grows up through the cracks in the sidewalk. The lawn is not a lawn. The garden is weed. Windows in the house are boarded or broken and the house needs paint. Pass inside through the bolted door. The smell is of mouseshit and stale air and plumbing

by Gordon Pengilly

gone sour. The linoleum has started to rise. A film of dust clings to everything. The proverbial cobweb hangs. Nothing moves. The lungs of the house are desiccant. When the house stopped breathing its people in and out the other process began. It began immediately. Oh, the land is still being farmed. The bank sold it off to a corporation from somewhere in Europe. Was it Dutchmen? Anyway they don't call them farmers: they call them *agri-conservateurs*. The house and the out-buildings will soon be removed, the way the farm family was removed before that. Upon leaving, the family tacked up a snapshot on the living room wall. The snapshot's still there though the faces have started to blue. It was taken that spring before the Old Man passed on.

2. How the YoungFarmer&HisFamily Came to Manage the Farm by Themselves

I'm as old as the hills, I can say anything I want to. The Old Man's last words before the butter&egg man came and took him away. He'd just finished telling his wife of forty-eight years how the government were a bunch of lying cheating intolerant sonsofbitches who didn't give a flying hoot for the farmer anymore and every last banker was no bloody better so screw 'em. His wife prescribed for him a nap. He went outside to change the oil in the half-ton and dropped dead in the yard to the sound of a bird going *tchew-wew pew pew pew*. His heart gave out like a tire. You could hear it burst all over the country. He farmed this farm for fifty-five years just to watch it going broke in front of his eyes. His wife had just prescribed for him a nap but she didn't mean a long one. The Old Man's last words before the butter&egg man came and took him away: *I'm as old as the hills, I can say anything I want to.*

Where do old farmers go when they pass?

Some contend they go straight into the very last thing they put their eyes on. Know a man who believes his daddy is the caragana bushes behind the house. Old boy must've lifted his head one last time and looked out the window. This man says when the wind blows those bushes ring like little bells and he's decided the old boy's in there engaged in the music. Others believe they all go straight to paradise, whatever that is. Still others say they just expire and go back to dirt. That'd befit.

3. The Old Man Drops Dead in the Yard and the Next Thing Y'Know He's Sitting on the Corral Fence Rolling a Smoke with the Butter&Egg Man. The Sun Is an Orange

Gosh darn. Guess I'm croaked, huh? Blessed with a quick one though. Woulda hated the hospital. Only time I was ever in there I couldn't shove that industrial food past my Adam's apple. Nurses were good, very good. No complaints there. Do they have nurses where I'm going to? Gosh darn, is that a Purple Martin perched up there? Haven't seen one of those on the farm for years. Barnswallow family. Glides in circles, a couple of quick flaps, then glides. Has a sort of gurgling song, deep in the throat. My daddy could do it really good.

4. The Old Man's Funeral Was a Big Affair

the butter&egg man was there & so was a blue-black swallow perched on the cross-beam of the old chapel's gallow

tchew-wew pew pew pew

& the choir sang pretty good, too

5. This Is What Grandma Said to Herself in the Moments as They Lowered Him Down

i

my boy love was a very good man

ii

he had a crop of black hair when I married him and hardly any when he died. he had big arms for a scrawny man from working so hard all his life

iii

he had a very fine sense of humour. not much ever seemed to get his goat and he never showed any violence. he hated cheaters and liars but I never saw him punch any one of those either. though I'd heard a few stories about some of his younger years

iv

he swore quite a bit. wasn't very religious. though i never heard him use any parts of the female anatomy for swearing. he had a way with women which I always admired though I never let on that I did

v

he really enjoyed his kids and any kids for that matter if they were any size bigger than babies. he'd go out of his way to help a kid in trouble if he could. it tore his heart out to see his oldest boy having such a tough time farming through really no fault of his own. his feelings of helplessness overwhelmed him in recent years and contributed to his decline

vi

he walked between buildings with a meadowlark on his lips. a long strider he leaned forward on his hips like a man on a horse without the horse

vii

he held the family together. (you can say anything you want to now my boy love)

6. Left Alone with the Current and Future Catastrophe of Farm Economics, the Farmer&HisPartner Struggle to Keep the Family Farm Together

Ask'em. Ask any of'em. Ask the farmer who's losing his farm through no fault of his own. He'll tell ya. They'll all tell ya how the government of this country has betrayed the small farmer. They all want to shoot somebody. They will tell ya how they've been forced into a state of *crisis management* where a combination of high interest rates, poor market returns, recent years of drought, and deteriorating cash flow are putting so many close to bankruptcy, and they dismay at the coldness of those institutions they thought were there to help them. Tragedy. That. After. Years. Of. Many. Government. Ad hoc. Programs. We. Still. Have. No. Viable. Workable. Agricultural. Policy. In. This. (Miserable) Country. They give farmers bandaids for wounds which require major surgery then have the gall to turn around and fault them for bad business habits when the bleeding won't stop. Well listen, folks: among farmers of the prairies are the sharpest businesspeople you're apt to find anywhere: they've had to be to cope with the scourge of present conditions and there seems no dawn forthcoming. STRESS. Loads of it. Ask'em.

7. The Farmer&HisPartner Had a Big Fight Today, Another in a Lengthening Row of Fights, and, as Always, Regret it Deeply, After. The Old Man's Balance Is Missed

Scene: Her damn dog chases the new colt through a barbed wire fence, tears the colt's throat wide open and nearly causes a marriage break-up.

—It's your damn dog too! Whenever he does something stupid you always turn and blame me!
—If it were my damn dog I'd put a bullet through his head!
—Put it through your own damn head!
—I just might!
—You kids get in the house!
—Good God, look at that poor little horse.
—I know!
—I'll try and catch him. You go call the vet.
—I love that colt as much as you do.
—Go call the vet!
—Stop screaming at me!
—Just do it!
—I'll get the gun too! You can shoot the damn dog then shoot me then shoot yourself and make us *all* happy for a change!
—Ssh, boy, ssh. Come, come.

8. The Farmer Sleeps Out on the Porch / Insomnia&Lullaby

can't sleep
again
tonight I
can't
for the life of me
sleep a-
gain

on windy april days farmboys with cowlicks
lie in the sides of haystacks watching the

clouds race while swallows make lazy loops
from barnyard to windbreaks like brush strokes

which erase bright suns and straight above
barns which creak the trees bend and farmboys

alone in haystacks are dreaming of sailing
ships like miracles through a sun haze they

angle through summerfallow brown and grey and
green and glide through barbed wire simply as

breath the wind gusts barn doors slam *they*
slam and cowlicks tingle to toes like waking

9. The Farmer&HisPartner Make Up over Breakfast

How do you give an apology?

Modestly. Mindfully. Fresh
frying eggs. Strong coffee.
Home-grown bacon and garden
potatoes. I'm sorry. Guess
I just lost it yesterday.
I've been losing it a lot
lately, eh? Can't seem to
control it. Feel it burning
up through my shirt and when
it hits my neck I'm a goner.
There are words in my mouth
I don't even know I have.
There are muscles in my face
I don't even know I have.
There are children within
earshot I don't even know I
have. When I scream at you.
When I scream down your pretty
throat I think I'm trying to
hurt myself in there. Please
don't let me do that in there.

How do you take an apology?

You just do somehow.
There it's taken. And I'm
sorry, too. Let's don't flog
ourselves, eh? Everybody
loses it once in a while.
Nobody's perfect. I'll talk
to the kids, they'll be okay.
Today's another day. And so
is tomorrow. We'll keep on
fighting for as long as we
can. If the bank calls in
our note it will not disgrace
our name. We're doing our
best, we still have each
other and I will
always
love
you.

10. The Farmer Wanted to Feel Good about Something

so he sat down at the kitchen table to dismantle&oil his favourite old rifle but the newspaper was lying there and it said that the price of wheat stands at roughly the same value as it was during the Dirty Thirties which was the last time prairie farmers had to turn their land back to the banks in mortgage defaults. The farmer wanted to feel good about something so he went to the fridge for a nice cold bottle of beer but the radio was on and a farmwife was saying that the day the bank manager told us to put the farm up for sale we didn't know what to do so we just went back to the car and we both started crying and the farmer wanted to feel good about something so he went outside on the porch to get a better look at the big fat rainbow up there after a nice little shower they'd just had but the rainbow just looked back at him with a kind of *so whatness isn't I pretty* and the farmer didn't know what to say, couldn't get very excited, so he just went back into the house and sat down again.

11. Spring

and flood:

a long winter running off
creating lakes
in the summerfallow
a sanctuary for wild birds

My God those swans

slow ballet of fans
and soft canes
recumbent
on overnight mirrors

hearts tipped over like little explosions

trumpets and drums
when frightened
off

The white of swans informing us
of a whiter world
somewhere else

12. The Farmer Goes to the Bar

It had rained. Never bitch about rain. Too wet to work though. So the farmer jumps in his half-ton and drives down the highway to the region hotel for a few draft with some of his neighbours who suddenly got the same idea. He drinks. But he doesn't seem to get drunk. None of them seem to, though they share enough pitchers to float a concrete boat. It's a mystery. One of them suggests they're all dead, embalmed, can feel no pain. And to prove his point this fellow walks into the pisser and puts his fist through the wall.

13. Meanwhile the Farmer's Partner Sits Down at the Kitchen Table to Again Go Over the Books. A Stack of Unpaid Bills Reposes at Her Elbow. She Composes a Letter Instead.

Dear Mr Prime Minister,

Crisis management seldom solves problems, and it's the result of several years of crisis that we farmers are facing today. Our cash is strapped; our options are becoming ever more limited. The opportunities to diversify are being strangled by your policies, or, I should say, by your lack of them. Many of us are so far in debt that our production is unprofitable even before we start spring planting.

It seems incredible that in one short decade so much devastation has been caused. Many farms in Alberta are third and fourth generation! The rural lifestyle is eroding and will continue to erode as small operators are forced to quit their land according to most current figures which say farming is no longer viable. No longer viable! How did it get this way?

Who can honestly encourage a spouse or a child to farm while asking them to assume the burden or face the risks that we are currently facing? There has to be something terribly wrong with a system when a farm can't pay for the groceries to feed the people who work it. As small farmers face their demise so go our rural traditions. What of our birthright? What of our heritage? It's not just the soil which is blowing away.

14. The Farmer Heads Home from the Bar for Supper

He decides to take the back road home through his pasture to check on his cows and he stops for a moment at the old junk pile to have a cigarette. There Lies Nearly A Hundred Years Of Sweet Discarded Humanity. Soup cans and oil filters, rotten lumber, old horse bones and bedsprings, the old coal stove and decades worth of licence plates. He sees a Purple Martin gliding high above him. He doesn't see the butter&egg man reclining in the rubbish though somehow he senses him. The farmer sits down on the old coal stove and rolls a fat one. He started rolling his own a few months ago to save a few dollars. His wife has quit completely and won't have it in the house anymore. She seems to have more willpower than he does in most things. If, for instance, they did lose the farm, he figures she could more gracefully start a new life than he could, elsewhere, somehow. She's had some university. The kids are both young, youth is resilient, they'd bear no serious scars. Life would go on. But what about him? Forty-three years old, no other training to fall back on, no real interest in anything else. Except for animals. Do love animals. Could open a pet store maybe. Run a kennel. Read in the *GraiNews* about a farm family who got out before the banker's axe came down and put together a little traveling zoo of cows & pigs & sheep & chickens and took it on the road in an 18-wheeler from town to town like a circus. A fairly noble venture. Nothing to be ashamed of. When Joe Louis went broke he became a wrestler. The farmer is suddenly drunk. And with that, he realises one of the more cunning properties of alcohol, the stuff coves up in certain brain cells and leaps out laughing when the mind itself becomes ridiculous, pathetic, and in the next moment he sees himself as a part of the junk pile, his and the horses' bones bleaching in the noonday sun, his entrails toughened like rawhide tangled in the bedsprings and he bellows at the top of his lungs. He climbs back into his truck and starts away.

15. Shouting Down the Cistern

rhymes my mother taught me
in the shape of a meadowlark's song
bouncing in the hard belly down
in the thick hot smell of water standing
and my face in a sky blue hole
like a penny looking up, I,

with brown shoulderblades
flashing in the sun,
marvel

at my voice going down
drop a note going down
like a stone dropping down
drop a stone down down

  and see my face break apart
and   drift into edges on the darkside
      of circles

16. A Quiet Supper by Recent Standards

The kids to bed early. She'd planned to read him her letter to the prime minister but decided against it because he seemed so lost and unsure of himself. She cleans up the dishes. He stands on the porch with his hands in his pockets. The moon resembles a clown. A star falls down.

—You should talk to me. Y'shouldn't keep stuff inside.
—I was down at the old junk pile this evening. I think I'll borrow a front-end loader and clean the whole thing up. It's an eye-sore.
—And put it where? In another pile somewhere else?
—Maybe I'll bury it then.
—That's a pretty big hole you're talking about. Why don't you just leave it where it is? The kids like poking around down there the same as you did when you were a kid. Keep talking to me.
—Look at that moon.

This Is What the Farmer Kept Inside:

Everything I own is turning into junk. My machinery's all on its last legs and I can't afford to upgrade. When Dad was farming he'd patch things up and make them work again. Or he built what he needed. Well I don't think my knack or my stamina or my brainpower has much to do with it anymore. Times have changed and I've simply been left behind. I'm just glad Dad died not to see it happen.

—Are you missing your dad tonight?
—Look at that star.

17. Sleep Comes Hard Again

The farmer tosses&turns. This way, that way. Maybe he should sell off some land, turn the rest of it back to grass and toss everything into a cow/calf operation. Industry projections for slaughter cattle are still optimistic. Yeh, right. Take all of your eggs out of one basket and put them into another. That's good thinking. This is the age of diversification. How 'bout some goats? Llamas are big. Ostrich? Would have to get an off-farm job to supplement the change-over. The wife's prepared to look for work in town. Shuffle the kids back'n forth between Grandma and school and day-care. Might pay for groceries but they'd never see each other and the car's worn out as it is. Ostrich are ugly. He finds himself praying for hail. There's a storm warning out. Too bad he couldn't afford to load up on insurance this year. Finds himself praying for crop failure in Europe and China and south of the border. Good God, there's something really sick when a man has to wish ill-will on the world to keep his livelihood.

18. The Farmer's Reoccurring Dream

the farmer's reoccurring dream starts out he's walking in the pasture toward the coulee which borders his land to check on his cows his feet feel very light today the sun is pulling up on the earth like it does somedays makes buildings the hills his cows his crops look taller than they really are he gets this feeling he could defy the laws of gravity if he wanted to so he jumps over a stone and sure enough the laws let loose just a little so he runs takes a leap he's flying he's flying it's easy as pie wonders why he's never tried this before he circles and glides a couple of quick flaps then glides swimming in the sky looking down at his land the coulee &hislungs&hisknees&hisbrain&his feet&hisarms&hiseyes are moving slowly clockwise round something deep inside himself deeper than he's ever known before and he does not want it to end his reoccurring dream

19. His Wife Has a Nightmare

Nightmares her husband in bed. It's clear that he's been in bed for a long time. So long his beard and his hair have grown like a hermit's. He's soiled the sheets many times and his teeth are brown. She tries to get him up but he won't. So she puts the kids in the car and leaves the farm with the table half set and dinner in the stove. It isn't clear where she's going. She tells the kids they're going on a picnic down to Writing-On-Stone. The driveway badly needs shaling. The road out hasn't been graded for a long time. It's gouged with ruts and the weeds in the barrowpit haven't been sprayed. Now she sees the Old Man walking with the dog in the summerfallow toward the house. She can't decide if this is a good sign or not. The summerfallow is dirty and the rocks haven't been picked. The Old Man waves. She waves back but keeps going. When she reaches the county road she turns the car south and speeds up. She sees her own hands on the steering wheel and remarks to herself how white her knuckles are. The kids start singing a song which Grandma taught them on a different picnic.

Come, butter, come,
Come, butter, come;
Peter stands at the gate
Waiting for his butter cake.
Come, butter, come.

20. The Sun Is an Orange

—What're you building, Dad?
—A martin house.
—What's that?
—A birdhouse, a feeder. It's gonna go up by the barn. It's for swallows. But not just ordinary swallows.
—What kind?
—Special kind.
—What?
—Purple Martins. There hasn't been any on the farm for a long time but one just got here.
—Where?
—Somewhere hiding but I saw him this morning before you lazy got up. We'll stand it by the barn and see if he takes to it. Be nice to have one stay for a while then maybe some others will come.
—Do you want me to help?
—Hold this board while I saw it off.
—Are they really *purple*?
—Kind of bluish-black. But they look sort of purple when they flap in the sun.
—What do they sound like?
—They sort of gurgle.
—*Gurgle*!
—They sing deep in their throats way down deep.
—Like how?

—I haven't practised yet. Grampa could do it really good.
—Grampa liked birds.
—He did.
—You like birds.
—I do.
—I like birds.
—Good boy.

21. Like a Garden Trying to Squeeze Through a Gate

like a dragonfly skimming over laundry
like a circle of stone which the Indians painted
the clue of a buffalo wallow

as crooked as a treehouse
the fury of a wasp caught behind a storm window
a cowbell in a manger   the barnswallows sleep

like a piece of cultivator crouching in the weeds
like rainwater in an old truck tire
tighter than a granary full of wheat and as nervous
  as the hum of a telephone wire
the dizzying height of a homemade kite
the secret of dynamite rock

like a jackknife in your pocket
like the good hot smell of diesel fuel
like shaking barley dust out of your shirt
like wearing your brother's workboots when they
  finally start to fit
like a farmboy   like a whirlwind

Tchew-wew pew pew pew

ANITA PHILLIPS • *EDMONTON, ALBERTA*

MERNA SUMMERS

In a country renowned for its writers of short fiction, Merna Summers of Edmonton is one of a handful of writers through whom that reputation has been gained. She has twice won the Writers Guild of Alberta award for short fiction and, in 1989, received the Marian Engel Award, given annually to a Canadian woman writer whose body of work has made a contribution to Canadian literature. She has also won the Katherine Anne Porter Prize for Literature (1979) and an Ohio State Award (1968). She is author of three short story collections: The Skating Party *(Oberon Press, 1974);* Calling Home *(Oberon Press, 1982); and* North of the Battle *(Douglas & McIntyre, 1988). Ms Summers was born in Mannville, Alberta. Her mother was an immigrant from northern Sweden. Her father was born near Edmonton, at Clover Bar, shortly after his family arrived from "Indian Territory," later to be named Oklahoma. Merna Summers has lived her life in Alberta, in the sense of permanent address, but has traveled extensively. She has visited Mexico twenty times and, in 1987, was a member of a Canadian writers' delegation to China. She is currently working on a novel that deals with American immigrant experience in early Alberta. It is titled* A Whole Bunch of Us Angels.

Many Thousands Gone

JERRY RARELY SPOKE TO RAYMOND ABOUT her work as a translator. When you spend your life moving from one language to another, searching for equivalences, it can give you habits of mind that seem fussy and obsessive to the unilingual. With Raymond she did not want to seem fussy and obsessive, but playful, on the move, light as air.

They were friends, she and Raymond. Just that. Their relationship had never gone beyond that for what Jerry thought of as "the usual reason." Raymond was attractive and intelligent and good company, but he lacked the one ingredient essential in a man. Interest. What Jerry found most attractive in a man was if he was attracted to her, which Raymond certainly was, but not in that way.

Jerry was thinking of these things as she swung her Toyota on to the down ramp of the University Hospital's parking garage. She was feeling pleased that the Lot Full sign was not flashing, and she was wondering which of their several languages she and Raymond would speak today. English, of course, since Raymond had no other, but which English? It was Jerry's belief that every person on Earth contained a whole population of selves, a whole opera of possible voices, one of which they brought out for one person, another for another. Depending on who you were with, you could be thoughtful or frothy, simple or complex. You could be sister, good buddy, sweetheart.

With some people you were able to be more than one person, speak more than one language, and Raymond was one of these for her. She had known Raymond for fifteen years—both of them, it seemed, were permanent fixtures in Edmonton—and she had shared all sorts of occasions and moods with him. But she had never seen him sick before, and it seemed to her that this might change things.

by Merna Summers

She took the parking card out of the dispenser, decided to let Raymond choose the language today. They could be serious or jokey, depending on how he was feeling. Flirtatious was also a possibility.

They flirted quite a lot, she and Raymond, but they did it only in play. It was a pleasant way of passing time, no more a way of getting to the real thing than Monopoly was a way of making a real fortune.

Why did they do it? Jerry wasn't sure. She recognized in herself a taste for keeping things on the brink of romance, for feeling that wonderful emotions were about to burst into being. And now that opportunities for flirting didn't occur for her as often as they once had, flirting with Raymond gave her something else: a feeling that she was still in there, a part of things.

She wasn't sure what Raymond got out of it, except that flirting was a thing he was good at. Maybe it was simply a capacity demanding to be used.

Sometimes Raymond kissed her good night, but he did it lightly, playfully, almost as if he were doing it in quotation marks. He "kissed" her. The first time he had kissed her, which was early in their friendship, she had not been expecting this.

They had been to the theatre. They had come in separate cars and afterward they drove, again separately, to a restaurant near where the Hello Deli is today. The play had been *Time of the Lilacs*, a well done version, and it had put them in a nostalgic mood. It had been raining, but the rain had stopped. When they came out of the restaurant, the air was full of exhilarating ions. Raymond walked Jerry to her car, which was parked in front of a furniture store with a brass bedstead in the window. She had her car keys in her hand when she saw that Raymond meant to kiss her.

She was not surprised. She had naturally considered the possibility that things might move in this direction, had perhaps even wondered what was taking them so long. And yet for some reason, she had not defined to herself exactly what it was that she was expecting, nor when it was likely to occur. It was simply not a thing she had put into words.

Raymond kissed her.

And then she knew.

How things were.

And how they were going to be.

She felt herself translating the kiss. It said affection, even great fondness. But there was also something of apology in it. It said *Sorry*.

No quiere, she thought.

In Spanish, the same verb serves for *to love* and *to want*. In English, the meanings diverge. At least they did with Raymond.

That was what his kiss told her: that while he might be very fond of her, whatever it was that Raymond was attracted to, it was not to her.

Afterward, it had seemed to her that Raymond had somehow managed to kiss her without touching her. She thought of the places on her body where his hands might have rested during the kiss, and came up with a sense of absence in each of them. Then she remembered. She had been wearing a white coat with wide lapels. Raymond had held one lapel in each hand while he kissed her.

More friendships die for lack of a format than do for lack of affection, and it had taken her and Raymond a little while to find a workable format for theirs. The one they had finally arrived at had as components loyalty, genuine affection, playfulness. But it was only when it was clear that she had properly translated Raymond's kiss that their flirtation was able to begin. "The Game," Jerry called it.

Because it had rules of its own, a grammar. There was to be no trembling on the brink, she understood, no waiting for the first faint ripple that could tilt things forward or back. The scales would have to be kept perfectly balanced.

At first it had been hard to remember that *No quiere*. She had been used to going with the flow, to letting one thing lead to another, and you couldn't do that with Raymond. But she had got used to keeping things in balance. If an emotion was inappropriate, you controlled it, substituted something that *was* appropriate. Single women did this all the time. Gradually Raymond had become like a brother to her. A flirty brother.

There were still, after all these years, areas of their lives where their friendship did not go. They had friends in common, and also separate friends. The future was another area that was off limits.

Most friendships, even very casual ones, involve some sort of ribbon of road leading into the future. People say things like, "We should do a bicycle tour of Ireland together," not meaning that this is going to happen tomorrow or the next day, but simply "I like you and expect to keep on doing it," or, "Wouldn't it be fun if . . ." Jerry had thought that everybody knew that. But talk of the future made Raymond uneasy. He didn't play that game.

Except for once. Sort of. The two of them had been to a wine-tasting party at one of the consulates, where both of them had done considerable tasting, and they were back in Jerry's apartment, in the kitchenette. Jerry was sloshing cognac from the Camus bottle into the snifters Raymond had given her for Christmas. Raymond was leaning against the refrigerator and looking elegant and tipsy. Jerry remembered him as an arrangement in black, white, and red. Black beard, black tux, white shirt, red cummerbund.

"Jerry, my sweet love," Raymond said—he liked to call her "my sweet love" sometimes—"the two of us should arrange to be buried in the same graveyard with matching wine glasses hanging from our headstones."

"At last," Jerry cried. "A future."

Then she put an arm around Raymond's waist and gave him a quick squeeze to show that she understood both what he meant and what he did not mean.

It was in some ways a kind of half-life, this flirtatious chastity, but Jerry had been brought up to believe that a half a loaf was better than no bread. The world was full of people who had less. She had her work—she liked being in control of her life, and her work gave her that—and she had a fairly comfortable lifestyle. And she had Raymond. Not all of the time, it was true, but he was there when she needed an escort or—the old-fashioned word expressed it—a chum. Things were easy between them. What was not going to happen between them had been settled long ago. There was no straining in the loins to make being together unbearable. "Goodbye, my friend, it's hard to . . ." She had never had to say that to Raymond. She had never had to turn herself into something tight and hard and solid to be able to stand being near him. At least she didn't think she had.

Sex?

Well, what you had to do, you did.

The parking garage was nearly full. It always was at this time of day. Jerry crawled the Toyota up and down between the rows of parked cars, hearing again the sighing sound that her motor had been making at low speeds, that she had been trying to ignore. Her air conditioning was on the fritz too. She hated to think what that might mean: that someplace deep inside her car, things were corroding and poisons were seeping out.

She found a parking space facing the doors that led to the elevators. The usual congregation of walking wounded, a cheerless gathering in blue hospital gowns and striped terry cloth bathrobes, were clustered around the doors. Some were in wheelchairs, their legs propped up; some were hooked up to I.V. poles. All were smoking. She could smell their smoke from her car. She was surprised—she was always surprised—at how far the smell of cigarette smoke traveled. Surely it didn't used to travel this far?

She switched off the ignition, and reached around for the present she had brought for Raymond, a bottle of hazelnut sauce in a Callebaut bag. It seemed to have disappeared. The stack of translations in manila envelopes that she had picked up from Andrea's office was there, fanned out on the seat, but not the Callebaut bag.

She knelt on the front seat facing backwards, and started moving the translations to the back seat. There goes my weekend, she thought. Andrea had said they were mainly government documents this time, all wanted by some time next week.

Andrea had organized the translation service that Jerry worked with. It did work for both government and private industry, providing mainly written translations, everything from Canada's Food Rules to bids on engineering contracts in Latin America. Andrea set the rates, took her cut, and passed the rest along to people like Jerry. Her stable, she called them.

Once in a while Andrea called a meeting to discuss the art of translation. She had amassed a fair collection of books and articles on the subject, and she was big on semiotics and whatever new theory she caught flying by. Jerry went to the meetings, pretended to listen, and paid no attention. You had to be in control of your own translation. You had to trust yourself, fly by the seat of your pants. You could no more try to make your work fit a theory than you could turn control of your car over to someone else when you were in the driver's seat.

Carmen, an older translator who had taught Jerry much of what she knew about her craft, used to say: "You have to look down on your work." By this she didn't mean, "Look down with contempt," but something else: look down as a master looks down. Trying to see the whole job at once. Taking control of it. Getting the feeling—sometimes slowly—that you *were* in control. That you could handle anything.

Jerry thought of Carmen sometimes when she was dithering, searching for a word halfway between *evergreen* and *conifer*. "Look down on your work," she told herself. "I'm the CEO around here." She had even written those words on a piece of paper and taped it to the wall above her desk.

Timidity, rule-following: these were things to be avoided. Timidity led to word-by-word, the music lost. The best translation, she felt, was a species of impersonation. You had more in common with Craig Russell than you did with the theoreticians.

The major part of her work, of course, did not even call these questions into account. An impersonal government document in one language became an impersonal government document in another. Canada's Food Rules became *Como preparar alimentos buenos para la salud*.

But the part of her work that she considered most important, the part she would have done all the time if it had been financially possible, was literary translation, and there you were always stretching, taking the best you could do and trying to make it be more. Her current project was a translation of *Pedro Paramo*, a strange and wonderful novel set in a town of the dead, by the Mexican writer Juan Rulfo. It had been translated before, but it had been done badly, and Jerry wanted to do it again, to try to make its music flow in English. She had felt reading the original the way she supposed musicians must feel looking at a score: an almost physical desire to feel the music moving through her body. She was approaching the translation that way: whenever there was any doubt about how a line should be rendered, she was letting the music of the language decide.

In the ten years she had worked as a translator, Jerry had translated hundreds of pages, thousands. Words and more words. Many thousands gone, and how could you know that they were always the right words? That the meanings traveled from the pen of the writer to the eye of the reader without distortions you hadn't even thought of? That they passed through her as through a clear crystal lens, neither magnified nor diminished nor turned into something it was not in their nature to be?

You couldn't, of course. You did what you could do. Jerry's mother had been a Matheson, and the motto of the Clan Matheson was Do and Hope. Jerry had that taped above her desk too.

The Callebaut bag had slid into the space between the car seat and the door on the passenger side. Jerry retrieved it, then turned to swing her body out of the car. *Oh-oh,* she thought. Because the tightness in her buttocks was there again, and the rigidity in the muscles along her spine. The ramparts had risen. Before she had even left the parking garage. Before she had encountered a single white uniform.

Jerry had found that it helped when visiting someone in hospital to have something pleasant planned for afterwards. Today she meant to spend an hour with Raymond if he was feeling well enough, and then to go home and have a swim in her apartment pool. After that she would heat up some frozen canneloni, and then she would get down to work.

You needed these things, ways of getting through things. Jerry's mother had been in this hospital for several months two years ago, and the experience of visiting daily, month after month, of discovering what hospitals were really like, had left Jerry hardened, equipped with survival skills she would rather not have had. Curiously, it had also left her intolerant of people who believed that they could not visit hospitals, and she had discovered that there were a surprising number of them. Poor sensitive creatures, she thought ironically. Today she had discovered that Andrea was one of them.

"Rather you than me," Andrea had said when Jerry told her that she was on her way to visit Raymond in hospital. "Those places give me the heebie-jeebies."

Jerry had been surprised to hear her own voice go high. "Nobody *likes* hospitals," she had said. "You go because you have to go." Her words came out in little short splats. "And you don't let things get to you, because if you do, you will be useless when you're needed. And it's certain that you will be. Things go wrong in hospitals all the time."

Andrea's face expressed something between alarm and the desire to laugh. She settled for a shrug. "You certainly had that speech all loaded up and ready to fire," she said.

It was true, and Jerry had the grace to feel embarrassed. Nobody had appointed *her* to straighten out the world, she thought. The truth was that she envied people like Andrea, the easy riders, more often than not. People who knew what they didn't like to do, and didn't do it.

At least she hadn't said the word *duty*, she thought. That was a notion that had gone out of fashion. And she hadn't gone into some song and dance about being there for your friends when they needed you. Self-righteousness was out of fashion too.

Jerry took the elevator up to the main floor, went to the information desk. Raymond was being moved to a different section of the hospital today, his father had said. There had been an explanation of why this was happening, but Jerry hadn't been able to follow it. She hadn't been able to make much sense of Lloyd's account of Raymond's illness either.

Jerry had phoned Raymond ten days ago to invite him to a choral concert, had left a message on his answering machine. Yesterday he had left a message on hers. "Sorry to be so long getting back to you," Raymond's voice had said. "The fact is, I'm in hospital. But if you'd like to send a message, phone my parents and they will pass it on." And then he had given her his parents' phone number. Jerry had been surprised that he had not taken it for granted that she would want to visit him.

Lloyd, Raymond's father, had answered the phone when she called, and he had sounded almost slap-happy. "I have just this minute come home from Raymond's garden where I have been bringing in his harvest," he said. "Now, apparently, I am expected to blanch Raymond's yard-long beans and put them in bags for the freezer. I thought that your children were supposed to take care of you in your old age," he said. "I didn't think you were supposed to have to take care of your children."

"How is Raymond?" Jerry asked.

"Tickety-boo," Lloyd said. "Well, maybe only semi-tickety-boo. But he's coming along."

Then he told Jerry that Raymond had had his operation, but that he seemed to be doing well. He said these things as if they were in quotation marks. "Had his operation." "Doing well."

"You know what Raymond's trouble is, I imagine?" he asked.

"Actually, I don't," Jerry said. "I just this minute learned he was in hospital."

There was a brief pause, and Jerry sensed that Lloyd was doing one of those translations that even the unilingual do all the time: choosing one word to avoid saying another.

"It's a kind of skin cancer," Lloyd said finally, "only instead of having it on his skin, Raymond has it on his lungs." His voice still had that curious bantering sound, a spoofing sound. It was as if she had caught him in the middle of a long, jokey party, and some sort of momentum was keeping him going.

But what did it mean: skin cancer on the lungs? And what about her sense of words unsaid?

It was like trying to translate minimalist writing, to capture the unsaid thing, the half-said thing. Change languages and these things can disappear. And why was Lloyd sounding so all-fired merry about everything?

Denial, Jerry thought. Raymond had come through his operation, and Lloyd needed to believe that that was *it*.

Now he was talking about medicines, about all the new medicines coming out, but he sounded as if the medicines were a joke on everybody. He was making the sounds a man makes when things are going so well that he can afford levity.

Denial, Jerry thought again. Because no one would *not* worry about cancer. Even a cancer that wasn't where it should have been.

Jerry had met Raymond's parents only recently, and she had been surprised to discover how young they were. It had been at a party in Raymond's backyard, and Jerry had seen a couple standing in front of the delphiniums, the woman in a Tilley skirt and espadrilles, the man in shorts and sandals. Her first impression had been of firm, tanned flesh. She was thinking of them as contemporaries, friends, until Raymond introduced them.

Raymond was wearing a loose shirt of thin Indian cotton, and when Jerry looked at him to compare him to his parents, she had been shocked to see how thin he was. There was a sharpness to collarbone, shoulderblades, hip bones, that reminded her of lightning cracking. One hand was resting on his mother's arm. It was thin, bony. The flesh had receded from it and the veins stood out in sickle shapes, crossed finger shapes, blue against the white of his skin. Even his feet, visible in sandals, looked skeletal. When had all this happened?

And his face, it seemed to her, had suddenly got old. The flesh had receded at the temples, as if some sort of suction from underneath was pulling it in. There was white in his beard. Raymond looked like an ascetic patriarch, one of the desert fathers.

For a moment it was like looking through a split-image viewfinder. It seemed to Jerry that she was looking at two faces. There was the face she had always known, and there was the new, old face that Raymond had somehow contrived to hide himself behind. Then the known face went away, and she was left with the new, old face. Raymond looked tired, but there was a certain serenity about him. He looked like a man whose days in the sexual wars were past.

Jerry knew—no, did not know; *suspected* would be the right word—that Raymond was gay. She always felt her mental pencil hover over the word, *gay*. It seemed to her a particularly inappropriate word for what it denoted, especially now. But she understood that the people it applied to had chosen it for themselves, and they surely had the right to create their own definition.

Jerry had never given much thought to Raymond's gay-ness until a few years ago. There was a time when she was between lovers—that was the way she had thought of it *then*, as being *between* lovers—and one day she was thinking about the men she knew, not auditioning them, exactly, but letting their faces pass before her in a sort of mental procession. Not finding much. Too young. Too old. Too philistine. And Raymond.

Well, no, she thought. Great for a symphony concert, wonderful at a dinner party, but not, as she had always known, *interested*. And knowing the reason why, but seeing no reason to put a word to it.

As if her mother might overhear her. Or her father. Good Lord, her father.

Words failed her father when he was describing a man like Raymond. "Sissy," he might say, if he were speaking of a child. "Old woman" if the man were older and given to keeping a tidy house. But her father had no words at all for any of the categories in between. It was as if they did not exist for him. Her father would never have said *homosexual*. And never, never *gay*.

"We had a gay old time," her father had always liked to say. Still liked to say. Resolutely turning his back on the fact that languages change.

Invertido. Maricon. Probably a newer word by now.

The woman at the information counter wrote Raymond's room number on a slip of paper, told Jerry which elevator to take, and Jerry headed out along the concourse, her high heels tapping out a message of authority. Ordinarily Jerry affected a rather Bohemian look—dirndl skirts, sandals—but if she had a consulting job to do or a hospital to visit, she dressed differently. She was wearing one of her consultant's outfits today: an expensive-looking print dress, a yellow linen jacket, high heels. The language of this outfit was authority. If she had occasion to speak up about anything, she wanted to be listened to.

The language of the hospital was garden, was shopping mall. Trees rose through metal grills, vines descended from tiers of walkways above. There were trellised archways and sidewalk cafés. Thousands of plants, all healthy. Someone must gather up the ailing ones and put them where they couldn't be seen. There was even a waterfall, a curtain of water descending in a controlled flow over a tiled wall. Nature under control: was that the message here? You were not in a place of sickness but a place of health, of burgeoning growth. Or perhaps the important message was shopping mall. People came home from shopping malls with more, not less. Shopping malls spoke of gain, not diminishment.

Jerry took a glass-sided elevator up to the fifth floor, found Raymond's room. The door was closed and there was a sign beside it:

ISOLATION PRECAUTION
Visitors: Do not enter without seeing nurse for precautions.

She went back to the nursing station. A young nurse was bent over her papers. The face she raised was helpful, pleasant, as empty of content as a window blind.

"I'm here to see Mr Wilding," Jerry said.

The nurse looked at her watch. "He's been sleeping," she said. "But I have to give him a medication in five minutes. So you might as well go in and wake him up."

Not a word about precautions.

Jerry didn't want to mention them.

She was hesitating, wondering what to do about the closed door, when she heard Raymond's voice. "I would prefer that you take the plant away," it said. It was louder than Raymond usually spoke, and also rather theatrical.

A door opened and a woman in a pant uniform came out carrying a drooping plant. She was followed by a scrawny man, the scrawniest man Jerry had ever seen. He looked like a root in a nightgown. His blue hospital gown was flapping, threatening exposure, and he looked as if bits of him might be about to fly off.

It was Raymond.

Jerry spread her arms wide, signaling a hug, but Raymond put his hands up to hold her off. *"Don't,"* he said.

She stopped. "I've got an incision up my back as long as your arm," Raymond said. "And if it isn't still oozing, it's still pretty damned sore."

Jerry decreased the dimensions of her hug.

She rested her hands carefully on the tops of Raymond's shoulders, touched her cheek to his cheek.

Raymond hugged her. "Look, I've got to go pee," he said. "Find a chair. I'll be back directly."

Jerry went into the room, put the Callebaut bag on his bedside table. There were three books there: John Fowles' *The Aristos*, Robert Bly's *Wildness And Domesticity*, something called *An Atlas of the Muscles.* She sat down in a naugahyde armchair in the corner. There was a laundry hamper beside it, white canvas sides suspended on a metal frame. It was filled nearly to brimming with used linen.

The sign outside the door must have some significance. Why had the nurse not told her what it meant, what precautions were called for?

Because she was careless, that was why. Because she just didn't give a damn.

When her mother was in hospital, Jerry had been appalled to discover how many mistakes get made in hospital, as a matter of routine, almost. Mistakes that no thinking person would make. She wasn't sure if hospitals had always made these mistakes or if they were a new thing, brought on perhaps by the twelve-hour days that nurses now chose to work.

She would sit in her mother's room dressed in her consultant's clothes and she would keep an eye on things. The nurses were always letting her mother's intravenous bag go dry, and that was one of the things she kept an eye on. When it was nearly empty, she would go to the desk and tell the nurse there, diplomatically, without a hint of blame, that the bag needed to be changed. In the hours when she couldn't be at the hospital, her mother's intravenous bag went dry again and again. Her mother had what were called "bad veins." They collapsed, evaded the needle. Once it had taken seventeen pokes of the needle to get her intravenous running again.

One day, approaching the hospital in her car, Jerry had seen four white uniforms at a street corner, waiting for a light to change. A wave of rage and hatred had washed over her, astonishing her. For the first time she had understood what racial prejudice must feel like. Had had to give up forever her feeling of superiority to people who could feel it. Had known that what she felt about nurses had reached the irrational level, but had been unable to give up feeling it.

Raymond came out of the bathroom, bustled, got back into bed. "The reason I've been moved," he said, as if she had asked him, "is that they've got me on a whole raft of new medications. The doctors in the surgical section don't know very much about these new drugs . . . Whereas the doctors up here are using them every day."

Oh, she thought.

There was a clock on Raymond's bedside table, a big old-fashioned style alarm clock of the type Jerry associated with summer cottages and refrigerator tops. The young nurse came in carrying a medication. Jerry looked at the clock, but she was unable to relate the time it showed to her own sense of how much of the day was gone. Raymond saw her looking. "Don't pay any attention to that," he said. "It gains fifteen minutes every hour."

The nurse gave him his medication. "This is new," she said. "It's a mouthwash."

A mouthwash? She had been going to wake Raymond up to give him *a mouthwash*?

"Why am I supposed to take it?" Raymond asked. He spoke very seriously, as if he was determined to know the whys and wherefores of every drug he was given. Which was a good idea. But just the same, for *a mouthwash*?

The young nurse, however, was as serious in her answer as Raymond had been in his question. "Some people get fungus infections in their mouths," she said. "This is meant to prevent that."

She took Raymond's vital signs, and then a blood sample. She was wearing rubber gloves and an isolation gown, and Jerry watched as her gloved hands moved efficiently, lining up the tip of the needle with the tip of Raymond's middle finger, giving it a sudden sharp jab, squeezing the blood on to a glass slide.

"They go through dozens and dozens of pairs of rubber gloves in this one room alone every day," Raymond said when she had left. He was pressing a square of gauze to his middle finger with his thumb.

He's trying to tell me something, Jerry thought. And then unthought. Because what message could there possibly be in rubber gloves? In translation you had to put in all the meanings that were there, but you also had to keep out the meanings that weren't there. You had to be wary of opening the door to the unstated, the possibly fraudulent.

Over the hospital's public address system, a business-like voice was asking a doctor to go to a third floor nursing unit, STAT. When the message was over, there were two young men standing in Raymond's doorway. "Mark and Paul!" Raymond said.

Mark, slightly older, wore a weathered brown leather jacket and blue jeans. Paul was wearing a red coat cut like a cape with its own fringed scarf tossed back over one shoulder. Both of them were slender; they had the bodies of dancers.

They were Raymond's friends, whom Jerry did not know. Raymond had a whole other life that did not include her. And now she realized that she had never tried to imagine Raymond's other life. Never. Not once.

Mark and Paul were gay; Jerry understood that. She had understood it even before they went up to Raymond's bed and bent, each in turn, to kiss him on the lips.

She had seen this before, of course. It was the routine social greeting of gay men. They did it as women embraced, pressed cheeks. But when, she wondered, had all this started? When had gay men begun to do this?

Last week Jerry had been in a feminist bookstore, and had noticed a basket of lapel buttons with an attractive design on them beside the cash register. "This is nice," Jerry had said, picking one up. "Is it a symbol of something?"

The woman behind the counter had looked embarrassed for her. "It's the seventh letter of the Greek alphabet," she had said. "Lambda. Like our L. It's a sort of symbol for gay men."

Oh.

But why gay *men*? Shouldn't an *L* be for gay women?

Jerry had felt embarrassed at not knowing these things, and cross at feeling embarrassed. It seemed to her that more and more she felt as if the modern age—her age—had got ahead of her. That her own experience, the life she had lived, was out of date. That "where it was at," as people used to say, was someplace else.

There were only two chairs in the room, and three visitors. "There's usually a wheelchair outside the door," Raymond said. "Bring that in."

Paul did, but there was a pillow on it, and some small confusion arose about where to put the pillow. "Here," Jerry said, pointing to the top of the laundry hamper beside her.

"*No*," Raymond said.

"The linen's contaminated and the pillow is not."

So Paul put it on top of the cupboard where the boxes of rubber gloves were stacked.

Jerry soon realized that Mark and Paul had also come prepared to let Raymond choose the language they would speak today. Surprisingly, what Raymond chose to talk about was the medications he was on.

"Pentamadine, of course," he said.

"Aerosol?" Mark asked.

"What else?" Raymond hitched himself higher on the bed and his knees looked like a child's drawing of mountain peaks under the sheets. "At least people don't die of PCP any more."

The three men were speaking a language that Jerry did not understand, but she felt that Raymond wanted her to understand something. He had said *Pentamadine* and *PCP* as if they were Rosetta words.

"Some of the drugs are for opportunistic infections, of course," he said now. "Unfortunately, I have a few of those."

For a moment Jerry felt as if she almost had it. *Opportunistic infections*. The words had a shimmer to them, as if they were suspended in heat waves arising from pavement. It was as if there was a road leading toward her, a great tongue of a road. But there were no travelers on the road; the words shimmered away. She would come back to them later, Jerry thought, as she often came back to baffling phrases encountered in translation.

The talk became general, but Jerry could feel Raymond, not *watching* her, exactly, but tuned in to her in some way. Gauging something. Preparing for something. "I had sixteen visitors last night," Raymond said finally, as if he were taking the plunge. "Unfortunately about half of them didn't know that I was HIV positive."

Jerry could feel a meaning moving toward her, but moving like mist, tumbling in the air, traveling so slowly that it seemed possible that it might never get there at all. She felt as if her mouth had been frozen. Her whole body felt like that.

HIV positive.

Aids.

Sida.

This was the meaning that had been coming toward her ever since she entered this room. Before that, even. Lloyd had been trying to tell her something last night, but either he had evaded it, or she had.

But she felt it had come too quickly. The virus was not airborne, she knew that much—at least they claimed to know that much about it—and yet she suddenly felt as if the air in the room had claws. She felt that nothing was holding her up but her consultant's jacket, that everything inside of it had turned into rags. She held her face carefully, as if it might run away if she didn't. She mustn't let Raymond see her real face. She didn't want him to have to cope with her shock. She wanted him to think she had always known this.

She saw his hands. He was still pressing his thumb to his middle finger, holding things in.

And then she felt her head rising. She felt her neck become a long, long stem, and her head rise up on it toward the ceiling. From there she could look down on all of them: Raymond, Mark, Paul, and Jerry. *There is another me down there*, she thought. *She wants to go away*.

I must get control of myself, Jerry thought.

And then she was back inside of her body again in the naugahyde chair, and what had happened hadn't happened.

HIV positive.

Lordy, lordy, lordy.

She knew all about Aids, of course. She had read the cover stories in *Newsweek*, in *Time*. She knew that thousands of people were dying in San Francisco, and tens of thousands in Africa. She knew that some countries might be totally depopulated. But this was Edmonton. Things like this didn't happen here. Or not to people like Raymond.

Raymond was still speaking. "Now I've got something a little more than that," he was saying, and he might have been telling her something he felt a gentle regret about. Jerry realized that no time at all had passed since he had said the words "HIV positive," that he was speaking now if not on the same breath, then on the one next to it. That all that had happened had happened in less than a second.

" . . . a little more than that . . . "

. . . *un poco mas que eso* . . .

Not just HIV positive then.

Raymond had full-blown Aids.

"Full-blown" used to mean roses.

I have to go on looking as if nothing has happened, she thought. I have to do that.

I will run away, she thought. She had always wanted to live someplace else for a year. To live there and work there and get to know that other place. I will run away and I won't come back until this is over, she thought.

Only she wouldn't. She couldn't. She couldn't do that. And knowing this her brain began to run in smaller and smaller circles. *Oh, shameful. Oh, shameful.*

Jerry made herself concentrate on what she could see and hear and touch. She made herself say the names of things. Blood pressure cuffs. Callebaut bag. Laundry hamper. But these things seemed to her like part of a jungle she had to find her way through.

Gradually she became aware that the conversation was continuing, just as if nothing at all had happened. She realized that she was the only person in this room who had never faced this situation before. Mark and Paul, she saw, knew the language of what was happening. They knew how to *be*. They were neither full of gloom nor stupidly reassuring. They were just there. Living it with Raymond.

"I am a sensible, intelligent, middle-aged woman," Jerry told herself, as she had often told herself during her mother's long illness. She waited for the transfer of strength those words ought to bring, but it didn't come.

Now I've got something a little more than that.

Raymond was speaking to all of them, but she sensed his words were meant for her. "I could be worse off," he was saying. "I could be a political prisoner in Guatemala."

That was true. Even if Raymond were to die . . .

Remove the subjunctive. Death was coming down the road.

But she couldn't do it. She couldn't take away the *if*.

Perhaps Raymond couldn't either. He spoke as if he were making a gentle joke. "Of course it could turn around," he said.

Yes, of course. Why not? Jerry felt an almost overwhelming impulse to bring him lies. To tell him about the asparagus cure, which was for cancer but might work here, or the broccoli cure. To tell him about visualizing. To counsel Chinese herbs.

She forced herself to keep silent. Not to trivialize. There had to be an answer, because nothing is ever as bad as it seems at first, but the answer would be something more subtle than asparagus: something as common as foxtail, perhaps, or some plant from the Brazilian jungle. Something nobody had ever thought of trying.

Lordy, lordy, lordy.

There was something else in the room, something worse than anything yet, but Jerry couldn't put a name to it. It seemed to have something to do with the naugahyde chair. She felt the muscles under the surface of her skin ripple, as a horse's hide will ripple when it is touched. She moved her back away from the chair. Then she noticed that her arms, through the linen of her consultant's jacket, were touching the arms of the chair. She moved them too.

Lordy, lordy, lordy.

It was quite a while before it occurred to her that she could go home, that she had stayed long enough, that she could come back another time when Raymond didn't have any company, and stay longer. She kissed Raymond on the cheek, shook hands with Mark and Paul, left. There was a washroom on the way to the elevator. She went into it. She washed her hands, using soap, doing a good job of it. Then she went to the toilet. But when she had finished she found that she could not wipe herself. She could not bear to touch herself there.

Oh, shameful, shameful.

That night Jerry dreamed that she was camping in the high country. She had a slide-in camper mounted on a pickup truck. It appeared that she had decided to bake cornbread, but when she opened the canister, she saw that it was full of weevils. They were crawling out of the cornmeal and oozing up the sides of the canister. She went to the door to throw the canister out, and then the bears came in. Two bears, three, four. She was trying to push them out with the broom, but the broom handle was made of some soft, malleable material. It was flaccid in her hands.

When she awoke, it took her a few minutes to realize that there was no broom handle.

The next morning, waking again, she discovered that a course of action had come to her while she was sleeping. What had happened yesterday was past, and she didn't mean to let anything like it happen again. Things were certainly very bad, and some things she couldn't do anything about, but others she could and would. The first thing to do, she thought, was to phone the Aids Information Line. More information was the answer to most things, and getting it was always a good first step.

She made a pot of tea and, still in her nightgown, went into her office, looked up the Aids Line number. She was not phoning out of fear—as far as she knew there was absolutely nothing to be afraid of—but because she wanted information, and this was what any rational human being in need of information would do: go after it. I am a sensible, intelligent, middle-aged woman in search of information, she told herself. She moved the translations to one side of her desk and began to jot down questions on her notepad.

What she really wanted to know was whether you could pick up the virus from contaminated linens or clothing, and what happened if an open wound oozed on to a hospital gown, but she didn't intend to ask the question that way. She intended instead to ask a series of smaller, more general questions that, when you added them up, would tell you the same thing.

The person who answered the phone was a nurse. She told Jerry so right after Jerry explained why she was calling. Jerry had decided to start out by saying she had been visiting a friend with Aids, had noticed a sign beside the door, and wanted to be advised about precautions so that she could do things right the next time. A calm interest in right action: that was the message she wanted to convey.

"I don't think you need to worry very much," the voice on the phone said. "I'm a nurse. I work with Aids patients all the time, and I never feel the slightest apprehension."

Well, bully for you, Jerry thought, but didn't say.

There were some questions she would like to ask about the virus, she said pleasantly. For example, how long could it live outside the human body?

"Oh, a very short time."

"Would that be minutes or hours?" Jerry asked.

"Something like that."

She had asked a specific question, and received a non-specific answer. The message, she saw, was *reassurance*. The nurse was not here to give you specific answers to specific questions—the facts—but to tell you how to feel about them. Whatever they were.

Probably she didn't even know the answers. Nurses, Jerry believed, often didn't read the research; they were content to pass along whatever trickle-down information came their way. The official story.

"The main ways of contracting the Aids virus," the nurse went on in her pleasant, reassuring voice, "are through sexual contact or contaminated blood, as when addicts share needles."

Does she think I'm an idiot? Jerry thought.

"Aids is actually a very difficult disease to contract," the nurse went on. "For instance, you can't get it by shaking hands with someone, or from ordinary social kissing."

Nurses, Jerry thought, were like radio receivers that were turned off. They were so busy transmitting that it got in the way of their thinking. And the message they were transmitting was always the same message: *Everything is under control. There is nothing to worry about.*

Jerry felt the need to break through this wall of reassurance. She put her prepared questions aside. "What precautions do you personally observe?" she asked.

She could tell that the nurse did not like this question. It was not on her list of messages to be got across. "Well, of course I wear rubber gloves, and I don't replace the tips on needles," she said unwillingly. "But really, what it comes down to is just basic good hygiene." Her voice indicated that Jerry's question had something reprehensible about it, that it told her something discreditable about the questioner.

She's making assumptions about me, Jerry thought. She's putting me into some kind of category. There is something duplicitous going on here.

The hell with it, Jerry thought. "What about a wound that is not completely healed?" she asked. "If it oozes on to a gown or bedding, is transmission possible that way?"

The displeasure in the nurse's voice was now palpable. "Theoretically, anything is possible," she said coldly. "But really, I don't think you have anything to worry about. As a rule there has to be prolonged contact for transmission to take place. Say twenty minutes or so."

Jerry had not known this. It was good news. "Instant transmission is impossible then?" she asked. She wanted to have this confirmed.

But the nurse was getting tired of her. "Theoretically, anything is possible," she said again, her voice tipped with ice. "But I'm afraid I don't understand your questions."

"Really?" Jerry said, and her own voice sounded as if she were translating a message from Antarctica. "I thought I was stating them very clearly."

There was no point in continuing the conversation and Jerry ended it as politely as she was able.

But she needed to talk to someone. She dialed Andrea's number.

She told Andrea at once. "Raymond has Aids," she said.

"God," Andrea said.

Then, "I guess that figures."

Ordinarily Jerry would have resented this, but she was feeling the need to talk too badly to permit herself resentment. She felt the need to tell Andrea—and then tell her and tell her again—everything that had happened.

But she didn't, in fact, tell Andrea everything that had happened. She told her a version of it, parts of what had happened in Raymond's room, parts of her phone call to the Aids Line. She found that she could talk about shock, and grief, and heartbreak, but she could not, for some reason, talk about the naugahyde chair. She would come up to some part of her story and find herself stopping, side-stepping. It was as if there were parts of the experience that she had not yet translated for herself, and she did not want Andrea translating them for her.

She became aware that Andrea was listening closely, that she was listening to the gaps, and she began to try to close them. It seemed to her that she could feel Andrea gathering herself, preparing to give advice.

Finally Andrea interrupted. "Look, Jerry, cut yourself some slack," she said.

"I don't know what you mean."

"Raymond's sick and you're sorry as hell. But Aids is not a carbuncle. It's certain death. So make yourself scarce. Take a powder."

I might have known Andrea would say this, Jerry thought.

Why had she called Andrea anyway?

And then she knew. She had phoned Andrea because she knew Andrea would say these things. She had wanted to hear them.

Oh, shameful, shameful.

Shameful, and also useless. Because if there was a world in which you abandoned your friends when they were sick, it was a world Jerry wanted no part of. That much she knew.

Well, it was worth learning that much.

She rallied. "The thing to remember," she said, "is that Aids is actually a very difficult disease to catch. There has to be sexual contact, or shared needles. And there has to be prolonged contact. Say, for twenty minutes or so."

"You sound like you're reading from a script," Andrea said.

"I'm trying to figure out what the risks really are," Jerry said.

"Well, good luck," Andrea said. "Aids is a new disease. About half the things we've been told about it so far have turned out not to be true. I heard on the radio this morning that now they're worried about deep kissing."

"There hasn't been a lot of that in my life lately," Jerry said. "Not that I planned it that way."

Jerry wished afterwards that she had ended the conversation then, on a joke, but Andrea was just getting up steam. "Nobody really knows how you can catch Aids," she said. "What about that dentist in the States? And what about those two nurses with the chapped hands?"

For the second time in two days, Jerry felt knowledge rolling toward her. "What two nurses with the chapped hands?" she asked.

"In Arizona or Texas or someplace," Andrea said. "They had been nursing Aids patients, and they contracted the virus, and the only thing they could think of was that they had both had chapped hands."

Jerry felt a shudder move over her body. She was sitting at her desk on a perfectly ordinary morning and looking at a sign that said "I'm the CEO around here." On her desk her answering machine was turned to OFF, its one red eye gone blind. She could feel the upholstery of her office chair prickling her thighs through the thin fabric of her nightgown. Her chair had wheels. She could feel it moving under her.

"Look, Andrea, I'll get back to you," she managed to say, and hung up the phone.

There was a shape swimming before her eyes. It was round, slightly longer than round. It looked like a head, or something that was melting. Then it changed, stretched out, lengthened, until it was the shape of a sickle. It was the incision.

She was looking at the incision on Raymond's back, and it seemed to her that she could feel it on her own. She had almost touched his back. Maybe she *had* touched it. How could you remember a thing like that? She had certainly touched his gown, and his gown had touched his back. Raymond himself had been concerned about the sheets in the laundry hamper.

And then the picture she was watching changed. She was watching herself embrace Raymond. Her hands were on his shoulders. As she watched, they slid lower.

Oh, do not ooze, she thought. *Oh, do not ooze.*

Lordy, lordy, lordy.

I must get control, she thought, but this time nothing happened. The Jerry who handled things was not there. The Jerry she was left with stood up, and she felt a rush of hot wetness on her inner thighs. She saw a spot on the carpet. She smelled a new smell. It was a hospital kind of smell. *Something is happening here*, she thought, and she tried to put a name to it, but it had no name. Only a feeling. With an enormous effort she translated the feeling into a word.

The word, she saw, was fear. Was terror. The last word before there are no words at all.

TREVOR STOCKING • *BARRHEAD, ALBERTA*

ARITHA VAN HERK

Aritha van Herk grew up on a farm near Edberg, Alberta. Her parents emigrated to Alberta from Holland in 1949. At just twenty-four years of age, Ms van Herk won the Seal First Novel Award for Judith *(McClelland & Stewart, 1978). To those who considered this a sudden achievement she pointed out that she had, by then, studied English and Creative Writing at the University of Alberta for six years. Within that life as a student, she worked as a secretary, a bush cook, a farmhand, and an editor. Since that time, she has published five more books, including* No Fixed Address *(McClelland & Stewart, 1986) and* Places Far From Ellesmere *(Red Deer College Press, 1990). Ms van Herk teaches Canadian Literature and Creative Writing at the University of Calgary. As a writer, editor, and professor, she works to maintain literature's place in contemporary life. Despite "a tremendous shift to the visual media," she believes that "language on the page is still the most transferable, transportable, and potentially meaningful of all communications."*

The Erased and Eroding Languages of Alberta

WHEN MY PARENTS DIDN'T WANT ME TO UNDERstand, or when they wanted to talk about serious matters unfit for the ears of children, they spoke Dutch. Their transition to the fluid syllables of that hotly descriptive language was effortless, without warning or consultation, a simple decision of the tongue. They were at home then, comfortable and joking in a way that they were not in English. English was a territory where they battled through complex clauses like poison ivy, confused tenses and agreements, mangled idiomatic prepositions.

Sometimes I would crouch out of sight, listening, and try to fathom their secret discourse. I could hear them through the window, their voices engrossed, interwoven, with the peculiar intimacy that was suggested when they spoke Dutch. I felt my lungs contract, my limbs shrivel. I was excluded, out in the cold. I could not understand. This was my first terror—being excluded from language. But I refused to believe that I could not understand them. I listened, time and again, crouched under the caragana hedge or above the radiator, I cocked my ear toward their murmured intimacy. I erased everything I knew, everything I had learned at Edberg Elementary School. Completely blank, my mind whistling high and tightrope as an Alberta wind, I believed then that I could understand them. They would be talking about the big war, the one they had survived, or about the crops, or the mortgage on the farm, enormous concepts beyond my grasp anyway.

But I realized that in order to understand my parents speaking Dutch, I had to wipe out, completely erase, every vestige of English. Language is palimpsestic, one layer grows over another. English was a concrete block covering my original language, the one I had heard while I lay curled in my mother's belly. The one I was convinced that I still knew.

by Aritha van Herk

This is a strange obsession for a child to hang onto. But it was replicated four years later, when some relatives from the Netherlands visited us. I made crazy mistakes, but I spoke, unmistakably, their language and mine, my first language, that had been buried under the imprint of a Canadian education. Since then, I have done everything I can to somehow maintain acquaintance with this difficult but mysteriously expressive first language. I've traveled to the Netherlands, I've taken Dutch language courses, I've read Dutch books. And yet, it seems always just beyond my fingertips, elusive and irretrievable, despite my yearning.

Perhaps this is the quintessential characteristic of a Canadian. Those of us who come out of non-English or non-French immigrations, whose families have not been here for generations, carry the recessive gene of a different bequeathment, the language we once knew. Between us, between me and my mother tongue, is the terrible intimacy of loss. This language knows that I long to know it well; this language longs for my inherited aptitude to shape my lips and to pronounce words deep in my throat. But I am an English speaker first, and Dutch is an obscure language slowly losing ground to more dominant discourses. Still, the potential of my knowledge is a secret that, though buried, I return to again and again. It explains my obsession with language; it explains my obsession with stories. In its absence, it explains everything.

Let us pretend that we know another language.

This is a dream we all have, a deep-seated desire. To switch from one tongue to another, easily, without thinking about the move or the lego of words and their intricate fitting together, without having to struggle to say something simple.

Impossible, the forked tongue that some manage to hone. Fluently bilingual, that's what we call it. Or trilingual. How many languages can hurl themselves against the glass panes of the encoding brain before it reaches overload? Language overload: a brain teaser valiant in tongue but perhaps fearful at heart. The impenetrable wordplay of the most proficient: we are all capable of committing a *Finnegans Wake.*

Still, do we know those languages we claim to know? Do we speak those languages we claim to speak? Or do we practise a resolute monolingualism, longing still for the strange gutturals of our presumed inheritance?

Genes are passed on. Languages lapse.

As children in the farming community of Edberg, beside the Battle River in the central Alberta parkland, we spoke pig latin, delighting in the mystery of the transposed words. Who invented pig latin, a language ripe for childish invention? Where did it come from? *Illkay the umbay,* we shouted, gleeful, swollen with power. A cloak for swear words, bad words, *itshay* and *amday*. A *secret* language, a code. The pleasurable wallowing in the delight of believing that no one else could understand. Every child inherits pig latin, without any effort. It is simply there.

And we all knew nonsense words, invented words, passwords to our dens and hideaways in the bush. Language and words were connected to access, entrance; they exhibited power.

When did inexplicable and other tongues become foreign? When did we refuse to mimic them, refuse their intrigue? Where do we learn to frown at a different voice, at people talking together in words incomprehensible to us? Where does our suspicion of what we do not understand come from?

The course of a language is like the course of a love affair, full of thickets and tanglements. It takes so terribly long to feel comfortable, naked. It takes so terribly long to sleep comfortably together.

Adopted languages (however adept the practitioner) are like second-hand clothes, retaining the shape of the former owner. They never fit quite right.

All my speculations and observations are borne out by the voices of the immigrants who speak, but who are heard with half our ears. Listening to their language stories, about loss and access, I found I could not distil them. Their voices are louder, clearer, than my own.

> *When we first came to Canada, English was a torture to me. I could not understand a word people said, even though I strained and strained, like I was hard of hearing, as if by concentrating I could somehow catch those quick and mysterious sounds.*

How does an immigrant learn English? The terror of this learning is beyond comprehension, impossible to imagine unless you too have been forced to learn another language.

> *Everyone spoke so quickly, the words were like water rushing past.*

Reach out a hand and grab it, quick, hang on for dear life, don't let go of the one word that makes sense, that seems to get results, use it as a shovel or a paddle, a saw or a hammer, a wooden spoon.

> *Potato. Please. Chili pepper.*

Is it necessary to start with necessities? What comes most quickly, asserts itself first? Food? Shelter? Money? The body and its betrayals? Those events which are needs or requirements, and so require language as instrument? Or simply the arena of emotion, connection?

> *It was English, English everywhere, that made me feel so homesick. If only I could have heard another person speaking my language, speaking Polish, I wouldn't have felt so homesick.*

The body is easy compared to the mind. The brain that insists that the sky is not sky but *lucht,* the orange is not an orange but a *sinaasappel.*

> *The boss used to sign for us what we had to do. If we had to saw wood, he would act that out, and mostly it was all right, but one day he wanted me to prune the apple trees, and instead I pruned the maples.*

Velocity, too fast. And volume, too loud. The sigh, the exasperated shrug, the eyebrow raised. The impatience of those who have never thought about the privilege of their knowing.

> *The woman we worked for would get impatient, she would talk louder and louder, as if we were deaf or stupid. We still didn't understand what she was saying, and we felt like naughty schoolchildren.*

The lash of words, beaten with language. Only the angels speak in tongues without effort or practice. And beaten by English, people went home to cry and cry, in Ukrainian, in German, in French.

> *When we had parties together, and we could laugh and joke, oh that was good. I think we talked twice as much and three times as hard to make up for having to struggle with this English, so knotted and mean a language. It wasn't any tongue to have fun in.*

The mother tongue is the language of joy and sorrow, emotion and company. The language of dancing and kissing, of taste and touch, of pleasure.

> *Sometimes my mouth felt as if it were full of cotton wool. English is a hard language to learn, inhospitable. It has no warmth, no expression, no* gezelligheid.

So, how does an immigrant learn English? In classes, where a teacher swings a pointer? At work, where a boss gestures toward a shovel or a sewing machine, a cleaning cart or pile of dishes? Stores, where the immigrant can point or rely on pictures on the packages?

> *Cereal was easy but soup cans were a mystery, I never knew what kind I was buying. I remember buying Cow Brand baking soda. I thought it was powdered milk.*

How does an immigrant give up her old language? Put her in a cold bath of English, English, every day, without respite, no escape from its everywhereness.

Language was given to people to conceal their thoughts.

The givers of language are tricksters. This is the terrible truth of all our attempts to articulate, communicate, explicate.

Lapsus linguae: a slip of the tongue, a mistake in uttering a word, or an imprudent word inadvertently spoken. These are easy to commit if you are translating, shifting words from one position to another, black and red checkers jumping over one another.

Translation acts not as gain but loss. Think of losing an integral part of your body. A limb? We never want to lose parts of the body—limbs cut off are drastic losses, truncations. Hair might be a good metaphor, but it grows back, effortlessly, reassuringly. Trying to shake yourself loose from a first language could be compared to successfully erasing a stutter or a birthmark, some curious shame to its imposition or occurrence on the body.

The aboriginal languages were robbed—forcibly taken away. Losing not a language but *your* language, the language that has occupied you from birth, its sounding and syllables a continuing comfort, a way of reiterating: I exist, I exist, I exist.

The divided tongue.

My grandmother still speaks Cree. I don't know it, only a few words. But sometimes, I think I can feel it in my throat, rising up to speak. The biggest thing I can't understand, that makes me sad, is why they didn't want us to speak our language to each other.

Yet others actively seeking to replace their mother tongue. Mother's tongue, the tongue our mother. Hacking away at its insistent retention, wild raspberry canes cleared back, pruned, so that familiar expressions and vocabulary are shoved behind a different set of vocalizations, ill-fitting and ugly. Replacing one set of signs with another—the new ones beating back the safe and comfortable old.

A new coat? A new house? Objects we fit around us, objects we expect will fit us, wearing into the contours of our bodies.

They all speak English there, you know. You'll have to learn to talk the way they do.

Where does it begin, this new language? An abstraction: English.

We went to take English classes twice a week. It sounded easy; we thought that we knew it quite well. But I had so many things around my head, planning to leave, that I forgot everything by the next morning. Tien remembered it a little better, but not much.

And English just one abstraction among many others: Canada, Alberta, winter, English. These are only imaginable when you are *in* them, when you are submerged. Now you are in Canada, now you are in Alberta, now it is winter, everyone speaks English. You do not understand a thing, not the geographical difference, not the climatic difference, not the linguistic difference. It is all *other* and closed to your comprehension. You are caught in a story, or a long and complex dream where you stand up to give a speech to a roomful of people and then discover, horrifyingly, that you must give it in a language you do not know. A strange language.

English a slippery pig that I chase, I bring him down every time. But it makes me tired, chasing that pig, through mud puddles, he is fast, greasy, I am tired of talk. Watsamatter, they say. You so quiet. I tired from chasing pig. English pig. Not like Cantonese, dancing light, easy. I learn to say nothing, listen, watch.

Silence as refuge, rest. The ambivalent cloak of quiet. A hidden alternative to a chase ludicrous and without dignity. Silence bestowing dignity.

Using English is not as easy as using new money. Not as easy as wearing different clothes. A torment to the tongue and the ear, a set of hieroglyphics impossible to undertake on the page. English using you, a huge hand wrenching you around. Another slip of the tongue.

The children go to school in English. In between the lunch buckets and the rubber boots, in between the repetitions of their chores, the children bring home their school books. *See Spot run. See Jane and Dick chase him.* The adults pore over them but know they are terribly inadequate, beyond uselessness. What's needed is a guide to speaking practically.

A pound of butter. My shoe has a hole in it. A hammer and nails. A sore throat. Can I get a stamp, please? My car needs gas. I would like to open a bank account. Sugar, flour, oatmeal. How much is that package of cigarettes? Where is the nearest watchmaker? A bag of rice. How far am I from heaven? Cantonese. Ukrainian. Dutch. Urdu. Please tell me where I am, I am lost. I think. Two pounds of ham.

Translated from the original desire in form and vision. The sizes are larger, the wrapping is brightly coloured, the prices are unclear, the content beyond control.

And then, the nightmare of fear or emergency in another language.

Temple. Hospital. Revenue Canada. You have cancer. Fire. Church. Police. Ambulance. Marriage. Rodeo. Silk. Grave.

Coming through the fire of incomprehension. Licences and laws and libraries: their rattling staccato, their quick impatience. Too fast to be held down or figured out.

He doesn't say much, that one.

I can't get her to say a word.

Cat got cher tongue?

Speak up, I can't hear you.

Patches of English to cover tattered holes, its clumsy needlework pulling together the lips of a tear in a pair of trousers or a hole in a sweater's elbow. Language's clothing outgrown, shrugged off. All knees and elbows.

But worse, the torment of being an educated and well-spoken person suddenly transformed to idiot: en-childed.

You busy?

You want bathroom?

You wait.

Unable to protest the complexity of your understanding with the pure idiocy of the language at your disposal, its slippery refusal to obey your constructions, your lips and tongue shaping what seem to be imbecilities, when the elegant and ironic intellectual phrases you've figured in your head wilt in their inarticulation. You content yourself with complicated thoughts, ideas acted out in the language that originated them, that thinks and speaks instinctively within you. A silent dialogue: interior.

Translation is impossible, the shift from one language to another a travesty. The very concepts that one tongue can formulate do not exist in the other; they are other concepts and require other words. Translation lies down like an old dog and pants in weariness.

The coat is buying the woman.

See the car drive Hans.

Look out of your eyes, and hold your head shut.

Transition.

And at some point, in this barbarous place, begin to find slipping away from you the language you have always, with ease and pleasure, worn. Your real language slowly turning its back, growing more distant as it is invaded by English phrases, a hybrid lost to its own purity.

> *I mix words up—so many English words close the same. I don't know I make mistakes, but my children tell me. And I do it again—old mistakes now, but people understand me. At my age, no matter.*

Here is a slough, no man's land. The barbed wire frontier between two languages, alien because it is neither one nor the other. The loneliest of language moments, hands outstretched to either side, encountering silence. No response to the tongue's babble. The apostasis of conversion, unsuspecting defections. Treason, renegation. Suddenly the word that suggests itself is not the old one, but the new one, and the old is inexplicably gone.

> *You know, the funny thing is I remember most the first time I couldn't remember the Swedish word for something—I remember the word even—it was so particular to me, it was the name for a kind of special pan that you bake cakes in, and all I could think was cake pan, cake pan, I almost went crazy, that my own word should have deserted me, that I had forgotten, and I couldn't remember, not for days. Finally it came back, I sat up in the middle of the night and remembered, and I was so relieved, as if I'd been forgiven for a sin, you see. It made me feel terrible.*

The insidious creep of desertion. The new language begins to take priority. Boastful, chauvinistic, it elbows up all the room, begins to push the old words off the edge.

> *I know that I talk a mixture, between both languages. I can't find a word, so I use the one that's handy. And there's English and Italian all mixed up together. Well, people are good. They understand me.*

Replacement. Substitutions. Threat of passing off one thing for another. Ersatz without deliberation. And this transition an underground passage of the tongue. Hoping to make it past Hades through to another side, another version, more complete, comprehensible.

> *The worst thing was the first time we went home. I was so excited, I hadn't seen my family for ten years—and best of all, I looked forward to talking without having to struggle for the right words. We came from the plane, and I could see my*

family there, waving behind the glass barrier, and I was so excited—I started talking English to the customs officer. He was scornful, he said, "You forget your mother tongue already?" And I was embarrassed, but it went that way the whole trip. My good Dutch was completely mixed up with English—English words always coming out, and I didn't even know. It was better after a couple of weeks, but I felt like the ground had caved in, because I always believed that I couldn't forget my own language. And it was disappearing right from under my feet.

Disappearing right from under the ground of the tongue. Oh, temporarily recoverable, but its pure intuition lost, contaminated by the tongue's new colonizer.

And you see, it isn't the way we talk, but the way we look. Because I am visibly different, people expect that I can't speak English, so they speak to me as if I were a child. I notice that if I wear a sari, people act as if I don't understand them. But if I dress in western clothes, jeans and a sweater, they assume that my English is good. English is my language too, and the way I dress has nothing to do with my ability to speak.

Transitions past human zones of transition, and language attributed to appearance. The reformation of the visibly different other by the imposition of language and its disapprovals. How to make alien an other—insist that they speak white, and not express their visibility, their difference. Racism by tongue. English, English, English. And French? That's another country too.

Why can't these people learn English? She's just pretending not to understand the teller. If they don't know English, they shouldn't let them into Canada. What's my name? Janek. Were my parents immigrants? No, my grandparents. I know what you're implying, but they learned the language, they didn't expect the rest of the country to take care of them.

The hegemonies of habit, of ingrained and casual knowledge, and the danger of expecting all others to be the same. Language as transformer, its presence revealing political position. Intolerance on the tongue. A waiting subterfuge. The final transition from the understanding to the understood, and beyond.

Accent and effacement.

What is left behind then, when the transition is accomplished?

Oh yes, I love hearing the West Indian rhythms of speech. My father, when we came in the door of the house, insisted that we speak English correctly, but it was so lifeless compared to the language on the street, so straight-laced and dull. The street language had colour and energy.

Not only English—and French—those two occupiers, but the many versions of English stalking the streets, the small towns, the countryside in Alberta. Australian English, Irish English, American English.

> *The moment I tell people that we come from Australia, they're very nice. They just seem to react if they think we're English English, and most Canadians can't tell the difference. I think too that my accent has softened a lot since I came here.*

Accent is the sinister twin of language. You show me your accent, I'll show you mine. Stress determines the nature of accent, the prominence given in speech to a particular sound, syllable, or word by means of stress. A mark, call it birthmark, accent carried for life, and only erased when the tongue lies still. Accent calls attention to itself, refuses to permit the speaker protective colouration.

> *We come in 1973. I hardly know English. We go looking, looking for some friends who are living in the country and we are so lost. What I know about township and range and meridian, nothing. In Yugoslavia, everything road have a name. I ask a farmer, but he no understand me. My accent so heavy then, so heavy, I can hardly understand myself. (Laughter)*

Accent's marking is the last claim of the mother tongue, its hold over the bearer. "You may leave me behind, you may forget my words, but I will be with you always, every time you open your mouth, they will know, your listeners, that I was your first language, the original inhabitant of your speech. You cannot erase me, not completely."

Finally cherishable, that distinctive accentuation. And the multiple voices speak together, a thorough confusion of sound under the Alberta sky, bouncing off the Rocky Mountains. Old languages and new, in their fierce mingling. Exquisite cacophony. Yes, this sky calls forth voices, the many different voices of the people of Alberta. And even if they bank and go to school in English, even if that chauvinistic language throws its cloak over all, under the skin of Alberta runs a river of voices, speaking in tongues as multiple and multifarious as grain.

Fable. The Persians say that Arabic, Persian, and Turkish are the three original languages. The serpent who seduced Eve spoke Arabic, the most persuasive language in the world; Adam and Eve spoke Persian, the most poetic language; the angel Gabriel spoke Turkish, the most menacing language (definitely the language of punishment). Fable further: the secret language behind immigration must be the most persuasive of all ancient languages, even more persuasive than the three originals. The language of immigration, despite its collusion with the language of loss, is the most enduring and secretly seductive of all.

Multilingual, those fables are. Alberta too.

(I want to thank all those people who told me their stories, who talked to me about language and immigration.)

DR. JUAN J. TERAN • *PINCHER CREEK, ALBERTA*

WEYMAN CHAN

Weyman Chan was born in Calgary in 1963. His Toi-Sahn Chinese parents owned and operated a restaurant in that city. In the 1980s, he studied at the University of Calgary, earning a BA in English. For the last five years he has worked as a Lab Technologist (Electron Microscopy) at a Calgary hospital. Mr Chan's short fiction has been published in NeWest Review *and* Vox. *His poetry was included in* Many Mouthed Birds *(Douglas & MacIntyre, 1991), an anthology of Chinese-Canadian writing. He won the* Calgary Herald *Short Story Competition in 1987 and was runner-up in the same competition in 1990. In 1987-88, he was a fiction editor for* Dandelion Magazine. *Mr Chan writes about the "dislocations between generations and the discovery of one's `place' at the juncture between cultures, languages, and genders."*

Just one moment, please. I'm trying to think of the best way to word this.

I watch Pyrus take their order. She bears the one-liners of these men who've brought their own beer and bathroom humour. They start off by calling her cutie or princess. Pyrus tells them to hide the beer or she'll take it away. The restaurant is not licenced, but at least we get a return off the empty bottles.

Mom's in the kitchen, chopping bok choy and suey choy, or deep-frying egg rolls. She's quiet like that when no one's around and Dad's out delivering in his '71 Plymouth Fury. On weekdays when all of us kids are at school and Mom's alone and somebody comes, what happens? Pyrus tells me that Mom will come out of the kitchen all smiles, hand the customer a Tasty Chop Suey menu and then walk away. Exactly three minutes later she'll return with an ordering pad. She'll instruct the customer to order by number. "Numb-buhhh!" If this doesn't work, she points to the menu. She won't be able to answer any questions about the items, she'll just smile, point to the wall clock and nod. All she'll be able to serve the person then and there are tea, coffee, coke, or water. She'll say "ohhh" to acknowledge understanding of these words. As soon as the customer finishes talking, she'll walk away, never looking back and never really noticing the patron's face, because they all look the same to her. People have been known to yell at Mom and storm out.

I think of Mom as I watch Pyrus defer to these four men, providing them with an extra one, two, three ashtrays.

"Thank you, Sister Cherry Blossom!" they'll say, or, "Can I order a squeeze to go with that?" Two bikers wear leather vests to show off their chest hair and to restrain their growing bellies. The other two wear John Lennon shades and black t-shirts with winged Harley motifs on the back and front. Whenever Pyrus serves them and walks away in her narrow jeans, they watch.

"Hey, flood pants. Keep reading those comics," one of the guys yells at me. I push my head lower into those colourful frames of Orphan Annie among desert caravans and jungle people, searching for her Daddy Warbucks, her lost inheritance. Behind me, the Joneses get up to leave. Pyrus and I clean their table and I hear the guys from the stall near the front guffaw. "Flood pants," they say.

"Say, honey, is that little nipper there your kid brother?"

"Yeah, so what's that to you?" says Pyrus.

"Get him something to do in the kitchen. I want a word with you alone."

Pyrus grins and flicks her long straight hair behind her back. She throws a dish towel over her shoulder. "My dad's coming back soon. Anything you wanna say to me you can say with him around."

"Yeah, big boy!" I yell and run into the kitchen with a stack of dishes. Pyrus follows. As soon as the kitchen doors swing shut behind her, she sets her plates down and slaps me on the mouth.

"Watch what you say to them! They just like teasing, they're harmless."

"If they're so harmless then why do you act that way?" I almost start to cry.

"Act like what?"

"Tough."

"Finish up here."

Pyrus wets the dish towel in soapwater and rushes out. I look down at the worn-out brown pants I've grown out of, and my grey socks, their elastic so shot that they glide down my ankles as soon as I've pulled them up. Flood pants. I want to be strong, the all-reflective surface barrier that Mom is to strangers. But I also want to be like Pyrus, powerful and new; and why shouldn't there be danger and fun and a price to pay for wanting to see the beauty in those you've been taught to fear?

You've got to understand the family psychology, of fitting in. Where all the answers lie within that structure. Some never manage to break out. Some never manage to be themselves.

It doesn't matter that Constable Bill has now entered the restaurant. It doesn't matter that he sits two stalls down from the bikers, looks down at his paper and pretends to care for no one. He seems accustomed to pig jokes, keeping his head down like that. Pyrus asks one of the bikers if they've eaten bird's nest soup.

"Screw the nest! Where's the bird!" they say. "It's all upside down and backwards and slanted with you guys, ain't it?" they say.

Dad's back. He enters from the back door and the first thing he does is light a cigarette. Then he starts the rice, throws on an apron and belches.

"Bikers, Dad! There's bikers out there."

He ignores me. He never panics, that's his way. Our Mom died of cancer in '66, and she died so slowly that Dad can recognize long, drawn-out disasters only after they've surrounded and swept him a ways. A raw, grey chicken gets split clean in half with the cleaver he wields. The pieces are tossed and rolled in flour and then a light batter. He really has no time for my foolishness. Minutes pass before he glances sidelong at the hands in my pockets, then into my face. My eyes beg him to acknowledge me.

"*Ne gong mh-da-va*?"

Pyrus flies into the kitchen and upstages me. "Dad! They've been waiting for nearly half an hour! Here's the order!"

Dad takes the order and reads it out loud in English, as if to check Pyrus's handwriting.

"And Constable Bill, he wants coffee."

Dad swears in Chinese. "*Thlee-nooi-gai!* Give him a coffee then! On the house!"

Pyrus has a way of tightening her jaw, just like Dad, and her entire face hardens while her eyes widen. It is a beautiful face, as I suspect Pyrus herself knows. As Leonard Ashwood knows, and will any man who ever dates Pyrus in the future.

"I'm tired of giving cops free coffee. I'm tired of yelling `on the house,' while other customers laugh at us!"

"Go!"

Dad hits her on the shoulder. She goes. Out in the restaurant, she sets down the cup filled to overflowing with straight black coffee and smiles her most alluring smile.

"On the house!" she shrieks. The bikers at the other stall giggle, and so do I. This is Pyrus's way of getting back at Dad, his palm striking her on the collarbone. I want to remember the way Dad struck out, not with words this time but physically, as if she was still a girl going on thirteen. His open palm caught her below the neck—did he aim for her face? Did he still want to love her? Who do you love when your daughter is no longer your little girl? Or, maybe he did it because I was there, watching her quirky grin get wiped clean off. Still, she wears that grin as she enters the kitchen. I help her bring out the egg fu yong, combination dinners, and won ton soup. The bikers ignore me but heap their praise on Pyrus. "Can she cook or what? Or what?"

Then I see it. One of the John Lennons sneaks out a gloved hand. The hand strokes by Pyrus's inner thigh. She walks away and I follow. Constable Bill, deep in his newspaper, grins for a split second. He could be exercising his dentures.

In the kitchen, Pyrus holds a piece of egg roll to her mouth; her arm is shaking. I want to tell her that I saw what happened, and should I call him bastard or just say "that biker?" Just how neutral should I be? I watch them juggling ashtrays out there under the red light shining through the front window, and I can see that Dad's listening. They're turning wild out there, shouting, "Suzie Wong! It won't be long! It's on the house!"

A loud smash and Dad rushes out to look.

"That cost you two dollars!"

Dad returns to the kitchen, points me toward the broom and mop.

"I'll do it, you go help Mom," says Pyrus, dragging the broom and mop out.

"No! You stay here, Pyrus. Eddie, go."

Pyrus raises her voice while I leave. These bikers smell fear on me, my itchy palms, armpits, and hands. I want to run away, but get down on my knees and sweep. Beneath their table, sugar and glass shards bend light around the sheath of a boot knife—boot knives on all four bikers.

"Hey, kid. Nothing personal, but your sister is a hell of a lot cuter than you. Get her to bring me a cheeseburger."

Back in the kitchen, Pyrus is crying. It's not the tears that bother me, it's the red face. She stares at Dad's back, opens and closes her fists while Dad's hand stirs the chicken batter. Did he hit her again? I watch Pyrus go sit next to Mom on a little stool at the back. Two whole buckets of prawns, dead grey eyes and long red antennae woven frozen; Pyrus's hands scour through the slush. Her nerves as dead as prawns.

"You listen to your father," whispers Mom. "Good daughters don't talk to *Lao-fun* strangers. You'll make a bad wife if you don't learn to cook."

"Leave me alone!"

I pull a burger patty out of the freezer and pat it down on the grill, watching Pyrus. Her head leans forward, she lets her hair slip over her ear like that, to form a curtain between us. Will she tell me tonight, after work, when she's finished shelling prawns and folding take-out boxes and we're both dead tired and there are no customers? Will we sneak out together and run through the cool fresh air of the Richmond Shopping Centre parking lot under those orange streetlights, shedding our kitchen grease smell? Then maybe she'll shout "Peggy's Doink!" and she'll start me laughing and then she'll talk about school and the dances that she always promises me she'll sneak out and go to.

Pyrus looks up. She sees me staring into her, hauling out her thoughts, displaying them. She throws a prawn onto the floor and runs into the storage room.

"Come back here, you whore! Finish up what you started!"

But Step-mom doesn't chase after her. Pyrus is too old, too stubborn for that. Dad normally would've thrown his ladle into the wok, torn his apron off, and dragged us back by the hair of our heads. This time, he minds himself.

The burger patty lands on the grill with a loud sputter.

"Who's this one for?" Dad snaps.

"One of the bikers," I tell him.

Dad flips the patty one more time before slapping it onto a bun. Then he coughs loud and horcks, opens his mouth over the steaming meat, and quickly lays a cheese slice over top. Dill pickle, lettuce, and tomato follow. Dad hands me the platter: a normal cheeseburger, and everything is what it seems.

Even as Dad stares you straight in the eye, you know what you must do. You feel the slow pull outward, to Pyrus's eyes hot on your back, to the bikers' scraggly, oily faces as you go out and see them picking at rice grains and egg tidbits, experimenting with chopsticks for the first time. What are they thinking? Every second that passes opens up possibility, a frame-by-frame exposure of yourself, letting go of silence and bursting forth a wisecrack, something Lucy might say to Charlie Brown. Except this would be real, enemy lines would be crossed, and there'd be something beautiful in that honesty. You'd be free of whatever delicacy your parents might have for *Lao-fun* customers and their buddy-buddy charm and mystique.

The cheeseburger speaks. The sweaty patty sizzles on the platter on your hand. Keep moving. The bikers stare at you. One of them—the one who stroked Pyrus's thigh—reaches out a hand. Reward him! Give it to the bastard! You have power over him, the means of heroic revenge—but this is not your revenge.

It belongs to Pyrus.

You see Constable Bill, reading the newspaper. He lets out the occasional yawn to convince everyone that he's ignoring them. Suddenly you are walking tall and visible, even smirking with pride. The restaurant's neon name shines red in your eyes as your feet take you over to his table.

"On the house!"

Constable Bill nods approvingly, cradles the burger in his sausage fingers, and eats.

Sometimes customers would tell my Dad, "Oh, it's so nice to see the whole family working together like this!" It looked nice from the outside. We had our good times. But we worked hard. We saw how different we were because of our Chinese parents, and this did a few things to me. It sensitized me; as a kid, I thought of myself as a freak. So I started going out more with my Caucasian buddies. I learned how to hunt and fish, and I play a wicked game of darts. I only eat steak and potatoes now, no rice, no fish. I'm like a banana—yellow outside, white inside. I'm glad it all turned out.

Don't say what the psychologists say: hyper-vigilant. On edge. Always compensating. Living two thoughts separately, and not really knowing it.

Only tell them, when you're angry, what Pyrus told you that evening, eighteen years ago, when you heard coughing and found her smoking a cigarette under a slivered moon out back, behind the lard oil drum. A broken moon, she called it. She never did tell you what Dad had said to make her cry. And you can't enter their heads to retrieve any messages in blown-glass bottles, because the words back then have changed over the years, settling out of memory, and the lonely desperate fears that first caused them to be uttered. It might've been a sly remark, a choice word or two in Chinese, but it's exactly these pieces of long-forgotten oral history that sink in deepest.

"We have to be sneaky, from now on," she said. "We're never given a chance to explain, or defend ourselves. When you're grown-up you can smoke too. Well, here. Breathe it in slow and deep. Now you'll be tough as nails. You wait and see."

MELISSA HOFER *(left)* **and MAGDELINA HOFER** *(right)* • *SMOKY LAKE, ALBERTA*

MARIE MOSER

Marie Moser was raised in Edmonton, Alberta in what she describes as a "strong French-Catholic tradition." Her maternal grandparents came from Ottawa in 1900 and her mother was born in the French-Catholic settlement of St. Albert in 1905. Her father came west from Sherbrooke, Quebec in 1915, a descendant of Nicholas Cantin, who made his home near Quebec City in 1637. In her writing and in her life, Ms Moser has worked to keep the traditional values of French Canada alive. Her first novel, Counterpoint *(Irwin Publishing, 1987), winner of the 1985 New Alberta Novelist Competition, explored the history of French-Canadian settlement in Alberta. She has raised her four children to be French-speaking, and has struggled to ensure that they will know the traditional songs and Christmas rituals of her people. Though she feels the modern world works against such a retention of culture, Ms Moser has found that children, "by nature, like traditions—they are traditional beings." As for the future, she knows it to be beyond her control. She can only hope that what she has handed on will be handed on by others too; that the gift will be received and passed on through future generations.*

The Last Lullaby

"I DON'T THINK THIS WAS SUCH A GOOD idea, coming here," she says. Paul and Lisette are sitting in his car stopped at the curb in front of the Heritage Villa for Senior Citizens.

"You want me to meet the relatives, don't you?" he says. He takes her left hand and adjusts her blue sapphire engagement ring.

"Of course I do. It's just . . . well, she's an old-fashioned French-Canadian lady, set in her ways."

"What did you say to call her? Ma tent . . . "

"Ma *tante* Elodie. It means `aunt,' even though she's really my great-aunt."

He jumps out of the car and hurries to her side to open the door. "After you, *mademoiselle*."

She holds onto his arm as they enter the bright lobby. Ferns cascade from macrame hangings in every corner.

"Her suite is over here," she says as she leads him away from the lobby. A lively piano tune and a chorus of voices fill the hallway with sound. The music stops for a moment and then the same line of the song is played again.

"That sounds like one of ma tante Elodie's songs. She still plays the piano. I think she turned ninety-one on her last birthday. When I was small, she'd sit me down beside her at the piano and teach me French songs."

"You never told me that."

"It's not that important."

The door of the suite is open. Paul and Lisette stand outside the door looking at the circle of four women around the piano. They are wearing identical black tams and vests over white shirts.

by Marie Moser

Three of the women hold up their music sheets while the fourth, frailer than the others, stands in her walker and looks over at another's music.

The woman sitting at the piano is noticeable for the pure white of her hair, pulled tightly to the top of her head in a pearl-coloured bun. The song ends with three loud chords. The pianist turns around to talk to the quartet and notices Paul and Lisette at the door. For a moment she does not recognize Lisette, then she smiles.

"We'll take a rest now, girls, and meet at half-past four for another rehearsal," she says. "I have an important visitor now: my great-niece. Come in, Lisette."

The four turn to look at her, smiling. She walks directly to her great-aunt, who is rising slowly from the piano bench, and puts her arms around the small woman.

"Ma petite Lisette . . . "

"Ma tante Elodie. I brought someone to meet you. This is my fiance, Paul Malory."

"Don't tell me! You're getting married!" Her dark brown eyes widen behind her glasses as she extends a thin hand to Paul. "I'm so pleased to meet you, young man."

When the last of the quartet has shuffled away out the door, ma tante says to Lisette, "*Mais c'est un très beau garçon!*"

Lisette cringes; she had been hoping she would not speak French. Quickly, she whispers to him, "She says you're very handsome."

"It's all right. I figured it was something like that. I really liked that song you were playing, ma tante."

"Your fiance does not talk French?" she whispers loudly to Lisette.

"Well, no . . . "

"I was simply asking. Welcome, welcome, Paul. Please sit down. I was reviewing a few songs with the quartet. We're having a concert for the villa tonight."

She lowers herself carefully onto a kitchen chair and faces Paul and Lisette on the couch. "And what do you do?" she asks Paul.

"I'm studying to be a civil engineer."

"You're going to work on the railroad?"

"No, ma tante." Lisette looks at Paul who is smiling broadly. "He's going to university so he can design bridges and roads."

"Oh my, isn't that silly of me?" She hides her mouth in a girlish gesture when she laughs.

"Not at all," Paul says. "My grandfather thought the same thing when I told him."

"You are lucky to get a good education. I wanted to study music when I was young but my father, he would not let me go. That's the way it was in those days." She takes a tissue and wipes her forehead. "Such a warm day. Would you like a glass of lemonade? I had some made for the quartet. Lisette, pour us three glasses and I'll get some cookies."

Lisette goes to the kitchen and sees a pink rectangular plate, with a pattern like tattered lace, sitting in the middle of the table. The sun shining on it gives it an iridescent glow. She delicately touches the scalloped edges. "Where did you get this plate? It's so pretty."

"It belonged to my mother—let me see—that would be your great-grandmother, wouldn't it?" She places some cookies on it and carries it out to the living room. Lisette hurries to pour the lemonade and follows her.

"Look, Paul. This is ma tante's mother's plate. Isn't that amazing?"

"Yes, yes it is," he says, peering at it and reaching for a cookie. "Did you come from a big family? Lisette hasn't told me too much about her past."

"She hasn't?" She frowns at Lisette. "But there are so many good stories—" She pauses and then brightens. "Then, I will have to tell you some of our family history."

She wets her lips as she thinks, then begins the story slowly. "My parents came west in September of 1905. We were six in the family. I had four older brothers and a baby sister. I was five years old at the time. My father had been a shopkeeper in a town called St. Scholastique in Quebec, and he left to start a new life on his own land. Too, he had many sons and thought he would have lots of help on the farm. My parents took the colonists' train to Calgary and then got on some kind of cattle train up to Strathcona, just on the other side of Edmonton. They had to hire some wagons to take their belongings up to Morinville where my mother had a cousin with a big house. It was a long journey in those days. I was young but I remember it started to rain and rain, and the roads turned to mud and one of the wagons overturned. Me and my mother and little sister got thrown into a ditch. We were pulled out soaking wet. It was terrible. We were close to my mother's cousin's house, but my little sister got sick from her fall in the water and . . . she died a few days later. You can imagine how my poor mother felt. About eight months later, your grandmother was born, and then six more children, three boys, and three more girls."

She sips from her lemonade and takes a bite from her cookie. She doesn't look at either of them as she appears to search her memory. "I'll show you some pictures."

She pulls out a photo album from the cupboard under the china cabinet and sits between them. The album is arranged chronologically, starting with her own parents' parents, and then the pictures of her family when they first arrived in Morinville. The first pictures are starkly black because everyone is dressed in mourning for the baby who died. Later, there are more joyous pictures of a picnic outside, with a long table set up with food. The last picture is a large one of the family standing in front of the new house, the girls with lace collars on their dresses and the boys in their Sunday suits.

"Look at the size of that family!" Paul says.

"Everyone had large families in those days . . . and yet there are only two people in that picture left living today."

"See, that's my grandmother there," Lisette says. "The one with the long hair on her shoulders."

"You look a lot like her, did you know that?" Paul says.

"Yes, yes," agrees ma tante. "Same eyes, same nose. I was thinking the other day that, of the one hundred and seventy-three people descended from my parents, there are only four families who have kept our traditions and our language."

"Things change, ma tante. It's not that important any more," Lisette says. She realizes what she has said when they both turn to her. Paul shakes his head slightly.

"Lisette, you too?" Ma tante says it quietly and then with a sigh closes the album and sets it back on the shelf.

"It's true," Lisette says, straightening. "It's not part of my life anymore."

Her great-aunt looks at her and then her gaze drops to her hands on her lap. "It's all right, Lisette. I understand how it is."

The conversation has been dampened and uneasy moments pass.

Finally, ma tante says, "But what am I thinking? I have to give you something for your engagement."

She looks about her suite pensively and her eyes settle on the plate with the one remaining cookie. "I will give you your great-grandmother's plate."

"Oh no, ma tante. I couldn't take that."

But her great-aunt has already removed the cookie. She opens a drawer, finds tissue paper and wraps up the plate. "I have lots of other plates. I told you she never used them. Well, neither did I, until recently." She hands the package to Lisette, pressing her hands around it.

Then it is time to go. While they are standing and exchanging goodbyes, ma tante takes Lisette by the hand and says, "Wait. There's something I want you to hear."

She sits at the piano, her frail hands searching the keys for the right chords. She begins to sing:

Fait dodo, bébé à maman
Fait dodo, tu auras du lolo.
Papa est en bas, qui frappe du marteau,
Maman est en haut, qui fait du chocolat.
Fait dodo, bébé à maman,
Fait dodo, tu auras du lolo . . .

Her voice is gentle but strong; the melody and words so familiar that she sings without thinking. "Your mother sang this song to you when you were a baby cradled in her arms. It is the song my mother sang to me and to your grandmother. No one knows where the lullaby comes from; it has always been in our family. I hope you will not forget it."

She stands up again and opens her arms. Lisette bends over to receive a last hug. "Please come and see me again and I'll tell you more stories, Paul. About my own family. Maybe about Lisette next time."

"Goodbye, goodbye . . . "

They walk down the hallway with the soft notes of the lullaby following them until they are outside.

As he opens the car door, Paul says, "What does that mean: `fait dodo?'"

"It means go to sleep."

He sits in and rolls down the window before starting the car. "What a big family. Two rows of kids—like a classroom picture."

"Now you know. I told you she was an old-fashioned French-Canadian lady."

"I thought she was very nice. Sharp too. Isn't it amazing how well she can play that piano?"

"I guess some things you don't forget."

On the drive home Lisette is relieved that it is all over. It doesn't matter what her great-aunt said. She unwraps the plate and looks at it, something her great-grandmother set on her table. Perhaps she too will pass it on to her children.

She sits silently in the middle of the seat, close to Paul, and tries to remember the lullaby. How did it go again? She has forgotten some of the words already.

She holds the plate close to examine the lace design and she sees that a tiny crack runs the entire length of the plate. She wonders why such an incredible feeling of sadness falls over her.

SYLVIE RENOIR • *EDMONTON, ALBERTA*

MARILYN DUMONT

Marilyn Dumont was born in Olds, Alberta in 1955. Her early childhood years were spent in lumber camps in the Sundre area where her mother worked as a camp cook and her father as a faller. Her family came to Sundre from the Kikino Metis Settlement south of Lac La Biche. When asked if she was related to Gabriel Dumont, the famous hunt chieftain of the Saskatchewan Metis and Louis Riel's general during the North-West Rebellion of 1885, Ms Dumont said that she was but that she was also a direct-line descendant of an earlier Gabriel Dumont, the Batoche Gabriel's uncle. This older Gabriel Dumont and his brother Isidore were famous hunters, men on whom early fur trade forts relied for meat. The older Gabriel Dumont was also involved in the establishment of the Metis community at Lac Ste. Anne. Marilyn Dumont was for several years an academic advisor for Native Student Services at the University of Alberta. Before that she worked as an employment counselor, a shipper/receiver, a tree planter, and a plywood factory worker. Her writing has appeared in numerous journals, including blue buffalo *(1986),* CV 11 *(1987),* A Room of One's Own *(1990),* Matriart *(1991),* Orbis *(1991), and in the NeWest anthology,* Writing the Circle *(1990).*

Squaw Poems

peyak

"Hey squaw!"

Her ears stung and she shook fearful of the other words like fists that would follow. For a moment, her spirit drained like water from a basin. But she breathed and drew inside her fierce face and screamed till his image disappeared like vapour.

niso

Indian women know all too well the power of the word squaw. I first heard it from my mother, who used it in anger against another Indian woman. "That black squaw," she rasped. As a young girl, I held the image of that woman in my mind and she became the measure of what I should never be.

nisto

I learned I should never be seen drunk in public, nor should I dress provocatively because these would be irrefutable signs. So as a teenager I avoided red lipstick, never wore my skirts too short or too tight, never chose shoes that looked the least "hooker-like." I never moved in ways that might be interpreted as loose. Instead, I became what Jean Rhys phrased, "aggressively respectable." I'd be so God damned respectable that white people would feel slovenly in my presence.

by Marilyn Dumont

newo

squaw is to whore
as
Indian maiden is to virgin

squaw is to whore
as
Indian princess is to lady

niyanan

I would become the Indian princess not the squaw dragging her soul after laundry, meals, needy kids, and abusive husband. These were my choices. I could react naturally, spontaneously, to my puberty, my newly discovered sexuality, or I could be mindful of the squaw whose presence hounded my every choice.

nikotwasik

squawman:

a man who is seen with, lives with, laughs with a squaw.

"squawman"

a man is a man is a whiteman until

he is a squaw, he is a squaw, he is a squawman

Helen Betty Osborne

Betty, if I set out to write this poem about you
it might turn out instead,
to be about me
or any one of
my female relatives,
it might turn out to be
about this young Native girl
growing up in rural Alberta
in a town with fewer Indians
than ideas about Indians,
in a town just south of the "Aryan Nations"

it might turn out to be
about Anna Mae Aquash, Donald Marshall, or Richard Cardinal,
it might even turn out to be
about our grandmothers,
beasts of burden in the fur trade
skinning, scraping, pounding, packing,
left behind for "British Standards of Womanhood,"
left for white melting-skinned women,
not bits-of-brown women
left here in this wilderness, this colony.

Betty, if I start to write a poem about you
it might turn out to be
about hunting season instead,
about "open season" on Native women
it might turn out to be
about your face   young and hopeful
staring back at me   hollow now
from a black and white page
it might be about the "townsfolk"   (gentle word)
townsfolk who "believed Native girls were easy"
and "less likely to complain if a sexual proposition led to violence."

Betty, if I write this poem.

HERMAN RESCHKE • *CAMP CREEK, ALBERTA*

CHERYL FOGGO

Cheryl Foggo is thoroughly Calgarian, having lived in Calgary all her life. She is also a third-generation Black Canadian on her mother's side of the family. Her great-grandfather was part of "a wave of Black farmers who arrived on the Canadian prairies in 1910." Her father is Bermudian. The name "Foggo" came "from an Englishman who was shipwrecked off the coast of Bermuda in another century." Ms Foggo has told her family story in the book Pourin' Down Rain *(Detselig Enterprises, 1990), a finalist for the 1990 Writers Guild of Alberta Non-Fiction Award. Ms Foggo's short story "Personal Questions" appeared in the 1990 anthology* Alberta ReBound *(NeWest Press). Like the story that follows, "Personal Questions" is set inside the world of Canadian Football League players and of the people whose lives those players intersect. Ms Foggo recalls that her first ever job was "selling hot dogs at McMahon Stadium," home of the CFL's Calgary Stampeders.*

Looking for Africa

I AM LOOKING FOR AFRICA IN THE HAIR of the people around me. It is difficult to tell.

Directly in front of me, two rows up, is a woman with long auburn waves, more than waves, crimps. Africa, I think. To my left and down one row is a man with a red cap, a baseball cap that says Hank's Trucking, turned sideways. He is devoting his full attention to the football game, his face is alive and his head ducks and juts along with the players' movements. He has stringy hair that might be blonde if it was washed. No Africa.

To my right sits my daughter Barbara and to her right are three young girls heavily made up. They are, all of them, wearing tight leather skirts, and all of them have Africa, in varying degrees of modification. I am thinking they could be the girls Barbara spoke of who come to these games because they are involved on some level with the players. Sometimes the players' real girlfriends or wives come too and there is a confrontation. They make me nervous for no discernible reason other than that they are loud. I don't ask Barbara who they are for fear that they will hear me.

It is mid-afternoon but dark. Ominous thunderclouds hang over the field and as far as I can see. I note that beer is now sold in the stadium, which was not the case when I last attended a football game, in 1976. Because her boyfriend Reggie plays, Barbara has free tickets to all the games, good seats too.

I try to relax. I don't wish to be here but I am here with a tight feeling in my throat. I tell myself to relax, and begin to breathe deeply. Barbara glances at me briefly, then back at the field.

I think about what I once read, that any curl in any hair is a gift from Africa, and go back to my search. There seems to be no one else that I can see, but there are so many perms. It is really difficult to tell for sure.

by Cheryl Foggo

Reggie is returning a punt. I know it is he because Barbara has told me that he wears sweater number 27. He looks like a child from here, a happy high-stepping child, dodging to and about, whirling, lifting his knees almost to his chest as he runs.

Many in the crowd are standing. He is nearing the end zone and we need the points to go ahead. Someone behind me shouts, "Come on, Bailey! Come on, man!" and Reggie renews his speed as though he can hear. But then he is caught by his left ankle from behind. He takes another step with his right leg fully extended and hits the ground just that way, with his left foot yanked backward and his right leg in front. Someone in a green jersey flies in from the side and crushes him against the turf. The referee comes, waving his arms and shrilling his whistle, and everyone gets up with the exception of Reggie.

The crowd is silent as Reggie lies there. In fact he doesn't move at all. A man who I assume is the trainer runs from the sidelines and bends over Reggie, then turns back to the Stampeder bench and gestures for help. As more men run on field bearing a stretcher, Reggie rolls onto his back. I believe that I hear him moan but I may be mistaken.

Barbara is on her feet, I notice now. When they lift Reggie to the stretcher and begin to carry him away, she crosses in front of the leather-clad girls and starts up the concrete stairway.

"Barbara," I say, "where will I meet you?"

She answers me without turning her head and I don't catch it.

"What did she say?" I ask the girls.

"She said she'll be back," the prettier one responds.

The trainers have stopped in mid-field and have set the stretcher down. They are examining Reggie's right leg. His back is arched as though he is in pain.

I feel the onset of a slight panic, partly because Barbara is gone. I have grown fond of Reggie, have grown to see through his American brashness. I have recently come to believe that he will be the father of my grandchildren.

The game has been delayed for some time now, because of what has happened to Reggie, and some of the people seated around me are growing restless. He is alive and that is good, they seem to feel, but let us now carry on with proceedings.

The trainers continue their ministrations. It is not their job to worry about a jittery crowd.

Someone seated in the same row as me, a man who I hadn't noticed until now, shouts, "Beer!" Those around him, his friends I would guess, laugh. He stands up.

"Hey, ref!" he bellows. "Throw him a watermelon. Let's play the game."

I am sitting alone in a football stadium. "Where has Barbara gone?" I wonder.

I ponder the inebriated man's remark—"Throw him a watermelon." Some laughter followed it. Do people laugh because they understand the symbolism of watermelon as it pertains to Black people, or because they don't understand but believe the remark to be amusing because it was uttered by a drunk? I wonder about this as I sit on the hard bench. Perhaps only he and I understand. The Black girls sitting beside me appear to be unfazed. They are talking about cassette tapes. One thinks she left her car unlocked with all the tapes inside in plain view and wonders if she should go now and check.

I lean forward to see around the people seated between me and the man. He is small and has acne.

I think for one small moment that I am going to weep. I wish again that Carl was alive. I don't want to be where I am. I don't want to be who I am. I don't feel like being Black today.

I decide that I will say something to the man. I will stand in front of him and deliver a zinger, I don't know what yet, then I will make my way to the parking lot where I will try to find Barbara's car.

I find that I am up, I am stepping over people's ankles, excusing myself. I am holding my purse and the paper cup of Coke that Barbara gave me.

I am in front of the man, but instead of speaking, I raise my arm and, with a violent motion that surprises even me, I hurl the contents of the cup into his bumpy face.

From all around I hear a gasp. The man stands up and screams at me. "What are you doing?" There is a moment of confusion. A girl tugs on his jacket as he glares. I don't avert my gaze, people are surrounding us and the man looks as though he is about to spit. Instead he snaps his arms and pushes sharply and lightning-quick at my chest. I tumble backward, knocking people down and am caught by the man in the red hat.

He sets me upright and turns to my attacker. "Are you crazy? This is an old lady!"

The people around us are looking at me and the man as though we are from the same circus, but different freak acts. Someone has summoned security and three uniformed but unimposing men are approaching, one of them having to hop over a banister. Two of them look frightened but the third speaks up.

"What is this?"

"Look at my jacket, man."

I believe the cola has ruined the leather. Many bystanders are offering their version of the story. The girl who was tugging on the jacket says, "Totally unprovoked." Someone argues with her. "He's been drunk for the last hour."

I am unable to speak, unable to catch my breath. My left breast is aching. The right breast, which was removed two years before Carl died, feels nothing.

A diminutive child is peering through her mother's legs at me and, when she catches my eye, she smiles. I feel obliged to smile weakly back at her.

I hear a lightly accented voice, which sounds nearly familiar, speak my name. I look around and my eyes settle on a Black face, which I am relieved to see among the faces of the large crowd which is now smothering me. It takes a moment to register that it is a face I know, the face of Gilbert Merrick.

Reggie has been transported to the Foothills Hospital. His leg is broken in three places and he has a dislocated hip.

Gilbert has taken me away from the stadium, after I and the man in the leather jacket have both declined to press charges.

Gilbert has found Barbara and explained what has happened, assured her that he would see me home. He has brought me to a Caribbean bakery and café which he apparently owns. He doesn't say this but I glean from the demeanour of the staff that it is so.

I am sitting on a stool at a corner table, drinking a very strong, sweet coffee. Gilbert returns from the kitchen with a plate of rice, chicken, and beans, wrapped in what he explains is a roti.

We talk about the things that have happened since we last were together. Gilbert's wife has been dead for longer than Carl, nearly six years. I am embarrassed that I had not heard of his café, and that I haven't eaten here before. He tells me that it is a successful venture. He does not say this boastfully. He has one child, he says, a daughter who, like mine, is dating a football player.

The food is very good, but I do not hurry. I am afraid that when I am finished Gilbert will offer to take me home, and I know that my house will be dark when I step into it.

I eat and at the same time study Gilbert's face. Except for two deep lines across his brow, time has ignored it. He still has brown eyes, he still has a long, narrow nose with flipped-up nostrils, he still has full, dark lips. He still has the blackest skin I have ever seen and hair that cries "Africa!" He looks beautiful and I am puzzled by this.

Gilbert is talking to me.

"Your daughter said `you're joking' when I introduced myself. Does she know me? Do I know her?"

I feel an immediate rush of heat from my abdomen to my scalp. "She would have recognized the name. I . . . I've mentioned you. To her."

"You've mentioned me." He is merciful and does not ask what I have said, but I know that he knows.

"Is your daughter serious with her Mr Bailey?"

I think for a moment about who Mr Bailey might be, before realising Gilbert is referring to Reggie.

"It would seem." I shrug. "He goes back to where he's from between seasons. Atlanta, I think. Barbara sees other people when he's away. I think he does the same. But they . . . well, by their standards, I believe it is a very serious relationship. What about your daughter? Who did you say she sees?"

"Rupert Price. Number 11. They live together. I have asked Sandy about their plans for marriage, but she is young. Sandy does more or less what she wants to do."

"Price. Isn't he white?"

Gilbert nods. "Yes."

A slight girl, possibly Africa, who has been serving the five tables near us, comes over.

"Can I bring you anything, Mr Merrick?"

"No, no, we're fine, unless—" He turns to me. "Eunice, would you like a drink?"

I decline.

"I remember that you are not a drinker."

"Today's events may get me started." I mean for it to be funny but my voice is trembling.

"I know it is easy for me to say, Eunice, but try to shake it off. People like that are everywhere and if you let them snatch one iota of your life's enjoyment, where will you be?"

His tone is so gentle and I am so exhausted, and my left breast aches and aches. I begin to cry.

"I would have done the same if I'd heard what he said," he continues. "I would have popped him one."

"And then you'd be just another Black behind in jail." I say this bitterly, louder than I intend. What I have said shocks Gilbert and he laughs.

I am laughing now too, bottled-up, overdue laughter that I can't stop. I am nearly hysterical. I recall a time years ago when I went to a concert where people were smoking marijuana and I didn't know why but I was dizzy and felt that the top of my head was floating away. I feel that way now.

Gilbert is laughing too.

I feel ridiculous, but better.

We stop finally and I want to talk some more.

"Your accent is nearly gone," I say.

He looks at me very directly. Seconds pass.

"You were always so concerned with accents and things, Eunice." He says this flatly.

I see from his face that forty years has not taken the sting from our last moment together, that he feels the pain, that my telling him to go away is as fresh as yesterday.

I am wrong about my house being dark. Barbara is there waiting for me when I arrive. She is lying on the couch with a cold cloth over her eyes and only the smallest lamp lit. She has a migraine.

"What's happened? Is it Reggie?" I ask this without removing my coat.

She makes the slightest nodding motion with her head. She doesn't remove the cloth from her eyes.

I am impatient for her to answer but too frightened to ask her to go on. Reggie has died, I feel certain. Internal bruising of some vital organ has killed him.

"We had a terrible fight up at the hospital. He won't play again this year. He's probably finished."

I feel relieved. "Why would you fight about that?"

"Well."

"Barbara, what's happened?"

"He said maybe we should get married."

"What's wrong with that?"

"I don't want to live in the States. How bad do I want to have brown babies and raise them in Georgia?"

"Well of course you'll live here."

"He says it's no better here. He says Calgary's a backwater."

I feel my back stiffen. "That is typical American ignorance."

"He says *we're* ignorant, that I'm making a judgement about a place I've never been. Which is true."

We sit silently for some time and I think about the day.

I am fifty-nine years old and have engendered my first fist fight. I am still shocked that the man in the red cap referred to me as an old lady. My former future son-in-law has broken bones and, worse than that, he has assaulted my daughter's sacred status as a fourth generation Black Canadian. And Gilbert Merrick has . . . has come.

Barbara speaks, as though she is reading my mind.

"I thought Mr Merrick was very nice, Mother." Her tone is scolding.

"I never said he wasn't nice."

"And you always called him Jamaican. Sandy's told me her dad is Bermudian."

"Who's Sandy?"

"Sandy Merrick. His daughter. She was sitting next to you at the game."

"You mean those three girls? Which one?"

"The pretty one in the dark green. But the point, Mother, is that he's not Jamaican."

I laugh a little sheepishly. "It was just a joke. Mom always referred to any Black person who wasn't Canadian or American as Jamaican. When Gilbert phoned she used to say `It's that Jamaican boy again.'"

Barbara carefully swings her legs to the floor and sits up. She removes the cloth from her eyes to stare at me. Now, as ever when I look at her, I am struck by her loveliness. She is like her father's family, golden-skinned, slender, Africa waving gently through her hair.

"I always thought of him as Mr Roller Coaster," she says. "I almost said that when he introduced himself."

I try to picture what Gilbert looked like forty years before, on the roller coaster. I remember his terrified expression and his cries to be let off. I recall my humiliation and my certainty that I would never love him. I recall that I didn't think him beautiful.

She offers to make black currant tea, and I let her, although I fear that it will keep me awake on a night when I don't want to lie awake.

She stays an hour longer, tells me that she still thinks I should press charges and asks me how my boob is. Then she says she is going back to the hospital to grapple further with Reggie. I watch her drive away.

I look at the clock—8:40. It is a tad early for bed.

I wonder why I allow Barbara to persuade me out of the house. She says continually that I mustn't retreat from life, I let her coax me, and then I return to my empty house and melancholia. I look up the meaning of the word "melancholia" in the dictionary. It says "mental disease characterized by great depression of spirits and gloomy forebodings." This seems an exaggerated description of the way I feel and I replace the book in the spot where it has been for twenty-two years.

I decide to go to bed and, to my relief, I sleep. I am dreaming that the man in the red cap who referred to me as an old lady is rocking on the swing on the patio. My dream is disturbed by the ring of the doorbell.

Startled, I sit up and look at the clock—10:12. I am terrified that at the door I will find the man who punched me in the chest. I am more afraid not to know so I take my robe and creep to the entranceway. I can see no one at all through the peephole. I turn on the outside light and call "hello" but receive no answer. My heart is pounding. I open the door to nothing.

This has frightened me badly. I turn on every light and sit on the couch to collect myself. I try to recount exactly what has happened.

"I have had an unpleasant day." My voice sounds unlike my voice, tremulous and low. "I have had a dream and heard the doorbell. The ring could have been a part of my dream."

I feel better to think that the bell perhaps did not ring. I go to the bathroom to fetch an aspirin for the pain in my left breast. While there, I open my pyjama top, to check for bruising, and am satisfied to note that a textbook contusion has formed, swollen and purple, and that I am not imagining the pain. I stare at my breasts, the bruised left one and the false right. I have always thought of them, referred to them, as breasts. No man but Carl has ever seen them. I imagine what it would be like to have a man see them as they are now, damaged. Gilbert.

I walk toward my bedroom but, in the hallway, am taken over by a feeling that I should not be there. I snatch my long coat from its hanger, slip into my shoes, and leave the house ablaze with light.

Gilbert's café—*The Caribe*, it is called—is dark. I am thrown off by this, finding no one there, and also by the realization that I am parked on a popular street wearing pyjamas.

I consider going to Barbara's apartment but it is a thirty minute drive from where I am. I think anyway that she will be with Reggie. I don't want to go home. I consider Motel Village.

A light flashes briefly inside The Caribe and Gilbert comes out onto the sidewalk with a young man and a young woman, not the one I saw earlier. They have just closed, I surmise, and this is confirmed when Gilbert locks the door behind them and waves as they proceed down the sidewalk.

I suddenly feel foolish, like I am a jilted lover in a really bad film. I reverse my car, intending to drive away before Gilbert sees me, but it is too late, he does see me. I smile and gesture casually, implying that I am there on other business. He is not fooled and comes to the window, looking terribly worried.

I feel that he is going to say, "Is everything all right?" and he does.

We are in the café. He has closed the blinds so that people won't see the light and think that it is open.

"Why were things like that so important to you?"

Gilbert is asking me about the roller coaster. I want to tell him the truth. It is minutes before I respond.

"It seemed a very foreign behaviour. I thought if you were a . . . a Canadian you wouldn't be afraid of a roller coaster. Or that you wouldn't show it."

Gilbert is rubbing the tabletop with the palm of his hand, very slowly. His knuckles are cracked. I recall only now, as he does it, that he bites his lower lip when he is thinking.

I feel that I should tell him everything.

"I think you were too Black for me. Then." I add "then" very carefully.

Oddly, he seems relieved to have me admit it.

"What did you like so much about me, way back, Gilbert?"

"When you are young, sometimes you like people because they are pretty. I wanted to be like you and your friends, in your world."

I nod. I know that he is going to say more.

"It was good for me, when you left. It made me stop wanting to be in your world."

He is happy to have said this to me, and I feel purged.

Gilbert asks me if I would like to dance. He pushes aside some tables and selects "Sweet Bitter Love" on the juke box. I rest my head on his chest. When I speak, I don't look up, and my voice is muffled.

"It's not just watermelon, it's everything else that's happening now."

He understands what I am saying and pats my shoulder gently.

We are driving in my car to the Northland Mall, hurrying to get there before midnight.

The lights of the carnival are still blinking and people are lined up at the roller coaster. We have not had time to go to my house for clothing but I tie my belt tightly around me and Gilbert says no one will notice. It is not large, as roller coasters go. Still, as I stand beneath, watching its highest point, my head is tipped all the way back. I am uncertain of the cause of my dizziness. Is it the aspirin or the action I am about to undertake?

We are called forward by the operator. Things are different now. We are strapped into our little car and this time I am terrified too.

We agree that it is a good place to start.

KIRBY SOON • *CALGARY, ALBERTA*

GLORIA SAWAI

Gloria Sawai of Edmonton was born in Minneapolis, Minnesota. At one year of age she moved with her parents to southern Saskatchewan. When she was in high school, another move brought her to Alberta: to Ryley and later to Camrose. In adulthood, the traveling continued: to Joliet, Illinois, to Minneapolis, to Japan, and back to Alberta. She received a BA degree from Augsburg College in Minneapolis and an MFA degree from the University of Montana in Missoula. Her short stories have appeared in several anthologies, notably Best Canadian Stories *(Oberon Press, 1982) and* The Oxford Anthology of Canadian Short Stories *(Oxford University Press, 1986). Her stories were also collected in the three-author anthology* Three Times Five *(NeWest Press, 1984). Her play* Neighbour *was published by the Playwrights Union of Canada in 1980. Besides being a fiction writer and a playwright, Ms Sawai has taught English in high school, college, and university. Her own writing has been influenced by the southern Saskatchewan prairie where she spent her childhood, her Norwegian Lutheran family roots, and a marriage into a Japanese family tradition.*

The Dolphins

BENEATH THE GENTLE WATER FOUR dolphins sleep. They lie belly down just below the pool's rippling surface. Their smooth humps rest like quiet hills in the green waves. A dorsal fin cuts the water's edge, and one dolphin slides up, into the air above, curving himself over the others, a slick grey arch dripping water like wet crystals, shards of fluid glass. The muscled lid on top of his head pulls open. He sucks in air, pushes the lid shut, and plunges down for another snooze. A short one. Dolphins have to sleep holding their breath.

In her narrow bed, under a white quilt, Elizabeth dreams of the vessels. Thousands of them. Glass containers that fill the shelves in rooms and corridors. Bottles, jugs, tumblers, urns, crystal cups as small as thimbles. And in one of these rooms or corridors, on one of the hundreds of shelves, hidden amidst all the glass, there is one secret vessel. In that one lies the answer. If she looks hard enough, if she is determined, if her will is strong, she will find the answer. Then she'll know. Then everything will be all right. She moves slowly down the narrow corridor.

She wakes, hears her mother in the bathroom. She's sliding open the mirrored door of the medicine cabinet, moving things around in there. Elizabeth hears the clinking sounds. She closes her eyes, pulls the quilt over her face. She sees her mother remove a small bottle from the shelf, pry open the plastic lid with her fingernail, shake a green pill into the palm of her hand, lift her hand to her mouth. Water gushes from the tap, splashes into the porcelain sink.

Elizabeth sits up and calls.

"Mother?"

"Yes?"

"I hear water running."

by Gloria Sawai

"I'm thirsty."

The water stops.

"Mother?"

"Yes?"

"Did he come home?"

"Not yet, but soon he will. Go to sleep now. Everything's all right."

Those are her words. That's what she always says.

"Everything's all right."

In the morning, her mother stands at the kitchen counter, fitting a pleated filter into the coffee maker. She's wearing a purple housecoat. Her hair is uncombed.

Elizabeth, in jeans, her hair brushed into one long sandy braid behind her back, pulls a chair out from the table, sits down, picks up the cereal box, examines the cartoon on the side of the box. Today's Saturday, there's no rush.

"So," she says, "will you drive us to the mall?"

Her mother doesn't answer. She's gazing into some private vision inside the coffee pot.

"You said you'd drive me and Hannah Shimizu to the mall to watch the dolphins."

Her mother stares at the bubbles rising in the plastic tube of the coffee maker, combs her tangled hair with her fingers.

"Well? Will you?"

Her mother covers a yawn with the back of her hand.

"Our report's due on the fifteenth. We've hardly gotten started. Mr Shimizu will bring us back. So will you?"

"I said I would, didn't I?"

Elizabeth shakes cornflakes from the white box into a blue bowl. "He didn't come home, did he," she says. It's not a question, but in her mind's eye she sees her father stumble into the house, slam against a chair. She pours milk over the yellow flakes.

"Don't worry so much," her mother says. Her neck reddens. Stiff muscles show beneath her skin. "Everything's going to be fine."

At 1:30 Elizabeth and Hannah are at West Edmonton Mall at the dolphin pool. They've paid their dollar and are sitting in the miniature grandstand that curves around one side, surrounded by noisy children, parents, grandparents, quiet lovers. On the mall's upper level, Saturday shoppers crowd behind a thick plastic railing and gaze down on the water, restless for the show to start. On the green bridge spanning the pool's far end, more shoppers gather. They're waiting for the trainer to fling open the door of his secret room beside the water, to run out onto the concrete shore and sound the whistle that will call forth the dolphins.

In front of them, through the pool's transparent wall, they see the quiet forms move slowly in the deep, and all around the moving forms, beams of yellow light shimmering, slim corridors of light flickering in the blue-jade water.

Suddenly it's time. Up they leap in perfect symmetry, four dolphins arched above the pool, grey backs glistening. Then down, head first into the waves. They swim in one long smooth and flowing circle. And swiftly up higher, higher still. Crystal sparks rise after them and fall glittering to the surface. For a moment they're suspended in mid-air, beaks straight up, pointing to the steel and plastic sky high above.

"Ladies and gentlemen," the trainer calls. "Meet our four Atlantic Bottlenose dolphins, here to play, have fun, show you their tricks."

He throws an orange ball into the water. In one slippery flash the dolphin has it on the end of his beak, is pushing it forward, swiftly, so smoothly, holding it steady with his snout. He flicks it off, twists, grabs it with his flippers and around the pool he goes, bouncing it up and down and up—

"Look at him look at him look at him go. See him dribble that ball down the court. He's heading for the net," the trainer yells.

Everyone claps and oh oh see that dolphin go. The ball slips, the dolphin swirls around, nips it with his beak, and pushes it toward the basket sitting on the edge of the pool. He eyes the hoop, flips the ball with his snout and misses. On the second shot the ball circles the rim around and around come on come on and falls just outside the net. Oh oh oh isn't that too bad. But on the third try the ball sails over the rim and plunks into the bucket. The crowd cheers. Someone whistles.

"Did you see that?" Hannah asks.

"My goodness," says Elizabeth.

"A slam dunk!" the trainer yells.

And the old woman in red boots says, "My what these dolphins can't do."

Elizabeth stays awhile at Hannah's house. They're standing at the kitchen counter spreading peanut butter on slices of white bread. They're swirling the mixture into hills and valleys on each slice, letting broken pieces of nuts emerge like jagged stones on the brown surface. They laugh at their clever designs.

Hannah's mother is also at the counter, at the far end. She's stirring rice in a large bowl. One arm circles the bowl, holds it tight against her chest. With the other she mixes the rice. The counter is too high for her. Her arm sticks straight out from her shoulder, bent at the elbow, like the stiff wing of a bird. She stops stirring, sprinkles vinegar over the mass, stirs again, then with her hand fans the mixture until it glistens. She does this over and over. She's making sushi for a family outing tomorrow at the Devonian Gardens.

Mr Shimizu is sitting at the kitchen table in the centre of the room. He's reading the paper and drinking coffee from a thick mug. The Devonian Gardens is his idea. He's a botanist. He's wearing sweat pants and an old sweater. He sits easy, seems to feel at home here, to like it here, in the kitchen drinking coffee and reading, not saying much of anything. Elizabeth notices these things. Upstairs, Hannah's brother and his friend whoop and thump at some game or other.

Hannah leans toward Elizabeth and says in a low voice, "My parents don't know anything about dolphins."

"Mine neither," Elizabeth says. "Well, I've told my dad one or two things."

Suddenly Hannah turns and moves to the refrigerator across the room. She moves in an arc, around her father sitting at the table. She stands with her back against the fridge, her hair sharply black against the white door.

"I would like your attention," she says. She stands straight, her hands resting on her narrow hips. She stands like Mr Murray, the sixth grade science teacher.

"Today I will teach you about dolphins," she says.

Her father looks up from his paper. "A lesson on Saturday?" But his eyes smile. Her mother looks up too, but she doesn't stop working the rice.

"We recognize the intelligence of dolphins by what they do," Hannah says. "One. They make friends. That's important. Two. They play and have fun. Not like some people I know—I won't mention names. Three. They take good care of their children. You may want to think about that for awhile." Mr Shimizu makes a face at Hannah, but he's enjoying the speech. Elizabeth can tell. "Four," Hannah continues, "they come to the aid of other dolphins in their time of need. They've even been known to help creatures not of their own species. Like humans. There's another, but I can't remember."

"They mourn the death of their friends," Elizabeth says.

"Yes," Hannah says. "They feel sorrow." She looks intently at her father, then at her mother. "In conclusion, these are the signs of intelligence."

Mr Shimizu claps. Mrs Shimizu stops stirring and wipes her forehead with the palm of her hand.

"I know something about dolphins," she says.

"What?" Hannah asks. "What do you know?"

"In winter, in the north, in Hokkaido, Ainu fishermen stand on the shore and look out to sea. The water's cold and black, and they stand there on the rocks and call out. *Iruka kujira*, they say."

"What's that?" Hannah asks.

"And sometimes," her mother continues, "these fishermen can see one of them way out there, alone, lost, left by the others, jumping up and down like they do, in that icy water."

"What does it mean, *iruka kujira*?" Hannah asks again, but her mother still doesn't answer. Hannah goes to her, leans her chin on her mother's shoulder, speaks loudly into her ear. "Mother. You can't just not tell us. What does it mean?"

"It means dolphin," her mother says. "Dolphin whale."

"Dolphin whale. Is that it? That's all it means?"

But her mother doesn't answer. She's standing alone on a rock somewhere in Japan, looking out.

Hannah's room is full of stuff—shelves of dolls, games, furry animals; a dressing table with photographs, little bottles of perfume, a long-handled mirror, a crystal bell. Hannah clears a space on the dresser, and Elizabeth puts the plate of bread down. Then she picks up a brown photograph in a silver lace frame.

"It's my grandfather," Hannah says. "My mother's father."

"He looks young."

"He was young." She turns on the red lamp suspended over her pine desk. "He died of leukemia."

"Really," Elizabeth says.

"After the bomb. A long time after. He lived in Nagasaki." She adjusts the light to shine closer to the clippings and coil notebooks that litter the desk top.

"Some blew up, some burned up, some just blistered all over. My grandfather got leukemia. Where do you want to sit, on the bed or on the chair?"

Elizabeth sits cross-legged in the middle of the bed, on a pink quilt ruffled and rippling like a small sea, Hannah on the chair by the desk. "I'm glad this war is over," Elizabeth says. The War in the Persian Gulf ended only short weeks before. "I don't think it did much good."

"Not for people, anyway," Hannah says.

"Especially kids."

"Or mothers either for that matter."

"Are there dolphins in the Persian Gulf?"

"I guess."

Hannah leans forward and raises her head. *"Iruka kujira,"* she calls. She reaches to the dresser for a slice of bread. "I told you, didn't I? My mother knows nothing about dolphins."

Elizabeth takes the long way home, following the Mill Woods ravine. The evening sky is overcast but strangely bright. A harsh light. It has an edge to it, like tin. It lies sharp on stones and dirt, on mouldy scraps of paper stuck on branches, on dead leaves packed in ditches. Scattered flakes of snow drizzle down on her. She buries herself in her jacket.

She thinks of the Shimizus at the Devonian Gardens tomorrow. She sees them walk among the trees and shrubs, stop to look at branches, to examine small buds. They comment, ask questions, make jokes. They don't hurry. Then she sees them sitting on a bench outside. They pass around the box of sushi and everyone takes and eats. Mrs Shimizu pours tea from a tall thermos into small cups without handles. They hold the cups in both hands, their hands like bowls. And everyone's there, not somewhere else. They take time, don't always look at their watches. Some families are like that.

When she gets home, the car is not in the driveway. Her mother must still be shopping. She walks around to the back, digs in her pocket for the key, but the door is unlocked. She pushes it open and climbs the four steps into the back hall. The light is on. She removes her jacket, hangs it in the hall closet, and opens the door to the kitchen. She stops. Her breath freezes in her chest.

Her father is sitting at the kitchen table.

He sits rigid, chin on chest, one arm stretched over the formica top, one hand holding an empty glass. Nothing else is on the table, just one thick empty glass. Elizabeth knows that somewhere in the house—on a cement ledge in the far corner of the basement, in the bookcase behind the encyclopedias, on a closet shelf—his bottles are hidden. She knows her mother will find them, will gather them up in green plastic bags and carry them to the alley. She will do this at night when no one can see her.

Elizabeth watches her father. Maybe if she moves behind him lightly, ever so softly, silent, like a robin's feather, her feet hardly touching the floor, she can get to the corridor and to her bedroom at the end of it, without his notice.

"Hold it. Just hold it right there."

He turns in his chair and, barely lifting his head, raises his eyes and looks at her. His face is lined with wrinkles; the whites of his eyes are pink threads. He's wearing his brown bathrobe, open at the neck, and his neck is very thin. "No greeting? No salutation?"

"Hi, Dad," Elizabeth says.

"Hi Dad? Is that it, hi Dad? I'm your father don't forget. Honour your father, don't forget, sneaking behind, creeping like a scared caterpillar." His Adam's apple swims and bulges under the loose skin of his neck. He leans back in the chair. Elizabeth shifts slightly.

"Hold it."

She breathes in thin strips of air.

"Where's your mother? What's going on? Who's in charge around here?"

Elizabeth shrugs. He lets go of the glass. It sits alone in the centre of the table. "Hey." He raises his hand to her, a limp benediction. "Can you answer the questions of eternal life?"

She's stuck. She knows her father's drinking pattern: first religion and poetry, then anger, more like rage, finally a whimpering self pity. The last is worst.

"Where did you come from? Why are you here? Where are you going?" He says the words slowly, over-articulates. He eyes her slyly. "Well? Answer me."

"I've been to the dolphin show," she says, "and I live here."

"God damn," he says, "I forgot about that. Oh, I *am* sorry. *Very* sorry. So so sorry. I do repent."

"It's all right," she says.

"The living womb of the sea of creation and I forgot. Come here. Give your father a kiss. Apollo was a dolphin, you know, when he carried poor damned souls to the land of the dead. Did you know that?"

"It was me who told you."

"Come. Right here. One kiss." He curls his finger, inviting.

Elizabeth goes to him and bends over him. His skin is yellow. She touches his forehead with her lips. It feels damp and cold.

"You're my dolphin," he says. His eyes are wet.

She turns to go.

"Hold it. Stay right where you are." His hands clutch the table's edge. He lifts himself up, lets go of the table, stands alone, straight, stretches tall. "They're whales you know." Slowly he slides back down onto the chair. "Stunted whales. Runts. Not in the big league. No leviathan."

His eyes slits, he gazes at Elizabeth standing quiet in front of the refrigerator.

"Canst thou draw out leviathan with a hook? . . . Tie a rope around his tongue and pull him out? . . . Well? Canst thou?"

"No," she says.

"Canst thou put a hook in his tongue and a chain in the hook and swing him around in the deep?" His voice rises. The veins on his forehead stand out.

"Canst thou pierce his skin with barbed irons?" He coughs, gurgling, and wipes his mouth with the back of his hand.

Elizabeth leans hard against the refrigerator door. Her hands are fists against her thighs.

"Hey, I asked you a question, Miss High and Mighty. Canst thou?"

"I said no, Dad. I already said no."

"Hold it. No talking back. Like Job, and gets God all riled up with canst thou this and canst thou that."

He shakes his head, puzzled. "But God didn't know, did he? The Heavenly Father, such a refuge e'er was given, just didn't know. He *thought* he knew, but he was mistaken. That's the whole problem right there. Mistaken. Isn't that the whole problem right there? Isn't that the trouble? That's it, isn't it?"

He sits up, makes his hand a gun, and points it at Elizabeth. "Ra-a-a-a-a-a-a—a," he croaks. Then he raises his head toward the ceiling. "Ra-a-a-a-a-a-a-a-a-a," he shouts to God somewhere above the roof. "Have you heard the latest?" he says. "We *can* fill his skin with iron. We know how to do that now. We can crush his big whale heart and smash his liver to bits." He tries to raise the gun, to point it up, to wave it in the face of God, but his hand falls limp onto the table.

Elizabeth is quiet, unmoving, watching.

He looks at the empty glass in front of him. His voice turns to crooning. "Don't cry," he says to God, now floating just above the glass. "Don't cry," he says, and strokes the rim with his finger, "hey, fathers make mistakes too you know, they aren't perfect, they have their weaknesses . . . we try our best." He sucks in his breath, makes small whimpering sounds, then large ragged sobs, his body shaking.

Suddenly he's up, his arm extended, his hand clutching the glass. He aims it at her. Elizabeth ducks. The glass smashes against the fridge door, falls in chunks, pieces, powdery crystals onto the tile floor. He walks slowly, only a little crookedly, very carefully into the living room.

"Fathers are a piece of shit." He groans, falls into the sofa, and snores almost immediately.

For now it's over. Elizabeth can breathe.

In the alley, she stands beside the back gate. She has emptied the dust pan of shattered glass, replaced the lid on the aluminum garbage can that leans against the fence. She is holding the empty pan in her hand and looking down the alley at the houses: at the roofs and doors, fences and gates, at the windows letting out the light from inside, at Borneman's next door, whose little kids run naked in the yard in the summer rain, at Hallesby's, where Sarah is probably right now practising her cello for church tomorrow, at the house at the end of the alley, with the huge kennel in the back yard, where sometimes dogs howl in the middle of the night. The sky has darkened. The rim of a narrow moon hangs below a grey cloud. The wind settles into quiet ripples about her, and Elizabeth turns back to her own house.

The front doorbell rings. Elizabeth doesn't answer. She's setting the dust pan on the floor in the kitchen closet. It rings again. She sits down on the edge of a chair beside the table in the darkened room. There's a knock on the back door, loud and persistent, then a voice.

"Anyone home?" it says.

"Are you there?" it says.

Gladness. Comfort. Hope. Elizabeth rushes into the back hall. Richard is back.

"How the hell are you?" he says, his big hand on her shoulder. In the dimness she looks up to where his face is, brown and shiny, to where his welcome eyes are, his smile.

"Hi, Richard, when did you get back?"

"Thursday," he says. "Can I sit down? Aren't the lights working? Did you blow a fuse or something?"

Elizabeth flips the switch by the refrigerator. The room glows. They sit at the table, facing each other.

"So. What's new?"

"Not much."

"Where's Papa Sam and Mary?"

Elizabeth jerks her elbow toward the living room and Richard strides into the room, his long feet gliding over the tiles.

Richard is a friend of her father. In the old days they were together a lot. They'd stay up nights—singing, talking, arguing. Later, fighting. Then Richard disappeared for a year and, when he came back two years ago, he was different. He returns from the living room. "I put his leg up," he says. "You can't sleep very well with one leg dangling. Where's the coffee?" He goes to the counter, pulls out the filter from the coffee maker. He empties the soggy grounds into the sink, rummages on a shelf for a clean filter and fresh grounds.

"When did you get back?" Elizabeth asks.

"Thursday."

"Did you like Australia?"

"Did I *like* it? Do I like blue skies? Do I like strawberries and cream? Do I like a warm bed in winter?"

"You're tanned. Did you see any dolphins? Me and Hannah Shimizu are doing a report on dolphins."

"Is that so?" he says. "Well, I'm sorry to say I didn't see the dolphins. I heard a story about one though."

"What *did* you see?"

"Fish." He plugs in the coffee maker and sits down across from her. "Water and fish. I learned to dive with one of those tanks on my back and a mask on my face. In the Pacific, that is. Deep, eh? And I saw fish. Huge, tiny, fat, skinny, pink, purple, polka-dotted . . . fish with spikes on them, honest-to-god like nails sticking out all over . . . and little yellow fish that looked like flat canaries, really cute . . . and *silver* fish. I'd hang there in the water, tons of it, thousands and millions of tons on all sides." He leans toward Elizabeth, his eyes intent and personal. "Water's so powerful you know. And there I'd be, suspended in all that power. Just hanging in it. And the fish would swim up to me, right up to my goggles, and they'd look in at me with those bulgy eyes, and they'd say hi Richard, and I'd say hi fish, and then they'd take off, who knows where." He gets up from his chair.

"What's the story?" Elizabeth asks.

"Story?"

"About the dolphin."

"Well." He pours himself a cup of coffee and sits down again. He holds the cup in his folded hands. "It's about this dolphin called Opo, not in Australia, New Zealand actually. People used to go out in the ocean and swim with her and touch her. She even let children ride on her back. They all loved her. But one day someone found her in a coral pool near shore. She was dead. And when the village heard, everyone became very sad. And that evening at dusk, some Maoris dug a grave by the town hall and carried the dolphin there and buried her. And they covered her grave with flowers." He sips the coffee loudly. "That's a true story," he says.

Elizabeth sits very quiet. She looks toward the living room, then at Richard. "Why can't he stop?" she says. "You did."

He stands and moves to the counter to refill his cup. "It's a mystery to me," he says.

For a moment she considers his words.

"I think it sucks," she says, finally.

Her mother is looking out the living room window, staring at something beyond the ravine. The television is on, her mother's favourite afternoon soap, "The Young and the Restless," but she's not watching it.

Katherine Chancellor, in more-than-living colour, is flicking her fingers about her face in little circles, long jeweled fingers glittering near her eyes, her cheek, her chin. Miss Chandelier, Elizabeth's father calls her, but her mother loves her. She loves her fancy house, everywhere huge bouquets of flowers in crystal or gold vases. She loves her maid Esther in her tidy uniform, and Katherine's own expensive clothes in colours to match the flowers, never the same outfit twice, and her hair graceful and stylish, even when she's sleeping, even when she's walking in a strong wind.

Elizabeth throws her books on the chesterfield.

"Get in the car," her mother says. "Your father's at the Grey Nuns."

The narrow bed. The square table. The ice water in a green glass. The metal dish, pewter kidney turned inward. The high pole. The bottle strapped to the top. The tube from the bottle dangling down, onto the bed, onto the blue sheet, onto his hand resting there, into the silver needle, the needle flat, visible under the skin, slim outline on a blue vein.

And Richard on a chair at the foot of the bed watching the form in front of him: the feet and knees smooth hills under the sheet, the chest a little field, the penis a small stone. Elizabeth stands by the high window. She looks at his face. His eyes are closed. The skin is tight over the cheekbones.

Her mother pushes the door open and backs into the room with a tray holding two cups of coffee and a can of Coke. The three of them linger in the semi-darkness near the bed, sipping, talking in low tones, their voices strangely clear, melodic in the stillness.

He opens his eyes and looks at them.

"Everyone's here," he says.

He looks at her.

"Hi, Elizabeth," he says.

"Hi, Dad."

Elizabeth tells Hannah about her father. They stand in front of Hannah's locker, bent arms weighted with 3-ring binders, glossy textbooks, plastic purses. They stand close, talking. The crowds in the hall are beginning to thin. The bell for the first class will ring in a minute.

"Do they know what it is?" Hannah asks.

"They're still taking tests," Elizabeth says.

Hannah slams shut the locker door with her foot. The metal rattles. "Will he need an operation?"

"I don't know." They walk quickly down the corridor toward their classroom. They walk close together, avoiding clumps of students who scuff and shove.

"It's not leukemia, is it?" Hannah asks.

"No." They reach the room just as the bell rings. Before they enter they stop for a second to catch their breath.

"Well," Hannah says, "at least it's not that."

Elizabeth dreams again of the vessels. She's standing in a long tunnel. Its walls from floor to ceiling hold the shelves filled with glass. She's waiting for the right container to reveal itself to her, to empty its secret to her. Then gradually, almost imperceptibly, the shelves begin to loosen from the wall, to dip, lean, bend. Pitchers, carafes, bottles, tumblers, are falling one by one, softly, slowly. They turn in the air, circle, glide, and finally land. Pieces of amber glass, and jade and ruby red, rise like fountains before her, then fall in piles everywhere, glittering heaps on the tunnel floor.

And she's standing by a streetlight on a road she doesn't know. It's evening. A small rain is falling. From the house at the end of the street a woman walks toward her. She's old and wearing boots that glisten. Elizabeth knows that when the woman reaches her she will stop for a minute under the light. They will look at each other. Elizabeth will say hello, and the woman will say hello. Elizabeth will say it's a nice rain isn't it? and the woman will say yes it is.

And in that instant, that one swift and slippery moment, circled in light, washed in rain, Elizabeth knows exactly what she needs to know. She knows nothing. She knows everything.

She turns in her narrow bed onto her left side, her cheek on the pillow, knees bent, her thin body curved into sleep.

In the Atlantic, north of the Hebrides, a mother dolphin nudges her calf through purple water into white spume on the ocean's surface. With her snout she pushes the calf into the cold clear air above the spray. The infant muscles on the baby's head stretch open, and the dolphin takes her first breath.

In the Mediterranean, off the coast of Tripoli, two dolphins swim close together. They nuzzle each other with their beaks, caress with the soft tips of their flukes. She opens herself to him, thin crevice in her slick body. And he is there, twisting himself around her. They turn and swirl in the foam. They dip and glide, and together plunge down into the ancient sea.

On a windy shore in New Zealand, a dolphin lies stranded. The muscles on his head are slack. Surrounded by air, no air enters. His pearl-grey neck and white belly blacken on the stones. In the ocean a family calls. Their whistling clicking cries speed through the rolling depths, the crashing surf. Where have you gone? Oh. Oh. Where?

At the mall in Edmonton the dolphins are playing. They're racing, leaping, turning somersaults, breathing. They're swimming around in circles. They're having fun, taking care, being friends, before they sleep.

RUTH REID • *EDMONTON, ALBERTA*

CLEM MARTINI

Clem Martini is a Calgary writer, playwright, and drama instructor. Except for two years in Montreal, he has lived his life in Calgary. When asked about careers beyond writing, he said that he was a father. "This is a career beyond writing. Sometimes it is a career beyond sanity." Mr Martini is married to the writer Cheryl Foggo, whose work also appears in this anthology. Mr Martini has written several plays. A Change of Mind *was produced by Alberta Theatre Projects (Calgary) in 1991.* Nobody of Consequence *also premiered in Calgary in 1991, at Lunchbox Theatre.* Life History of the African Elephant, *winner of the National Playwriting Competition, was produced by Lunchbox Theatre in 1989. Mr Martini also wrote* Shattered Dreams, *a 1989 National Film Board documentary. Between his wife's Black-Canadian background and his own French/Italian/German/Danish one, Mr Martini feels his two young daughters will have "an interesting diversity to choose from."*

Conversations with My Neighbour's Pit Bull

(I)

HER EYES ARE SEARCHING MY EYES. SHE wants to quit Tai Chi classes, she says, so that her Saturday afternoons will be freed up. She needs that time, she tells me, to meet with, go out with, guys. To date guys. It's time, she says. Past time. Everyone her age, apparently, is doing it. In trying to answer my twelve year old daughter's question as to why I do not want her to begin dating, I begin with a parable.

"Two Zen monks are walking," I tell her. "The younger says, when will my training be complete? The older says nothing. They walk. Years pass. Again the younger monk asks the same question, again the older monk says nothing. Decades pass. The older monk dies. The younger monk leaves."

I endure Ellen's basilisk-glance a long moment before she says, "Excuse me, Dad, but that is . . . I don't know *what* that is. That is an incomprehensible pile of shit, is what that is."

I comment that *that* is not a very mature reaction, she retorts that it is a very mature reaction to a really obscure story, I conjecture that it only seems that way to her because she doesn't understand it.

"I think I do. Are you telling me I have to wait till you're dead before . . . ?"

"No. I am telling you that you are, that you will be ready when you are . . . ready. It's not a, it will not be a matter of someone telling you."

"Okay, and I'm saying I'm ready."

"And I'm telling you you're not."

"That's so . . . unfair!"

She turns and walks away. Before she reaches the long hallway she pivots and says evenly, "Mom would let me go."

by Clem Martini

I respond something to the effect that she shouldn't use her mother when she isn't here to speak for herself but by then I'm talking to the air. She's out the door, down the street, and away; away from her home and her lecturing philosophy professor father. I can see the neighbour's Black ceramic figurine grinning over at me like some malevolent wood spirit even as she goes, though. I see it even as Leslie mounts my porch, holding a piece of paper in front of him like a catcher holding his glove hand up to receive a particularly hot pitch.

(II)

"What is it?" I enquire.

"It's a form saying you don't mind what I do with my property as regards any changes I make. The city requires that I go to all my neighbours and get their signatures." He pulls out a pen and hands it to me. "I'm rebuilding the house." He says this with a sweeping gesture which expansively includes his house, the sky, and the rest of the universe. "I've had an architect look over the place and draw up some plans." He fishes another piece of paper out of his pocket. He doesn't offer it to me, it's merely Exhibit A. "It's going to be nice. Garage. Right over there. An atrium there . . ."

I'm shaking my head. Leslie stops.

"No," I tell him and hand him back his pen.

"No?"

"You need my approval, my signature, before you can initiate this, is that correct?"

"Well, ah, *need* may be too strong a word, the city would like . . . What do you mean `no?'"

"Not while that Black figurine sits there."

"You're joking?"

"No, I'm, ah, I'm not. And. And. And, I want you to get rid of . . . Thunder."

"What?"

(III)

For the purposes of this tale please keep these things in mind:

1. a terra cotta figurine of a Black jockey;
2. a half dead tree;
3. a twelve year old girl, Ellen, my daughter;
4. a black pit bull terrier named Thunder;
5. and the whole weight of the Western world since the time of the Roman Empire at least.

In the dark across the lawn up the steps sits the terra cotta figurine. In my house and down the hall in the smaller bed, under the sheets, returned from her walk, lies my daughter. Down the hallway out the back door over the fence into my neighbour's yard once again, across the lawn and into the small hut, the chained pit bull terrier, Thunder, as dark as a rain cloud, as loud as his name. And winding through my mind like a water serpent, the entire history of Western civilization: corrupt, monolithic, dark, decadent. The dog flashes from his hut and stretches the chain taut as a stretched elastic band and barks defiance at a Siamese cat which streaks away. The terra cotta garden ornament grins dimly from the stoop. The tree dies quietly. My daughter shifts a lock of her dark hair from her forehead, looking for a moment very much like her mother, then grips her pillow harder and mutters in her sleep, "How much? How much more time?" And Western civilization whispers its own inarticulate imprecations on the wind.

(IV)

The tree is a fine looking *prunus persica*.

"Have you had a look at this bush?" Leslie calls.

"It's a peach tree."

"It's dead."

"Perhaps not."

"It's spring and there's not a leaf or bud anywhere."

"Certainly I'd agree that it looks dead, but is it dead? That is the question. You postulate that looks, that the appearance of death equals death in fact. But is that true? Common experience tells us that the appearance of death may be replicated by sleep, by a condition of unconsciousness, by feigning death. The actor on stage appears dead, but is not in fact dead . . . "

"What do you think it's doing?"

"Sleeping perhaps. Suspended animation."

"Look," he says and snaps a branch, "dry as burnt toast."

"Don't snap the twigs! Goodness, how would you feel if your fingers were ripped off while you lay asleep in your hammock . . . ?"

"It overhangs my property. I could help you take it down. Wouldn't take long."

"No."

(V)

The Black figurine is a garden gnome of some ancient sort, a jet-black jockey created in a day when racial sensitivity was yet unknown and perhaps even undreamt of. Its lips are immense and red. Its countenance is black as a raven's wing. Its eyes are wide and leering. All in all, the finished product is as insulting a stereotype as ever existed. I protested its installment the day that it appeared, but Leslie would brook none of my liberal rhetoric. "You're making a mountain of a molehill," he told me.

"No, no, no. I am, I think, looking very realistically at this, ah, piece. It's a symbol, Leslie, a symbol."

"It's a lawn ornament, Robert, a *lawn ornament*."

"No, it's more than that."

"A simple bit of decoration."

"I'm afraid, I can't agree. It's an insult and I think you should . . . throw it away."

Leslie refused, and later, responded negatively to my attempts to buy it away as well, leaving me no choice and no leverage. So, it is in the loneliness of my home, late at night, as I peer out the back window listening to Thunder barking, and pondering my neighbour, my daughter, and life in general, that I am struck, as though by lightning, by a blinding bolt of clarity.

How might I handle things differently?

Leslie is an immovable object and inflexible to any already tried solutions. By using this image I am able to frame the whole premise differently.

When the possible solutions are exhausted, what remains? The unlikely and the improbable. Thunder howls all the louder. Who has influence over Leslie? Who has his ear? Who does he have chained and entrenched in his backyard?

Man's Best Friend.

(VI)

Which is what brings me to the backyard of my neighbour, at three in the morning, carrying texts and tracts of Mohandas Gandhi, Martin Luther King, Mother Teresa, Albert Schweitzer, and a three-pound slab of bloody steak meat. From my vantage atop the fence between our properties, I drop the texts and meat to the growling canine. He devours first the books, which I take as a good sign. The steak meat follows. All the while I try to explain in calm, low tones my intention to share ideas, network, and perhaps use his inestimable influence to sway Leslie. After an hour of crouching on the ground with Thunder eyeing me mutely, I come to a profound, if on the face of it, somewhat obvious realization: I am acting like a lunatic. You can't reason with a dog. I stand, and slowly back toward the fence.

"I have given this my best shot," I tell him as I step back. "I've been accused in my time of having some idiotic notions and, I suppose, this is an example of one of them." Before I climb over the fence, I gaze at Thunder one more time. "You are unsightly, unaffectionate and, I presume, deadly. Why oh why would anyone purchase such a creature?"

Thunder rolls, stretches (sinews and muscles twitching with each separate movement) opens his mouth and intones, "Testosterone."

"What?"

"Gun collections, expensive cigars, fast cars, and fighting dogs," he continues, cocking a shaggy eyebrow at me, "all the same thing—I'm just an extension of my master's penis. How did you want me to use my influence, and have you any more steaks?"

(VII)

I'm crawling into bed, it's four-thirty in the morning. The sheets are cold and limp. I pull them over my head and try to forget, but am brought back from forgetfulness by the feel of the back of a hairy hand against my cheek. I toss the sheets up. "What the hell?"

"Sorry," Leslie says, rubbing his eyes and sitting up. "I was waiting for you but I must have drifted off. Geez, you keep late hours at the university."

"In my *bed*? What are you doing here?"

"I wanted to make sure I didn't miss you. I just brought over the plans for my renovations," he says, moving the quilt aside and laying the papers out for me to see. "You can see what a terrific boost this is going to give the property values around here."

"Leslie, I'm not . . . "

He reaches under the bed and plunks something heavy next to the plans. "This is the scale model. The architect almost went blind putting in the detail in the washroom here. Look at the tile flooring."

"Can't we talk about this some other . . . ?"

"Can you see how he poured himself into this thing? If I wasn't, you know, having the rebuilding done myself I think I'd love to have this thing standing in my hallway, that's how nice it is. You can just imagine the architect, hunched over, tracing those lines late at night probably, somewhere in some little architect's office. You're not the kind of person to let a little ceramic figure get in the way of an architect's dreams, are you?"

"Go home, Leslie."

"I'm not a man to beg," he says, getting on his knees by the bedside, "but please reconsider this."

"All you have to do is remove the . . . "

He stands up suddenly. "A man's home is his castle, Robert, his *castle*—and that extends, you know, right into the front yard all the way to the furthermost edge of the property line. That's a sacred thing. You can't honestly be expecting me to compromise my principles?"

"You expect me to compromise mine."

"Fine," he snorts indignantly. "If that's the way you want to be." He stands and leaves. On his way out he hands me a sample of the colour swatches he'd had picked out for the exterior paint. "Just have a look at them," he pleads.

"For goodness' sake, Leslie, it's not just the figurine."

"What is it then?" he asks earnestly, his face beaded with sweat, lit from the top by the outside front door light.

"It's the total lack of understanding about what the figurine means."

"What?" he asks, almost doubled over with the desire to learn. "Tell me. What?"

"You don't really want to know."

"I do. Tell me."

"You don't."

"I do," he repeats fervently. "Honest. I want you to tell me."

"Can you not understand that someone could be hurt by that figure?"

"That's ridiculous!"

"Leslie! You just asked me!"

"Who? Who could be hurt?"

"Me!" I shut the door and return to my bedroom, climb into bed. Almost as quickly, Leslie scrambles in through the bedroom window.

"Why?" he asks. "There's no one Black on the entire block. No one will see it."

"There is."

"No, there isn't."

"Believe me, there is."

"There isn't, I've looked."

"My daughter is Black, Les. My wife is Black—and that is beside the point. Can't you see if someone Black could be offended, then *I* could be offended."

"Your daughter doesn't look Black."

"Ah!"

"But she doesn't."

"Exactly! She doesn't *look* like your preconceived notion of what a Black person should look like. That statue is your notion. But she is. Half Black."

"Oh. And is she offended?"

"Les!"

"Ask your wife then."

"I'm not going to . . . "

"I'd ask her myself but I've never seen her. The two years I've been here I've never seen your wife. I assumed you were divorced. Are you?"

"No."

"She travels a lot or . . . "

"She's in the hospital. She's been there since before you moved in."

"Oh. I'm sorry. What happened?"

"She was in a car accident."

"That's terrible," he says, for the first time that I have known him looking like he might truly be penitent about something. "I'm really sorry."

"That's all right. It's not your fault."

"Maybe you ought to take this and the figurine out to her and find out if she would be offended first, though. You could borrow it if you wanted."

"That's not possible."

"Why?"

"Just take my word for it."

"Can't you take stuff in on a visit?"

"Leslie! She can't talk. She went into a coma following the accident. She's been that way ever since. She's totally dependent upon machines to remain alive."

I lead him to the door once again. "Couldn't she just nod, or . . . ?" I shut the door.

"Go home, Leslie."

"Blink, even?" he asks through the closed door.

"Go home!"

(VIII)

"I have a solution," Thunder says. We've just finished viewing *Gandhi*, the film, against the back wall of his doghouse. Now I am lying flat on the soft grass outside his doghouse. Above me, the stars are bright and vivid. It's a perfect spring night. "You want me out of here. I want me out of here too. Lemme go."

Thunder has just chewed an armchair to pieces. His lips are curled back, he looks like an Egyptian sculpture resurrected from some ancient tomb, majestic, carved from granite, then magically animated.

"You think I like it here? Come on, Rob, give us both a break. Unhook my collar."

"You're joking."

"I'm dead serious."

"How could I? What would you do if I got you out?"

"What would I do? What does it matter? There are a thousand things. I mean, you have a word for those appetites related to the reproductive urges. You know, `animal desires?' Well, *I'm an animal!*"

I look at Thunder, all that muscle, all that animal quickness. "Noo, I don't think so."

"Come on, Robert, come on! I'm a he-dog, I want to meet a she-dog. What's so strange about that? And if we're talking strange, this whole business is unnatural. I mean, I'm already bent because of all the inbreeding, but I'm doubly bent because I'm trained to do exactly what my disability inclines me toward: fighting."

I try to back away toward the fence but Thunder keeps on coming. "Why on Earth would I let you out? I approached Leslie in the first place to get rid of you because I thought you were too wild."

"Not wild, Rob, crazy."

"I never said crazy, Thunder."

"Of course I'm crazy! But it's craziness I never asked for, it's not a craziness of my own making. I mean look at me, look at who owns me, look at the situation. Wouldn't you be crazy too in the same place? I live to fulfill one function, *one* function, Rob—to terrorize. That's hardly a way to make friends."

"I can't do it," I tell him, but he's not taking no for an answer.

"Humans and animals haven't got the same sense of scale, Rob, the same needs. I need to be outside and that means not just out of the house on a twenty foot dog run, but outside the fence."

"You're always snapping at the postman, the newspaper boy. You'd be a threat."

"Sure, if I'm locked up and I escape, I'm a threat. But if I'm let out, Rob, if I'm released . . . " I'm flat against the fence now, and Thunder is looking up at me with desperation in his eyes. "I'd leave the block, leave the city, you have my word of honour. I'm a dog, I'd find a way to survive. I'd become a symbol, a myth, a patron saint to other pit bulls. Take a chance, Rob, come on. Come on! Isn't this what you're talking about all the time? When the logical solutions have all been tried, what remains are the improbable ones. Looking out for the underdog. I *am* the underdog. Just undo the collar, the clip to the collar, that's all, I can take care of the rest. Please."

He's straining against the chain, each separate metal link utters an agonized tiny moan.

"I suppose the word of a pit bull isn't exactly a sure thing—but doing nothing, doing nothing is taking a chance too, a different kind of chance. Let me go. Please."

No sooner have I undone the collar than he hits the gate like a shot. The latch springs up under the force of the impact, the gate torques, opens, and he's gone, a sinewy dark India rubber creature bouncing down the alley, a dot against the white grey gravel, a blot against the already dim horizon, and then nothing. He's gone.

(IX)

Dreams carve through my sleep like screaming chainsaws that night, leaving me dopey and dazed when I awake the next morning. I go to the front door to retrieve the newspaper. I look out from the front porch . . . and can see. The view used to be obscured by branches. I pad down the steps and out onto the front lawn. My peach tree is gone. I close my eyes, open my eyes, look at the stump where the tree used to rest and feel my skin begin to sweat. I feel dizzy, as though the Earth has shifted. Then I look up and see Leslie, smiling as though he had just cut me an enormous bouquet with his electric saw. I look at the Black ceramic jockey, and it grins its big red grin back at me.

"Don't thank me," Leslie says.

"What have you done?" I ask.

"I've kinda pruned your tree back."

Pruned it back? There's nothing but a short white stump left.

"Why?"

"Well it's partially on my land. I know you're not the handiest guy, and there's, you know, your wife in the hospital. So, I thought I'd do you a favour. How do you like it?"

He continues smiling humbly at me and I realize that he really is waiting for me to thank him, pat him on the back for being such a good neighbour.

"Leslie. I could look at this tree, and wonder if one morning I might not get up and see it in bloom. While this tree stood, I could imagine that something could appear that lifeless, and still conceal life. And you cut it down."

"You're not happy."

"Do you ever listen? Do you ever think and listen? Do you understand what you did cutting down that tree, do you?"

"No, I don't. I don't understand you."

"You destroyed something precious."

"A dead tree!"

"You think that it means nothing because to you it means nothing, because you, like your idiotic garden gnome, lack a brain. You think it doesn't insult anyone because it doesn't insult you, and everyone you meet and everything you read confirms that opinion." I pick up the saw. Bits of bark still cling to the blade.

"How can I make you understand? I wrestle *every day* with how to represent my wife for my daughter, how to deliver the . . . knowledge, the strength, she had so that Ellen can recognize fools and bigots and sexists, but . . . how do I get her to recognize you? Because you don't stand out, you look like anyone, but you maintain all these, these, these . . . notions and ideas and symbols, and you never ever think about them, which makes them untouchable and you unreachable, and which makes you, Leslie, the enemy."

"What are you talking about? What are you doing?"

There is a hallucinogenic moment when all things happen at once. I raise the saw and turn it on at the same time that Leslie steps forward, at the same time that I hear my voice called, at the same time that I swing the saw forward. The saw performs a quick arc through air and time, a high-pitched *zzzz* rises and falls and the head of the lawn ornament tumbles out onto the flat green surface of Leslie's lawn. Leslie, howling with fury and bounding like an antelope, seizes both the cord to the saw and my arm simultaneously. He unplugs the cord, then in an almost balletic movement draws back his arm to strike me. Then—a miracle. As his arm and fist move resolutely toward me, he himself seems to slip away, descending back from me, where he spins and collides against the railing of his porch. He doubles over clutching his Adam's apple and drops to his knees. There, standing in front of me looking shocked, embarrassed and apologetic all at once, in her pj's, is . . . Ellen.

"I heard shouting," she says, blinking. "I just did what we do in Tai Chi. I hope he isn't hurt too bad. What was going on?"

Leslie rises, holding his throat, his face red. In a thin, choking voice he croaks, "Go," and points across the now almost invisible boundary between his and my yard, beyond where the peach tree stood.

(X)

Light has begun to spill over the edge of the horizon like bathwater over an overfull tub. I think of the electric saw and wonder what I have done, what I might have done. Ellen leads me by the hand to our lawn. "Follow me," she instructs, and begins a series of intricate Tai Chi movements. I follow as best I can.

This, she explains, as she steps forward and thrusts, is the time her instructor recommends for practising. The rising sun supplies an abundance of *Chai*, or energy.

"Remember," she asks me, "how you said if you had something to tell someone, but couldn't tell them, the next best thing might be to tell their best friend?"

"Yes. I recall."

"How come you don't have a best friend?"

"I do."

"You do?"

"You. You are my best friend."

She steps back and raises her arms effortlessly, then pivots. I step back, raise my arms and, somewhat less gracefully, pivot.

"How can I tell your best friend something that I can't tell you, if your best friend is me?"

"Tell yourself."

"Okay," she agrees after a moment, then begins speaking aloud to herself as she completes her exercises. "Ellen," she says, "I think . . . it's a good thing that the dead tree is gone. It was giving me the creeps. I think you should tell your dad that. Tell him that hanging onto anything too long is probably a mistake."

She finishes a routine and begins it once more, seamlessly, a loop on a machine, spinning around and around.

"Tell him that I don't want to visit my mother, hooked up to all that stuff at the hospital, anymore. It's been two years, her there, and you and your dad waiting for something to happen. It's not going to happen. She's gone."

I raise one foot and step forward. "How do you know?" I ask.

"I just do."

"How will I know?"

"You know already. *You know.*"

"Tell my daughter that I worry that she'll forget her mother. I worry that I'll forget her. Tell her I don't let her mother go because I don't know that I'm up to the job of being a parent on my own. The world. It's violent and cruel in small everyday ways, and I don't have the same instincts or compassion or common sense that her mother had. I'm scared and I lack confidence in myself. There's so much I don't know."

Ellen moves slower now, and I faster, so we are almost together, almost in sync, my movements barely shadowing hers. "Listen," she says, "tell my dad this story. There're these two Zen monks, walking. The younger says, when will my training be complete? The older guy says nothing. So they walk, and, you know, months pass and again the younger monk asks the same question, and again the older monk says nothing. Years pass. The older monk dies. The younger monk leaves."

Postscript

An interesting story appeared in the newspaper the other day, part of the silly season, I suppose. According to the article, buried on the fifth or sixth page, dogs all over the city are disappearing and heading for the woods. It seems they are being called or *wooed* away. Farmers, who always claim to be more canny about this sort of thing, maintain it's the work of coyotes who entice the dogs out to the edges of the city with the promise of sexual favours . . . then devour them. Maybe. Still, no one has actually *seen* this coyote nor have any bones ever been found; and oddly enough, the majority of the entranced dogs appear to have been . . . pit bulls.

MARIO MASCHIO • *BLAIRMORE, ALBERTA*

YASMIN LADHA

Yasmin Ladha was born in Mwanza, Tanzania in 1958. She has lived in Calgary, Alberta for the last thirteen years and is presently at work on an MA in Creative Writing at the University of Calgary. This fall, NeWest Press will publish her collection of short stories, Lion's Granddaughter. *As an East Indian from Tanzania whose adult life has been lived in Canada, Ms Ladha finds that her literary work is influenced by a variety of sources. Tanzanian politics, particularly the rejection of Asians from that country, translates into a "persistent turbulence" in her work. Her writing has also taken her on several excursions to India. "My feelings are Indian," she says, "but my language, my creative tongue, is Canadian." She seeks "a balance of both homes: Indian and Canadian." Ms Ladha has discovered that to have a biography such as hers and to be a writer in Canada results in a particular categorization. "I am viewed/branded in Canada, first as an ethnic writer and then as a woman writer. This kind of `ethnic' vision pressed upon me is tiresome." If she must be put in a slot, she says, she would rather it be one labelled "woman story-maker."*

Two Friends

(FOR SATWINDER PAUL)

The first time I learn the shape of a rooftop is in a prairie parking lot.
A rooftop is woman
and Saturday night dreams.

My friend and I
catch *barish* rain
in a prairie parking lot
fingertip drops
light as
hair/strand/chatter
turns furious on trees
green webbing
tangled impossible
like hair just washed.
In this thick spring
she and I have
no crocus thought
or sober rain
for the farmer.

Instead
we catch
bunchy *barish*
on rooftop elsewhere
the baked earth hisses
sprouts grass
glaring
as green chili

then

by Yasmin Ladha

my *sakhi*-friend and I
crave for roadside *paratha*
so brisk and round
and hot, hot *chai*
(out of steel tumblers)
in a prairie parking lot.

Teastall *chai*
thick as maple syrup
she says.
Thick as Golconda Ruby wine—
vineyards in Goa? Andhra Pradesh?—
can't remember label
but the Ruby
tasted of cream-soda.

Coyote, Atwood, maple red on white
(haven't ever had saskatoon berries)
bears out there
wear bells
rocks run blue
after their blueberry feast in fall.
At the conference in Delhi
how I filch
credit for the Rockies,
my warm host beams
"how you say, from Canada, eh? No?"
C'est moi
international poster. Seducer.

But on rooftop the dance is round/an elephant's gait
and milk poured on dreams
to placate gods
there are dreams on rooftops
heavy as thighs.

a mustard veil sails by
romance is flushed bangles
windy giddy with colour
clutches another veil
pink as restless feet.
A rainbow tangle
on rooftop

and

one slender flute.

Readerji, the flute reminds me of a mercury dancer in a gym, dancing alone. She has thin collar bones . . . doomed, exiled. And like the flute,
apart. The slender flute is blue Krishna's
mistress. But Krishna is Radha's. Her
devotion to him, torrential.
On the rooftop all know without Radha there is no
Krishna. So what
if he is a god? Yet it is the bamboo mistress who shares the intimacy of his breath.

Story of flute on rooftop:
She is flute
sealed between her lover's
grasp
(a lover's grasp
tough as mother's womb)
the lover has forgotten
other shapes. All.
"That kept one"
Radha sniffs.

Everyone knows
without Radha
there is no Krishna
Radha bina Kanu nahi
but even Radha
said to her Kanu
"tear that wretched bamboo
from your mouth
place *her* at your foot."

Bamboo flute/other/eternally
torn from siblings
holed in peak flesh
for one beloved's breath.
When he billows inside her
her breast holes sting
she reels
higher than bells

such is romance
out of rooftops
full of tears   succulent.
It is on rooftops
a lover is made
most perfect
then pressed behind eyes
and the wind on rooftops
is sweeter than chinook.

A bride draws a map:

Don't know why
I turn shy
when my *sakhi* tells me.
On campus
our backs turned, slunk
from starers, joggers
thighs pressed in secrecy
she shows me his photograph:
        he wears an earring
        collects Sher-Gil
        (from now on we call him *Sher-Gil wallah*)

                romance, romance, romance

                Walking across the snow field
                after 3 bottles of vino
                my *sakhi* and I holler hot words
                a pile up:
                your brother-fucker
                from your
                mother's sister's side
                mathematical intoxication/freedom
                romance is loving yourself thick
                and
                come home to serve tea
                to guests from Edmonton
                one, a world-wide matchmaker
                her coast-to-coast including
                Punjab, UK, Amrika
                (how she says it)
                home base—Canada
                wobbly hips
                but eyes like planted feet

Like parents
we want them
full of science:
fed on doctors and engineers
day one in Canada

Immigrant dream
persistent as polyester pants
straight to laundromat from school
on birthdays
no funny socks with lipstick kisses
but university fertility
now a double-barreled passport to freedom
an East Indian's frontier

(This one's not bad
a lawyer who collects Sher-Gil
not the earnest engineer
living room full of drilling manuals.)

But there is another bride who turns bitter:

Great Lakes on her palm
at the Delhi Conference I strut
her Rockies personally as breasts.
Her family tea with monarchy
postcard Mounties
1st of July . . .

Readerji
this familiar postcard map
but I draw another
of Canada as a woman, a bride.
She is an arranged wife
selected by immigrant husband
landing her "unsizeable virginity"
someone wrote
sturdy haunches and a lush dowry
his anguished North bride asked:
(Readerji, I map her pain
on rooftop space.)

Never to ask me, ME
an arranged wife
your hostile giving
to my dowry
a dark blue passport
(my immigrant husband
no longer shuffles
in Third World queue.)
Dominant husband
(immigrant in name)
between you and I
egg shell virginity
mosaic hymen.

A woman looks down
one hefty foot
on the boundary
of her rooftop
bellows to the pale northern bride
in adjacent verandah
"what you cooking?"

I have a rooftop here
I swear
bracketed, dreamy:
(Trudeau or Pierre? Shy choice. But I fetch you
[collars dashed up] green trench coat, colour of powdered henna
in the pink city of Jaipur. Red rose).

Readerji, My sakhi has gone to the tailor's for wedding measurements.
The limbs are differently thick now, that's why we call them
wedding measurements.

Sher-Gil wallah's mum says to my sakhi:
I laav you
her *moi* is full of French shoulders
not like "my" in English: lukewarm at the same time possessive
Punjabi-French *moi:* a burst
heart/soil/chipped nail/rose
ooi moi changi-girl, *moi soni*-girl
all jaunty praise in Punjabi
but I laav you
Sher-Gil wallah's mum says in English
and
sakhi and the Sher-Gil wallah
continue their romance:
"you are my kiker tree's shadow so cool"
"you are my tube-well's sweet, sweet water"
"you are my canola flower"
"Oh my buffalo's manure." (mushy *sakhi* bored)

Why is their romance in a Punjabi field not in prairie snow?
A pale bride accused her husband:

Between you and I
egg shell virginity
mosaic hymen

Not always, dear bride:
I left a love note on a birch bark
beside your fallen hairpin.

I know of spring flowers
not Kamasutran laden
but crocuses and buffalo beans
growing out of the armpit
of a brown prairie spring
whose murky colour like *guruji*'s eye
warming in pleasure
snow gone soft these days
old-timers tell me
but I don't let go of
winter boots till early May.

I laav you sakhi:
At her wedding I gave *sakhi* an exiled flute, a familiar landscape
in a woman's
map and milk-tipped strawberries (gods must be placated).

Many greet her milk and son wishes
I heap baroque henna:
    sakhi, sakhi, sakhi, salut—
    here's an uncircumscribed rooftop
    unending as a hair line
    and restless feet
    full of Saturday night dreams.

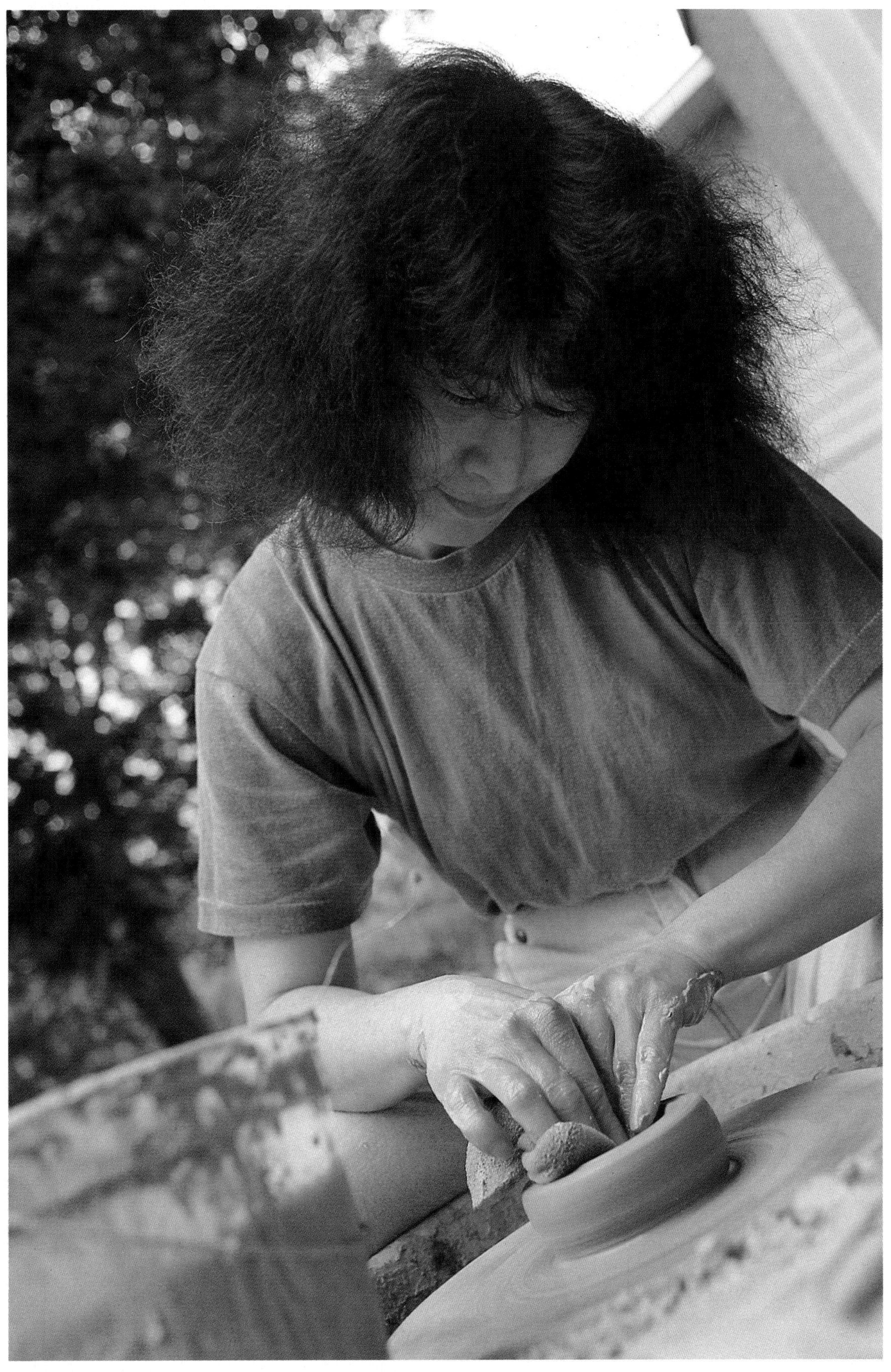

AKIKO KOHANA • *EDMONTON, ALBERTA*

WILLIAM PASNAK

William Pasnak is a well-known writer of juvenile and children's fiction. His titles include Under the Eagle's Claw *(Douglas & McIntyre, 1988),* Mimi and the Ginger Princess *(Lorimer, 1988),* Exit Stage Left *(Lorimer, 1987) and* In the City of the King *(Douglas & McIntyre, 1984). He received the Writers Guild of Alberta R. Ross Annett Award for both* Under the Eagle's Claw *and* In the City of the King. *He has also written many educational television programs for Alberta's ACCESS Network. Mr Pasnak was raised in Edmonton where, he says, "the ethnic variety made different cultures seem as normal as sunshine." His own family roots are Ukrainian, and British "via Upper Canada." In his early twenties he spent two years in Japan, learning, "while still impressionable," what it feels like to be "illiterate and linguistically isolated," to be "a minority, albeit a privileged one." After eight years in Calgary, Mr Pasnak moved to Vancouver in 1991.*

MacLaughlin's Dinner Party

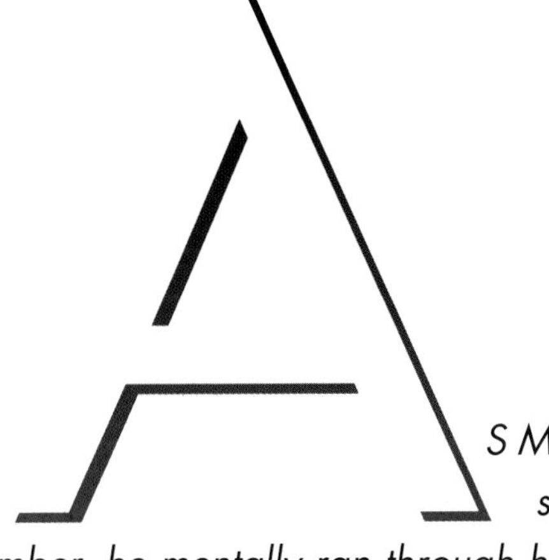

S MACLAUGHLIN DROPPED INTO THE LOW-slung leather telephone chair and dialed Beth's number, he mentally ran through his closet of identities and decided to combat her inevitable terse message as a laid-back, Caribbean existentialist. "De sun is shinin, an de sky is blue, mon. If you want to commun-i-cate, what you got dis machine ting foa?" Yeah, foa. That was good. Or something like that.

He was startled into his own identity when Beth herself answered on the first ring.

"Yes?" Beth hated to answer the phone. She felt it to be demeaning and, under certain circumstances, a vector for communicable diseases.

"Don't hang up, Beth. It's me, Mac."

"Oh, hello." Her tone shifted from guarded to neutral. They had been going out for over a year now, but Beth steadfastly maintained her independence, partly by showing very little enthusiasm for him except when they were making love. At least, that was how Mac generally read her behaviour. Sometimes he suspected she just didn't like him much.

"What happened to your phone machine?"

"It's broken. Sucked up the tape like soggy linguini."

"I told you it needed cleaning. When it starts to warble like that, the pinch roller needs cleaning."

"Don't give me a techno-junk lecture, Mac. I'm not in the mood. Donna called and I have to cancel her yogarobics class because the old ladies keep seeing black spots in front of their eyes."

"What about if they did it in the pool?"

"And then what would we call it? Yo-quati-cise? Sounds like something rude you do with ripe fruit. Besides, if they tried a full thigh stretch in the water, they'd drown."

"Black spots in front of the eyes would be preferable," he agreed. "Listen, I've got to tell you something. I bought a table."

by William Pasnak

"A table?"

"A rosewood dining table. With a filet of bird's eye maple inlay." He took a breath. "And a dozen chairs."

"A *dozen*? Migawd, Mac. Where are you going to put them?"

"Around the table, I guess. It's a big one."

"It must be the size of a shopping mall. Have you got room for it?"

"I think so. They're going to deliver it tomorrow morning. It's one of these unfinished jobs."

There was the short silence MacLaughlin always interpreted as her considering whether unexpected news should annoy her. "But *why* did you buy it?" she said at last. "No one but me ever comes over. You eat in front of the tv, or at that dinky little fold-out thing in the kitchen. You don't need a dining table."

"I think I want to entertain," he said. "When I saw this table in the store, I realized that I long for the stately ritual of many courses served on crisp linen, and the music of thoughtful minds engaged in passionate conversation."

"It must have cost a fortune and you don't have room for it."

"You're probably right, but indulge me. Let's give a dinner party anyway."

"Let's? Let *us*?"

"Beth, you know I couldn't do it without you. You're the gourmet cook with the class-one licence for the Cuisinart. I can't even make jello. And look, we ain't talking weenies and beans here. I want class. Trifle foie gras and duckling à l'orange."

"Truffle foie gras."

"My point exactly."

There was another short silence while she weighed the compliment, and the opportunity to sculpt a gourmet dinner from start to finish, against the actual work involved. "All right," she said finally, "but it can't be this weekend. I'm going to a women's tribal poetry retreat."

"That's okay. I have to finish the table anyway. How about next weekend?"

"Next weekend I have a goddess-style management workshop."

"The weekend after, then."

There was a pause. Mac could hear her flipping the pages of her appointment book. "Fine," she said at last. "I buy, you pay, I cook, you wash. Any dispute about the menu, my decision is final. All right?"

"Great. Thank you," Mac said. "This will be the start of a new era."

"Maybe. Who are you going to invite?"

"I haven't figured that out yet," MacLaughlin said. "A carefully matched and balanced set of guests who will sparkle with wit and intelligence."

"Oh, right," she said. "Good luck." And hung up.

When the delivery men had left, Mac very carefully slit the cardboard away from the satiny-smooth, sanded tabletop that now seemed enormous. He screwed the legs in place and then looked around to see if there really was anywhere to put it. An hour later, he was hot and dusty, the bookcase was in the hall, and the china hutch was, if not actually in the living room, at least out of the dining room. Gingerly, he tipped the table up into position in the dining area, set the chairs around it and stood back to study the effect.

It fits, he thought triumphantly. It fits.

Tentatively, he slid into the chair at the head of the table. A broad plain of gently fragrant veneer spread out before him. Beyond it, through the window, lay the magnificent view of the city that made Mac pay too much rent and risk his life on the icy hill roads every winter. Yes, he thought. Yes.

He glanced around the table, taking in his guests. "Moira, Tom," he said out loud. "More wine? Shelagh, can you . . .?"

He stopped. Shelagh, who the hell was Shelagh? Shelagh, can you pour some more wine for our guests? He didn't even know any Shelagh. Come to that, he didn't know any Moira or Tom, either.

But he would, he thought, as he pushed himself up from the chair. He would.

Two days later, as he was painstakingly scrubbing down the fourth of the twelve chairs with triple zero steel wool, and Vivaldi was riding across the Danish oil fumes like a skater marking new ice, there was the sound of a key in the lock. Beth walked in. She must have just come from the gym; beneath her parka, she was wearing sweats with the company logo over one breast, and her dark hair was circled by a bright yellow terry headband. Under one arm she carried a neon-green looseleaf binder.

"So this is it, huh? God, Mac, it looks like an aircraft carrier."

She was chewing gum and Mac had a sudden, unreasonable fear that she would park it under the edge of the table. "You see," he said defensively, "it does fit."

"Oh, yeah, it fits all right. A bit extreme, though. It looks—I dunno, like it belongs in a boardroom somewhere."

"It is a *dining* table," he insisted. "They said so in the store."

"Yeah, I know they—aw, forget it. It's just so damn big, Mac, that's all. Look, I want to talk menu." She dropped the binder on the table and flipped it open.

"Not here," he said, plucking the plastic off the table with a small sucking sound. "This isn't dry yet."

"Oh, gee, I'm sorry. Will it mark?"

Mac leaned down and sighted across the table. "Not once I've put a couple more coats on. Come on, let's try the kitchen."

When Mac had cleared the remains of breakfast off the small white scrap of Formica bolted to the wall, Beth opened her notes again and said, "All right, I'll just run through this and then you can tell me how much you love it." Her eyes were bright. "We start with Gorgonzola croustade and a carrot-ginger vichyssoise garnished with candied violets. Then a cellophane noodle salad with fresh shrimp, fresh water chestnuts, and a Szechuan dressing."

Mac groaned appreciatively.

"It gets better. Oh, and don't forget, you're going to need a different wine for each course, Mac. For a dozen people. It's going to cost you."

"With different shaped glasses for each wine," he confirmed, gently pounding his thigh with excitement. "Worth every penny."

"You can rent the glasses, you know. You don't need to buy them unless this insanity is permanent. But I'll have to consult Philippe at the Golden Goblet. Like, I mean, is there really a white that can stand up to Gorgonzola croustade?" She shrugged. "Okay, anyway, after the salad, we hit the main course, which is smoked pork tenderloin in a red currant sauce with braised fennel Dijonnais and garlic-roasted potatoes. Then a lime sorbet to cleanse the palate, and—"

"Wait a minute," Mac said. "There's a problem."

"What do you mean?"

"Beth, you know I die for your pork tenderloin. Your smoking loin is of the tenderest."

"Yeah, yeah," she said. "Spare me your coarse male humour. But?"

"But I'm inviting Dave and Brenda."

"Rosenberg? Oh, shit." She frowned at the page in front of her, then rummaged in her purse for a pen. "They're really kosher, too. That means no veal either unless I change the dessert."

"Hunh?"

"Meat and milk," she explained to him over-patiently. "You can't seethe the kid in the mother's milk. And I've got a cassata cream in chocolate shell here that I'm not giving up. All right, I know what to do—lamb."

"Lamb?"

"Rack of lamb Marrakesh. We swap the fennel for grilled eggplant and the rest can stay as is."

"Lambs don't drink milk?"

"Not cow's milk. And with the lamb, I can throw in that mango salsa Betty-Jean told me about." She made a note. "Okay, then we finish with the cassata and the usual—fruit, cheese, coffee, and liqueurs. Ah, for the fruit, that's chilled cherimoya with zest of lime and freshly grated nutmeg." She put her notes down. "So what do you think?"

Mac stared into space for a moment, letting the image of fine china, crystal, and Beth's gourmet cooking beguile him. The guests were radiant, witty, and, apparently, well-fed. "It's wonderful," he said at last. "It sounds perfect."

"Good," she said, favouring him with a rare smile. "I knew you'd say that. Now, who's coming to eat it all?"

"Ah, well, Dave and Brenda—" He fumbled in his pocket for the list.

"With you and me, that's four. And?"

He smoothed out a crumpled sheet of paper. "Fardad and Faryal."

"Good, they love my food. By the way, I saw Faryal at the store the other day and I think she's put on weight. So, that's six."

"Art and Connie Leung."

"Who?"

"She works at the office. Personnel. I've met him a few times. They're nice."

"Yeah, but . . . they sound Chinese."

Mac laughed. "No kidding. They look Chinese, too."

"But . . . "

"You've got something about Chinese? You've got a Szechuan dish in the menu. How would having Chinese people at the table be a problem?"

"But that's just it, Mac. If they come, I'd be embarrassed to serve them a Szechuan salad dressing. I mean, it's probably not even authentic or anything, and if it is I probably make it wrong. But—this is even worse—what if they thought I was, you know, trying to make them comfortable or something? I mean, how condescending can you get? It's like, `Oh, you're from Canada, how nice, here's some maple syrup for your burritos.'"

"All right, all right. Take it easy. We'll put Art and Connie on hold for a minute. Let me finish the list, and then we'll see."

"Fine. Who else then?"

"The Khans."

"With the Rosenbergs? They'll kill each other."

"I don't see why. Dave and Brenda are about as political as cocker spaniels."

"If they bother keeping kosher," Beth said emphatically, "they've got opinions, believe me. And the Khans are definitely Muslim."

"Well, what do you think Fardad and Faryal are?"

"Migawd, you're right. That's even worse. They'll gang up on the Rosenbergs and tear out their livers on your brand new table."

"Look, Beth, I really don't think that will happen, and anyway, one of the things this dinner is all about is a free exchange of ideas."

"Fine. It's your debacle. Who else have you got?"

"Shauna."

"But she's vegetarian."

"We've got vegetables."

"But not just vegetables. I mean, how does it look, Mac? `Here, have an alfalfa sprout while we eat this dead animal.'"

"She came to your place and didn't bat an eye that time we ate oysters that were still squirming. Just scoffed all the crackers and Brie and drank most of the wine."

"Okay. Have it your way. Shauna."

"Good. Then, Phil Kazantzakis."

"Oh, well, if you're sold on Shauna, you can forget him."

"Why? Because he eats meat?"

"Because he's a scientist, that's why. She's got this thing right now about technology tormenting nature."

"Phil's a geologist. Studies unmoving, unbreathing, unwhimpering rocks."

"So we can rape Mother Earth for material profit, right?"

"But—"

"And another thing she won't like, Mac, he's Greek."

"Oh, she's an ethnic bigot, now, too."

"She isn't a bigot. It's a carefully thought-out position."

"And she has carefully thought out that she hates all Greeks?"

"I'm just explaining to you, Mac, that Shauna isn't very happy these days about Greek mythology."

"Are you serious? Phil was born in Lethbridge!"

"It doesn't matter. It's in his culture, it's in his blood, it's what moulded him. And it's a mythology that is completely unenlightened about women's issues."

"It's a mythology that moulded some Bronze Age hill tribes three thousand years ago. If Shauna blames Phil for that, I say *she's* unenlightened."

"There's no point arguing with *me* about it, Mac. I'm just telling you, it's either him or her."

"All right, her then, against my better judgement. We scrap Phil and insert Mario."

"Mmmm . . . "

"Now what? Mario's got a great jazz collection, he's fluent in five languages, he's not a scientist, and he's not Greek. He's a perfect dinner guest."

"Just don't sit him near Fardad—or Faryal, for that matter."

"Why?"

"You weren't at that Grey Cup party at Cindy's, were you? Mario drank a yard and a half of tequila, got numb from the neck up but not the neck down, apparently, and made this outrageous pass at Fardad. Which would have been bad enough, but Faryal was sitting right there, and she did *not* think it was very cute."

Mac sat back and ran his hands through his hair. "Mama. This is harder than I thought. Can I rent some decent guests with the glasses?"

"Look," Beth said, scooping up her binder and getting up, "it's no different from a menu. Just needs work. A little planning, a little work. But I'll call you, okay? I have to go now and do the yogurt cleansing intro."

When she was gone, he stood for a moment, irresolute, and then, leaving the list on the kitchen table, he went back to the dining room and picked up the steel wool.

There seemed to be an almost infinite surface in need of oil and polishing. For a while, as the weekends and evenings slowly passed, Mac tried to calculate the number of coats times the number of square centimetres, but the figures mounted up as fast as video game scores, and became just as meaningless. Instead, he considered the vision that the chairs and table represented.

He knew the furniture stood, in his mind, for a finely made and leisurely eaten meal. But it was not *just* a meal, it was the occasion that surrounded it, a stage set of, of harmony and excellence, yes, in which people could be—what? Relaxed. Graceful. Electric. Intimate. Themselves.

Intimate.

By the time he was half-way through the third coat, it occurred to him to wonder where, after all, this vision had come from. He had never had a dinner such as he envisioned. In comparison to the luminous conception wrapped around the table, his life was stodgy, if not downright squalid, an insipid concatenation of office work, pizza boxes, videos with Beth, and laundry.

He tried to trace the vision back, to see where it had first arisen. Was it something from his childhood? His only memory of Sunday dinner at home was of bread side-plates that nobody bothered to use, and of Misty his dog, a sad-eyed sentinel, watching every bite disappear into his mouth. What, then? Was it psychological; some Jungian archetype, perhaps, slumbering in his subconscious, that erupted synchronistically (whatever that meant) when he walked into the furniture store? The grain under his fingers pooled and rippled like flowing water, but did not bring him an answer.

"How's it going with the guest list?"

Mac cradled the phone against his ear and realized he was still holding a paint brush dangerously full of Danish oil. He perched on the edge of the chair, holding the brush out carefully. "Ah, so-so, I guess. Turns out Mario's gone to Peru for a couple of months."

"You're better off without him, believe me. What about the rest?"

"And you're off the hook with the Leungs. I sounded her out at coffee yesterday and they've got a wedding to go to."

"I wonder if they'd take me with them. They always have all that good food at the banquet."

"I doubt it. Anyway, I think it's a round-eye wedding."

"Oh, forget it, then."

"But I thought I could replace them with that couple we met at the gym that night. Francine and what's-his-name, the photographer."

"Oh, right, you mean that half-dressed tramp that was all over you."

"She wasn't all over me, she was just being Latin."

"Suit yourself."

"But that still leaves the list short and unbalanced. I don't know who else to ask."

"Well, you can balance it by getting rid of Shauna, if you haven't asked her yet."

"Then it's even shorter." The idea appealed to him, though. He had only included Shauna because she was a friend of Beth's. Personally, he found her as enjoyable as a bottle-brush up the nose.

"So, it's shorter. Mac, you don't have to use all twelve chairs just because you bought them in a fit of delirium. Why not start small and work up to the whole thing? Besides, you'll save on the wine."

But I don't care about saving on the wine, he thought, when he hung up the phone a few minutes later. I don't care about the cost. Still, it seemed like Beth was right. Revise the vision, then. Get smaller. Even more intimate. Not a symphony, but a sonnet. Or whatever a musical sonnet would be. A lieder? A gavotte? A riff.

"Damn." Halfway back to the table, a single drop of oil fell from the brush and soaked into the broadloom. Mac went for a cloth, but he knew with unhappy certainty that the round, dark stain would never, ever come out.

With less than a week until the dinner, Mac at last acknowledged that he had become obsessive about rubbing down the table, and that he was avoiding inviting his guests. Perhaps he had been put off by Beth's objections to practically every name. She liked playing with food, and she did it well, but she really didn't understand his dinner. Or maybe, he thought, she didn't understand people. Certainly she didn't like them much, especially once she got to know them. Beth, he thought, left no fault unstoned.

Reluctantly, he put aside the oil, got out his address book, turned the telephone chair so he couldn't see the oil drop on the carpet, and got to work.

It took him all evening to go through the list. Francine and her photographer husband Clement, he discovered, had only been here on a short-term grant. They were back in Montreal now. The Khans, on the other hand, were free, but Sayeeda was having allergy tests and could only eat a few, unspiced foods—preferably white rice and steamed carrots. Fardad and Faryal would love to come, but Fardad would have to arrive late because he would be flying back from a meeting in Saskatoon; perhaps they could keep a plate of food warm for him. Dave Rosenberg mumbled evasively in response to the invitation and finally told Mac that he and Brenda were having problems right now. They would rather not come together. When Mac at last hung up the phone, he tallied his guests: Dave—or Brenda, Faryal and half of Fardad, Masud, and half of Sayeeda. It wasn't what he'd expected. He phoned Beth's number, left a message on her new machine about the revised guest list, and then, even though it was late and his arm ached, went back to rubbing the table.

The table was becoming magnificent; Mac could find no other way to put it. At least, that was how he thought of it during his good moments. During more pessimistic moods, he wondered if there was really a perceptible difference between the eighth and ninth coats of oil. When he took a break to ease his back, or to make himself a cup of tea, he would turn away for a moment and then look back, trying to glimpse the table as his dinner guests might: rich, warm, inviting, generous.

Inviting.

"I hope to hell," Beth's voice gritted through the earpiece, "that you like lamb. I've got enough to feed the whole city." It was the evening before the dinner party and Beth had just learned of the reduced guest list. Apparently, her new machine had malfunctioned.

"But you told me to scale down," Mac said. "It was your advice."

"But you should have told me!" she exploded, and she would not believe that he really had left a message. "I'll cook it," she said at last, coldly. "There's nothing else I can do with the damn stuff, anyway. But I'm not sure I'll come. This is turning into a farce."

"I don't see why," Mac protested. "So the plan is different. At least we have a few congenial people to come together with open hearts."

"*Open hearts?* Mac, you can get open hearts with beer and nachos. You said you wanted *class*! And now you've got steamed carrots and people dropping in like a cafeteria!"

But, can't you have both? he thought, as he went back to the table for what he swore would be the last coat of oil. Both heart and class? That was the point. Maybe the people weren't falling into line the way the food and the table were, but you had to start somewhere.

The trouble with Beth, he thought darkly, as he swabbed on the oil, was that she didn't allow for the—he groped for the right word—individuality of people. She wanted everyone to be the same. He looked at his chairs. By now he knew all twelve of them intimately, and knew that each had its own slightly different personality. What about people, then? But Beth, he knew, had a sense of rigour that was offended by the irregularities of people. It wouldn't surprise him if she did cook the food and then leave. Facing that thought, Mac realized that sometime soon they would probably break up. Not because of the dinner party, but just because it seemed inevitable.

It was late that night, somewhere between two and breakfast, when it finally came to him how the whole party had gotten started. Worn soft as old rope from his labour, and light-headed from the oil fumes, he had a lucid moment like that false sobriety that sometimes comes after drinking until sunrise. As a detached observer, he saw himself walking down the tiled shopping mall, turning into the furniture store to take a short-cut to the car, and coming to a dead stop, not at the sight of the table, but at the sight of—Shelagh.

Slim, auburn-haired, with high cheekbones and hazel eyes, wearing a soft cream blouse and a tweed skirt, one fine-boned freckled hand poised as lightly as a bird on the tabletop, she was looking back over her shoulder as someone called her name. Which, he was certain, must be Shelagh.

He could not explain how this vivid memory had remained unexamined, but as soon as he saw her, he understood that the table, the chairs, the dinner party, and the endless coats of oil to make the wood glow like a tropical sunset were all for her.

Fascinated by the mystery of his own unpredictable mind, he re-ran the memory. Mac entered the store; she turned. Listened for an instant. Walked away. Leaving the table magnetized. It took, he thought irrelevantly, less than fifteen seconds, but a car crash took somewhat less, with just as much change in a person's life.

It was not, of course, that he would somehow get to know her through the sympathetic magic of a dinner party; Mac knew that. In any case he was almost certain he remembered a wedding ring on her hand, and if there wasn't, he wanted there to be one. Buying the table was not the displacement of desire for her, for Shelagh, even though he found her tremendously desirable. No, it was his response to an aching openness, an openness to . . . what? The order and beauty of . . . her home. Her unseen, completely imaginary home.

Mac stared down at the wad of steel wool he was holding in his dusty, oil-stained fingers, and then looked around him. He was surrounded by a giant hamster's nest of torn newspaper and generations of discarded take-out containers from the Silver Dragon. There were tea cups and empty beer cans on every available surface. He was a complete fool, he thought. An exorbitant piece of furniture, all this work, and a half-assed dinner party that was going to cost him as much as the table had—for what? For Shelagh, whom he had never met, and a home he had barely imagined. Mechanically, he began again to rub.

But why not, he demanded savagely, as he scoured the wood. So he wouldn't sit down opposite Shelagh, Saturday night. If Beth was still pissed off, he wouldn't sit down opposite anybody. But he could want that, couldn't he?

Couldn't he?

Early the next morning, Dave phoned to tell him that both he and Brenda were housebound with violent stomach flu. Neither one would be coming. Mac knew he should immediately relay the news to Beth. Instead, he gathered up the acres of newspaper and spent a couple of hours cleaning and vacuuming. The table and chairs now stood revealed, alive and expectant. Mac felt peace settling over him. Beth would be here about two, with everything, and this evening, the dinner party would finally take place—not, perhaps, as he had envisioned it, but at least a beginning.

Then, about noon, the walls gave a small shudder as wind slammed in from the northeast. Soon afterward, it began to snow. The towers of the city disappeared. By one, Mac couldn't see a hundred yards through the whirling white. At a quarter past two, the phone rang. "I can't get up the hill," Beth said.

"I'll come and get you. I've got a four-wheel-drive."

"Don't bother," she said flatly. "It's a blizzard and it's going to get worse. Even if we did make it, no one else is going to get there."

"But—"

"Face it, your dinner party is cancelled, Mac. I'll freeze what I can and drop it off when this clears. What you do with it then is your business."

Much later, as darkness fell, Mac sat at his table, gazing out at the storm, with a bowl of instant noodles cooling on the placemat before him. He had no wine—that was still with Beth—but as a ceremonial gesture, he had found a candle and placed it in the mathematical centre of the table. It stood too far from him to throw much light on his meal, but it was something, he thought, of which Shelagh would approve.

"Tom, Moira," he said softly, "have some noodles." And began to eat.

DEXINE SARA • *BLAIRMORE, ALBERTA*

JOAN CRATE

Joan Crate, currently of Red Deer, Alberta, has led a well-traveled life. She was born in Yellowknife, NWT, and has lived in Vancouver, Quesnel, Victoria, Calgary, Cranbrook, Kamloops, Regina, Sarnia—and "a few other places for less than a year." After dropping out of high school, Ms Crate found her way eventually to the University of Calgary where she completed a Bachelor's Degree in English and a Master's Degree in English and Creative Writing. She has taught at the University of Calgary and at Red Deer College. Her first novel, Breathing Water *(NeWest), and her first book of poetry,* Pale as Real Ladies *(Brick), both appeared in 1989. She is currently at work on a second novel and a second poetry manuscript.*

The Wedding of My Sister-in-Law

IT WAS A NEW EXPERIENCE FOR ME, SITting at the table that early afternoon with my live-in boyfriend, as he and his family communicated in boisterous Arabic. Despite the familiarity of his voice and his occasional smiling glance, I was lost. Oh, I could make out the odd word in the conversation. Khalil called his sisters habibti, *which I took as a personal affront since that's what he always calls me (being the feminine form of* my love*). And there were other words I understood that cropped up in the conversation, English words such as "pornography," "silicon chip," and "hamburger," but as far as assisting me in understanding the conversation, they were of little value.*

I drank a cup of coffee that one of his three sisters had brought me, a concoction with the consistency of gravy and the impact of a Molotov cocktail served in a doll-sized cup, and I smiled at the children running in and out of the kitchen until they suspected me of being in the latter stages of dementia.

Suddenly Khalil turned to me. "Well, what do you think?"

"Whaaa?"

"About—oh." He looked back to the others, his three sisters, a brother-in-law, and one very soon to be brother-in-law. (The impending marriage was the reason we had traveled from our home in Calgary to Edmonton.) "We better speak English. Joan can't understand Arabic."

I had never met any of Khalil's relatives before, though I had overheard him talking on the phone to Samira, the bride-to-be, on numerous occasions. The first telephone conversation went something like this:

—Her name is Joan. I met her at University.

—That's because I'm usually at her place. I'm going to be moving in with her next month.

—Well it's easier. She has two kids.

by Joan Crate

After that the conversations were in Arabic. Yet there were words I could make out. Names mostly. Women's names.

"Leila?" Khalil would cry. "Tamara? Zenobia? La! La! La!"

Three sets of sisters' eyes now turned to survey me. After several seconds of uncomfortable silence, Samira began. "So, you're coming to the wedding?"

"Yes," I replied. "I'm looking forward to—"

"No," she corrected. "Only two witnesses are coming to the wedding. And Sahid's mother once she arrives from Lebanon."

"Yes, I know that." Khalil had explained that Samira, herself a Christian, was marrying Sahid, a Muslim, and because of Christians not wanting to enter a mosque and Muslims not particularly wanting them there, the ceremony itself was to be small. The real celebrating would take place after the wedding. "I'm looking forward to the rec—"

"No," she interrupted. "You think the Lebanese are strange people."

"No," I replied. "No stranger than—"

"Yes! They are. Unlike Canadians, the Lebanese take marriage seriously, both Christians and Muslims, isn't that right, Sahid?" Sahid nodded obligingly and the two other sisters joined him, dark eyes trained on me. "Family is very important, the most important thing of all." Samira fixed me with a withering gaze. "You're divorced?"

After an effective pause, she continued. "The Lebanese are very generous people at weddings. Beautiful wedding gifts."

"That's nice."

"No! They expect you to prepare a feast for them, all kinds of food, ten times what will be eaten. Materialistic people, they notice what everyone's wearing, talk about it for years after! That's the way the Lebanese are."

"That's too bad."

"No!"

"No?"

"Yes." Samira leaned closer. "Now, what kind of a dress did you bring? Was it expensive?"

The next morning when I awoke in the double bed in the spare room at Azizi and Latif's house, I was alone. The closet door was ajar and in the hallway I could hear the voices of Khalil and his three sisters.

"It's fine!" Khalil was saying rather heatedly.

"*Habibi*," Samira told him patiently yet firmly, as one would explain something to a simple child. "It's a sports jacket and a pair of pants. It is *not* a suit." There was the sound of dry cleaner's plastic being shaken fervently.

"Not for a wedding!" Azizi agreed, and Rima, the youngest sister, echoed obediently, "Not for a wedding."

"Your sister's wedding."

"Why don't you go buy a nice suit?" Samira insisted.

"Your second-oldest sister in Canada, one of only three sisters in this God-forsaken frozen wasteland they call a country," Azizi continued.

"One of only three sisters in this God-forsaken frozen wasteland," Rima chorused.

"Sahid!" Samira shrieked. "Come here! Let's take Khalil down to buy a nice suit."

"I can't afford a nice suit!" Khalil bellowed. "I'm a student!"

"Yes!" Samira affirmed, "you can." The conversation continued in Arabic, and the only phrase I could make out was "convenient monthly payments."

I dressed hurriedly amidst the commotion of limbs being forced into boots and coats at the front door. If decisions regarding Khalil's and my fragile finances were to be made, I knew I had better be there. Khalil burst into the room. "Hurry!" he gasped. "Or it will be too late!" He grabbed my wrist and pulled me out the door toward what we both feared to be impending bankruptcy.

Into Sahid's and Latif's cars we piled and soon arrived at a men's clothing store. The salesman began valiantly by showing Khalil the various suits in his size, but he soon found himself deferring to Samira and her extraordinary vocabulary of frowns, grimaces, and bursts of hilarious laughter. Finally, he retreated altogether and watched as the mob buzzed around the size 44 rack. A decision was reached eventually, though to this day I do not know how, and Khalil ended up with a garish, striped suit that he and I each assumed the other approved of. Only upon returning to the calm of Azizi's spare bedroom did we realize how untrue this was; we both detested the suit.

Cheeks flushed, Samira stormed into the living room. Sahid's Aunt Nadya had just called. She had heard from her sister-in-law, whose niece had been over to the house of the cousins who were preparing the wedding feast, and she reported that their parsley was limp and the tabouli was sure to be a disaster if new parsley was not found. She had not even wanted to mention the eggplants which looked as if they were suffering from a highly contagious disease—contractible only in this frozen wasteland they call a country, she was quite certain.

"*Habibi*," Samira ordered Khalil, her jaw tensed, "drive Sahid to the airport to pick up his mother. I must take our car to the market!"

Sahid followed Khalil and me to our decrepit Toyota parked down the street—dusty, rusty, dented, and blotched with body filler on the outside, grimy and worn inside. "Is this your car?" he nervously inquired of Khalil who was seating himself behind the cracked steering wheel.

"Sit on the newspapers," I comforted. "That way the springs won't do too much damage."

In the airport parking lot, Sahid's mother, wearing a pink veil that covered her head and neck, gave Khalil and me a salutary scowl as Sahid helped her into the back seat. Unfortunately, Khalil and I were so intent on finding room in our trunk, on the roof, and in our laps for her luggage, we forgot about the rusted-out hole in the floor right under her feet. Once the car started, Mamma began coughing into her veil. "Go faster!" I urged Khalil, but with the increased speed, the rumble from the tail pipe became a reverberating roar. Soon, Mamma had retreated fully into gasping, cursing folds of pink.

By dinnertime, the woman had still not managed to regain her composure. A supplicating Samira served an enormous meal, but Mamma waved the elaborate dishes and their inappropriately Christian creator away, indicating she had entered into a profound state of shock that was not conducive to the digestion of food. She wanted only to be delivered to Nadya, her Muslim hostess, and a large, soft bed. She held her head; she rolled her eyes to the heavens, and muttered, implored, moaned.

The next morning I again awoke to the rattling of dry cleaner's plastic, this time just a few feet away. I opened bleary eyes on the three sisters huddled around the bed, my dress caught up in their hands.

"No! This is no good," Samira informed me. Rima and Azizi shook their heads dismally.

"I'll be getting married in a suit," Samira informed me.

"Yes, I know—"

"No! You don't," and she marched out of the room and returned with a garment bag. "This, I will wear for the wedding photographs and the reception!" She tugged at the zipper and the bag split open to reveal gushing layers of tulle and lace, scalloped and adorned with beads, sequins, silver and gold thread, seed pearls, and almost every other ornamental frivolity known to woman. I was stunned. "Now you see why your dress is no good?" Samira grinned triumphantly over me as all protest died on my lips.

That night, a party was being held at Nadya and Mustapha's house. I knew it had the potential to be interesting, possibly even fun: clothing, cultural, and religious differences most likely cast aside for awhile, Mamma perhaps cajoled into a good mood, abundant food and connubial jokes abounding—but I didn't want to be there. "You go," I urged Khalil. "I'm exhausted!" I shut the door on the tangle of Arabic in the hallway and collapsed on the bed as everyone fought their way out into the winter air. Before the definitive slam of the door I heard Samira remark to Khalil: "*Habibi*, what kind of shoes do you have for the wedding? Were they expensive?"

The next day was the wedding. By the time I forced myself to leave the calm of the bedroom, Samira, Azizi, and Rima had already been to the hairdresser's.

"Your hair looks very nice," I ventured, and Rima and Azizi responded with half-nods, though Samira disagreed.

"No! It doesn't and I don't have time to fix it!"

Samira and Azizi (who was to be her witness at the wedding) sped off to different rooms of the house to put on their similar cream-coloured suits. They were glamorous suits, I had to admit, Samira's form-fitting and with an exquisite fur collar, Azizi's looser, as she was pregnant, with a satin collar. Rima left for Nadya's cousin's house, to inspect the final state of the tabouli, since Samira hadn't been able to locate acceptable parsley. She would not even mention the state of the eggplants.

I was hungry and inexplicably cranky. I banged cupboards and the refrigerator door looking for something to eat. "Bread," I told Khalil. "A toaster. I want a normal slice of toast with a normal bit of butter and strawberry jam on it." He handed me a piece of pita.

"This is bread?" I demanded. "No, this is something you use to shovel olives, cheese, and chickpeas when you're not acquainted with the concept of cutlery!" I couldn't believe my own words. I had always considered myself a tolerant person. Khalil stormed off into the living room to watch the hockey playoffs. "Beirut on ice," he fondly called them at home.

From the bedroom, a hideous wail arose. It was Samira's. Sahid had just called to inform her that his mother would not be attending their wedding. Samira fled to the living room where everyone clustered around her. She raised her arms to the saints and declared she no longer had any use for them: one, because she had converted to Islam in order to please Sahid's ungrateful mother, a woman who had flown halfway around the world in order to snub her; and, two, because they never answered her entreaties anyway. She collapsed weeping on the couch.

"Stop it. You'll ruin your make-up," Azizi counselled wisely, but Samira sobbed that she was not wearing make-up because Sahid had told her that his mother, a woman who throughout the entire pre-nuptial party the previous evening had flagrantly ignored Samira, would fall prostrate on the ground if Samira so much as looked at a tube of lipstick. Then she turned to Khalil, all her big-sisterly love and patience suddenly broken, and a stream of angry Arabic spewed from her colourless lips. All I could make out of her tirade was the solitary English phrase, "carbon monoxide poisoning."

I continued to slam cupboards after Azizi and Samira left for Samira's wedding, and Khalil continued to studiously watch the game on tv until a high-pitched warbling cry, as one might expect exotic birds to make while mating, dying, or doing both simultaneously, shattered our self-imposed silence. Khalil threw open the front door on Azizi. Next to her, an unfamiliar man with ginger-coloured beard and hair was throwing confetti on the newly-wed Samira and Sahid, but the bride and groom were oblivious to the festivities. Samira screamed vigorously at Sahid.

"You never told me that my sister, one of only two sisters in this God-forsaken frozen wasteland they call a country, would be considered half a person," Samira crowed, "that to sign our marriage certificate, we'd have to pick some stranger off the street!"

At this, the ginger-haired man shook his head as if casting off a burden of praise. "No, no. Quite all right. Glad to be of service," and he followed the small procession into the house.

"The Lebanese are strange people," I placated.

"No!" Samira seared first me and then her husband with her eyes. "Only the Muslims!"

Just then, Sahid remembered that he should go plead with Mamma to appear in the wedding photographs. He darted out the door and Samira plunked herself on the couch, sobbing fitfully.

I left the room to get dressed. Rummaging through the closet, I found the dress I had planned to wear. It appeared to have been taken out of the dry cleaner's plastic and rehung precariously on the hanger, but what was immediately apparent to me was that the back zipper was broken.

"Oh no!" I moaned.

"Anything wrong?" Azizi appeared beside me. Miraculously, another dress was in her reverent grasp. It was cream in colour—Samira's favourite shade—and was in fact the dress that Azizi herself had originally planned to wear to the wedding, she said, before Samira had discovered a sale on the $500 suits with the fabulous collars. Azizi generously proposed, since the zipper on my dress was tragically amiss, that I wallow through the wedding reception in the rich layers of cream. I agreed, and then she mentioned "convenient monthly payments."

Khalil stepped into the new shoes that had mysteriously appeared in his suitcase that morning along with a neatly folded Chargex bill, and we left for the wedding reception, our Toyota rumbling and belching the prescribed distance behind the profusely decorated wedding cars. As we entered the hall, I became aware of how Khalil's shoes squeaked and my slip rustled, of the sound of our own breathing as we found our seats.

The Muslim guests were on one side and the Christian guests on the other. No one spoke. The bride and groom entered and sat at the head table smiling tensely to both sides of the hall. The food was served and heads bowed solemnly over plates. At one point a particularly imaginative little boy, with an impressive talent for sound effects, made a rattling sound like machine-gunfire that caused several guests to dive under their chairs. But after that disturbance, the hall regained its funereal atmosphere. Only the voices of Samira and Sahid were loud enough to be overheard from the head table. "Are you sure I don't get half a serving of food?"

"Why not take your usual three?"

After dinner Khalil and I found a few Christians guzzling liquor under the back steps, and we were soon joined by other Christians, and then by wayward Muslims. When we returned inside, the dancing had begun. Samira and Sahid had begun their first waltz as man and wife and, as I saw the determination with which Samira was staring into her husband's eyes, attempting in spite of inadequate clothing, limp tabouli, and a hostile mother-in-law, to create at least one romantic moment in her wedding day, I actually summoned sympathy for her. I had already learned what she too would soon know, that the most a bride can expect of her wedding is that it be enjoyable for other people, that frequently and perhaps inevitably it can't live up to her expectations, particularly those of a Lebanese bride taught from birth to look forward to the day as the pinnacle of her experience. Yet I had believed that too. Once. When I was a little girl I dressed in my mother's lace slip, put a doily on my head, and marched through the living room on the arm of a groom taller than my father, kinder than Santa Claus, more handsome than Ben Casey. I spun under his adoring gaze, bathed in the admiring smiles and cheers of a room crowded with well-wishers. But no one cheered Samira as Sahid held her stiffly in his arms. The wedding of the woman I now call sister-in-law was failing miserably on all counts.

The waltz finished. Samira danced with a self-conscious Khalil and Sahid with his mother, and then as the music ended and the partners began a desperate search for new partners, Mamma strode to a table filled with relatives. She cuffed a few young men across the head, pointed out some pretty girls giggling on the other side of the hall, shrieked Allah only knows what, and before anyone knew what had transpired, Muslim men were asking Christian women to dance, Christian men were asking Muslim women, and, most surprising, women from both camps were asking men—they cared not who in the euphoria of their new found liberation—to dance.

They waltzed, they hopped, they waved white linen napkins, hooted, whistled, and shrilled. Mamma kissed both of Samira's cheeks, Samira and Sahid beamed, and then, amidst thunderous applause and kamikaze bird-calls, they walked arm-in-arm out into the cold Canadian night. Azizi reached for Latif's hand, and Rima stared into the blue eyes of the ginger-haired stranger and felt all vestiges of girlhood flee from her bursting woman's heart. Khalil told me he loved me and that weddings weren't so awful after all, were they? And perhaps we should have one.

"Yes," I readily agreed. "When we've finished paying for this one. In about ten years."

On the way back to Calgary, we encountered a snowstorm which increased in fury the closer we got to the city. For the last twenty miles or so, the visibility was almost zero, and at one point we went off the road and drove into the ditch. I clutched Khalil's arm as he steered through the blinding snow. It wasn't that we were lost so much as we just couldn't see where we were going, what lay ahead. I wondered if Samira and Sahid at their hotel bridal suite could feel the shuddering wind. Or if, in each other's arms, it's possible to be oblivious.

LESLIE NOGUE • *EDMONTON, ALBERTA*

MARY HOWES

Mary Howes is an Edmonton poet, born in Kitchener, Ontario, who moved "out west" twenty years ago. Except for a brief sojourn "back east" she considers the West her home. She writes: "I like the dictionary definition of the word `west' as `the part of the sky where the sun sets.' And the words `west' and `frontier' have come to be interchangeable. It's all wide open—no boundaries. No wonder writers go crazy out here experimenting with new ways of writing. What's to stop them?"

Ms Howes has published three books of poetry: lying in bed *(Longspoon Press, 1981),* QHS *(Greensleeve Publishing, 1989), and* Vanity Shades *(Red Deer College Press, 1990).* QHS *won the bpNichol Memorial Chapbook Award in 1990. She wrote the text for* The Beginning, *an experimental film by Calgary intermedia artist Jane Evans, which was nominated for two Alberta Motion Picture Industry Association Awards. In 1991, an independently produced audiocassette titled "Evidence I Was Here" was released, featuring spoken word by Mary Howes and original music by the Edmonton-based alternative music group, Guerilla Warfare.*

Howes' first theatre piece "I Can't Take It Anymore" was produced at Catalyst Theatre's "WRITE ON THE EDGE CABARET" in May 1992.

the part of the sky

where the sun sets

her eye's on a

c l o t h e s l i n e

where it breaks

sky
into
land
into
sensible squares

tea towels diapers pillowcases

white flags to signal
surrender
to the same day
beginning

wooden stoop
2 steps up
mouthpegs
one after the other
hook last square
to next & so on
down the line

by Mary Howes

reel life starts here
the proper way
to hang it all
where neatness counts & counts

oiled pulleys cut noise
so there's just the shush
wet sheets
& overhead
vee screech southerly
snow geese & blue

to pastures east
white postage stamps
stuck on neighbour's line

her eye's on mine

monday morning
the same day
beginning

our lines semaphore
to the border

c o o k i n g l a k e l i n d b r o o k t o f i e l d

r y l e y h o l d e n b r u c e v i k i n g

k i n s e l l a i r m a f a b y a n

w a i n w r i g h t

ropeswing
over prairie creek

glacier fed
a sudden chill

queen anne's lace
northern bedstraw
sweetvetch
in the blue-eyed grass
where i watch

one son on the arc
one son on the bank

they swing
they catch
they take turns

alone in this wandering hour
alone with runaway thoughts
catch in my throat

mayday
mayday

one by one
they drop in

pennies in a stream

each drop lasts a century
snap of straw word
too brief to read
after the letting go

this is the hour of severance

past the ropeswing tree
where prairie creek
turns into
swan
to the foothills where a redtailed hawk
becomes a plane
heading east

west on the yellowhead
to a silver onion church
planted by a pond
so blue
it smells of sky

on second glance
a field of flax in bloom

in the old days
planted & sown & spun & woven
by women who lifted their skirts
exposed their genitals
implored the infant flax plants

grow this high

inside the church
the beast screams
into the mirror

where is she

and she appears
over his shoulder
behind him

or

lost in the glass
beauty

to dream
you are a bunch of sticks
loosely held together
about to fall apart
scatter
every witchway
any moment
now

take the cutoff
to enchant alberta
follow the breadcrumb trail
through the woods
where white & red flowers
grow on the same tree
around the bend
to the gingerbread house

inside
the witch stirs a big pot
of orange goop
with a paddlespoon

it's alphagetti

i stir & i stir
& i can't make any sense of this
she says
not one word

headlong
down mt edith cavell
on my back
bandaged to my chest
a baby boy

black crack beside us
arm's length
i monitor
with fingertips
steer us clear
all the way down

temperature
pulse
respiration
tattoo of his heart
cold breath
on top of mine

whoosh
on white ice
our bound bodies
in gauze tunnel
transfusion

no cues
but the white
behind his head
on either side
the white ahead
i cannot see

we're picking up speed

to wake
from a cold white dream
to feel hot
wet

granite woman

shoulders
the responsibility
shrugs off all comers

she stays put

big sky woman
spreads the word
the air turns
blue
page
white

milk river woman
slashes through
the old story
bellyful of stones

grasslands woman

grinds to a halt
snowlines
in
summerfallow
spring
to attention

white pine woman
pitches a curve ball
spikes in her trunk
invisible to the saw

bonfire woman

flint-eyed
2
sticks

re(m)embers the first time

snow fence woman

bellies up
to the barbed
wire
chews
thru
to the next section

foothills woman
never any older
never any closer

vague blue

breast
rump
thigh
keeps her distance

northern lights woman
now green
now pink

the hiss & spittle
écriture writ(h)ing
her body

highway #2 woman

flicks the dial
to country western

(i gotta go cuz the road's
my middle name)

her eye's on

the vanishing point

a phone on tv is ringing & i answer mine
ray milland strangles me from behind
this is a rerun ray remember the scissors

i cut out the part that would hurt you most
lick the envelope & go out a little after 4
to mail it the blond guy on the corner

says jeez i thought i knew you & waits
while i slip it thru the slot my name's
will & i want you to come home with me

at the all night esso ruby's locked the door
she's vacuuming chocolate bars oh henry mr big
you've got an eating disorder i buy smokes

& a bonnie raitt tape head down the dark alley
a 4x4 roars up behind me hey baby wanna party
icy ruts no tread on my boots when i get up

i see the windshield on my car's broken tiny
blue cubes in the moonlight only thing gone
a christmas parcel i was sending to you

inside i eat a handful of cheerios you bought
the day before you left the dried apricots too
will looked a little like you

what i remember of him standing in the middle
of the intersection 99th & whyte just before
the light changed & the bronco hit him

the bananas are black smell too much like
black bananas i dropped one at the intersection
old vaudeville caper grace kelly's neck

is flawless unmarked her eye's on the dial
distorted body image in the mirror i am
blonde about to become a princess i hook up

the answering machine in case you call go out
to hang a red blanket on the clothesline it's
the signal for help on the prairies

don't know if it'll work in the city

KELLY A. GOULD • *ARDROSSAN, ALBERTA*

BARBARA MULCAHY

Barbara Mulcahy lives in a farming community south of Manning in Alberta's Peace River country. She and her husband and three children live in a stackwall house on land they have cleared, the latest generation in a long line of Alberta homesteaders. Ms Mulcahy's years in Manning (1978 to the present) represent most of her adult life and her longest stay in any one place. She was born in Trinidad and had lived in India, Greece, the United States, and Israel by the time she was twelve years old. Her first memories are of Greece; Greek was her second language, long since lost. Prior to moving to Manning, Ms Mulcahy lived in British Columbia for four years. Her poetry has appeared in many literary periodicals, including Prism International, Quarry, *and* Grain. *She is a librarian for the Manning Municipal Library.*

Hunting Season

1. The Town, Surrounded

The northern town nestles into the bright varying shades of fall. The highway, coming from one place and going to another, passes through the town. Here and there, in the fields of barley and wheat, flocks of geese light. In the bush all around the town, the bush that goes on and on into BC, the Yukon, the NWT, and Saskatchewan, the deer, elk, and moose go into rut. Males sharpen their antlers on willows; they rub off the velvet vascular skin, polish the tines. They urinate in wallows and lie down there, roll back and forth. Their neck muscles bulge. They have lost interest in food. A female calls and the males battle. The antlers rattle, clash.

In fall, in the Peace River country, when the air turns, gets a bite to it, and the strangulated leaves go gorgeous, when the wind comes, tears at the leaves until the trees are left naked, when the drakes have come out of their eclipse plumage and the ungulates go snakey, stop hiding, start bugling to each other, when the animals recognize what is more important than food and safety, when the whole forest is alive with the sense of gathering winter, of darkness and cold—that is hunting season.

2. The Hunters in the Town

Some of the hunters wear camouflage and some wear fluorescent orange. Some just wear their ordinary jeans, a plaid shirt, and a jean jacket. Some of them drive new four-wheel-drive pick-ups with the bodies jacked up so high you could almost walk under. That's so they can drive through man-sized ruts. They have a winch on the front so they can winch themselves out of mud-holes. Others drive rusty old trucks. Sometimes a man with a good truck, but a bad conscience, will drive an old truck in hunting season because the fish and wildlife officer, the fish cop, has the right to seize any vehicle used in the commission of a wildlife crime.

by Barbara Mulcahy

In theory, there are two kinds of hunters: outsiders and locals. Sometimes it isn't possible to tell one from the other. If it is possible, it's usually because the outsider has more money and even a guide, which he has to have if he's not Canadian.

If you look at it another way, there are all kinds of hunters. Goose hunters and duck hunters, trophy hunters (the ones that want a huge rack or a big bearskin), meat hunters. There are liars and wildlife enthusiasts. There are poachers and stalwart citizens. So this whole hunting thing is a lot more complicated than you might think when you drive into town in the fall. Then the town waits. Cartridges and a four-foot Canada Goose in a storefront window beckon, reminding a hunter of things that he might have forgotten to pack.

3. The Hunter with a Rationale

You see these teeth? They belong to a meat eater. The incisors, the long, sharp fangs? They're made to tear into flesh.

That's why I hunt. I was built for it.

4. The Old Hunter

When I was young, this Indian took me hunting. The morning after a fresh snowfall we'd walk till we found some tracks. We walked through the bush, quietly. Me, following his footsteps as best I could. We picked up our feet, no scuffling. Noise—that's the white man's way. Not look where you're stepping, make a lot of noise. You have to pick each foot up and know what's underneath where you're gonna step. You can walk on a green branch, it'll bend, but a dry twig'll snap. When I wasn't careful, that Indian'd stop, look back over his shoulder at me, glare.

Now they go in their four-wheel-drives on bush roads. Drive till they come to a cut line. Then they get their quads down out of the back and drive on the cut line. Drive. What do they care about noise, branches? It's driving, that's all.

5. The Young Hunter

It's fifteen miles back to prime hunting. Quads and trikes give the hunter an advantage. You can get through with quads. With a truck, you have to stop at the line. Also, it's fun to run up and down the cut lines. There's a trade-off. Now we don't camp any more; it's too easy to drive home and get in your own bed.

We still have the best thing though—the campfire. There's nothing like it—tea with leaves and bark. Tea melted out of snow. Garlic sausage on a stick. Toasted peanut butter sandwiches. Lies and jokes.

We drive around a block. Look for tracks that go in and don't come out. Then we go in, into the wind. So they don't hear us or smell us. Windy days are best. Even if you've got two people flushing and one guy waiting where it's clear, they can get away. They know where you are. Just have to step aside to be clear of you. They don't have to run at all.

If they do run, there's the thrill of the chase. They're strong. They're used to running, being scared up and running. They either get shot or they're away.

6. A Poacher

When I saw that deer standing there in the road, staring me down, I said, "Thank you, Lord," and I plugged him. I knew I'd better hurry before some namby-pamby Nosy Parker called the fish cop about firing after dusk. I threw him in the back of the truck. I was halfway home when I looked in my rear view and I see the bugger is trying to stand up. I only stunned him. Now, how the heck am I going to shoot him out here in the open? I swerve real hard, try to knock him out against the side of the truck.

That's when I got off the pavement and, when I tried to pull up off the soft shoulder, that's when I rolled. Totalled, and broke my ribs. But that deer is dead meat now.

7. The Butcher

Ravens are the garbage trucks of the North.

They hang out by the back door. I put the bones and the scraps in the garbage. If I turn around before I close the lid, they'll grab a leg and take off to the top of the grocery store. They all fight over it there. The dogs come around too, but there's no point in giving them any. The ravens take it away. The roof of that grocery store must look like a graveyard. No, in a graveyard the skeletons are covered; the grocery store roof is a boneyard.

The difference between domestic and wild meat is in cleanliness. A domestic animal is clean when they bring it in. No trim. You can eat the outside. But some hunters, especially early in the season when it's hot, they want to get the hide off as quick as possible—before the meat starts to rot. They don't put any plastic down. Just roll the meat out of the hide into the dirt and the leaves. Then they tie it on to the back of the trike and head off, usually through fourteen mud puddles. Or, if they're on horses, it's horsehair, and horse sweat along with the dirt and the leaves. When they bring it in like that, you have to reskin it, trim off up to an inch. The dirt and leaves dull the knives, too.

Once in a while, someone'll bring one in with the hide still on. Just hacked the head off with an axe and pulled some of the guts out. Leaves the heart, the esophagus, and the arse-hole with three or four turds.

There's even people who like their meat rotten. They leave it hang two weeks. When it's sticky on the outside, they bring it in. They say that's when it's tender.

There's all kinds. I just try to keep it clean. I cut and wrap it however they want.

It's a rush job, hunting season. There's blood and ground-up bone-dust and fat everywhere. We spread sawdust on the floor to soak it up. The freezer gets so packed with quarters and halves hanging on hooks, there's hardly room to get something out.

8. The Goose Hunter

First you got to spot the geese. Drive around, look for them or for coyotes. Where there's coyotes, there's geese or ducks. If the geese are in the air, you glass the sky, see where they're headed or where they're coming from.

Once you've spotted them, you wait till they're gone and then you go back to what they're feeding on. You want to find out what field they're using now and what part of it. Fresh soft droppings mean they fed there today; hard droppings mean they fed there before.

You dig your pit so it's facing where the geese will be coming from. They always come in into the wind. You want to face them.

Sometimes you're digging at night by flashlight. And the ground is hard. You need a good, sharp shovel. It's a lot of work and you have to be finished before dawn. You have to set out decoys, too. Because geese like to be together. Then you wait, listen. You can hear them first. And you have to be still. That's what they're watching for, movement.

Just when they're lighting, you pick out your goose. You can't shoot at the flock. You won't get anything. You pick out your goose and you have to lead it. There's all the factors: the wind, the goose—how fast is it flying and how far away is it?—and is it flying towards you or at an angle or what?

After you get the first flight, you go out and retrieve what you've shot. If you want, you can get a forked stick and prop a goose's head in it and make it into another decoy. But quickly, because you have to hide for the next flight. When there's no more time, you pack up and clean up and go to work. After work, it's the same thing—out, trying to sight geese, and up half the night digging pits so you can get up early and do it again.

It's not every time the geese come. Sometimes you dig twenty pits and all you do is wait. But there's something in that too, in the wait, in the cold, when the sky is just starting to light up, and the way you have to be still and listen so carefully.

It's like gambling or drinking, it's a fever.

9. The Cop

Hunting season: drunks. Driving too fast or too slow, or in and out of the ditch. You stop them, recite the whole thing: "It is my duty to inform you that you have the right to retain and instruct counsel without delay. This means that you may call your lawyer or get free advice from duty counsel immediately. If you are charged with an offence, you may apply to legal aid for assistance. Do you understand?" What does the guy say? "Wha? Wha'sat you say?"

"I am arresting you for impersonating a life form" is what I want to say.

10. Another Poacher

I come from a long line of poachers. Maybe even from Robin Hood.

You know why they regulate hunting? It's not for the wildlife. It's for the money. There's enough meat here for all of us but they want to keep it for the rich guys that come up from the city and pay a guide to show them where they can pull a trigger.

I'm not ashamed of it. It's Robin Hood against the crooked king.

There's still ways to outwit the king.

11. The Fish Cop

I can't show it to you. But it looks real from the road, at twilight, or in the dark. We catch a lot of poachers with it. It used to be called a decoy moose or deer but now we call it surrogate wildlife. That's a court term. The judges didn't like the word decoy. It made it sound like we were doing something illegal, something like entrapment.

It's made of plywood. It can turn its head, flip its tail up and down, fall over.

We move it from place to place. Put it out at dusk, eighty yards off the road, at least. And not just in hunting season. There are lots of things people do wrong when they see it. Road hunting. Night hunting. Spotlight hunting. Closed season.

See, the trophy animals are wary. They only come out at dusk. They come out together—sometimes feeding on the willows by the side of the road.

If you wound them at dusk, you can't track them. So there's wastage.

If they use a prohibited weapon, I can seize it. Even the truck if they've used the headlights to spotlight the animal. Because these animals freeze when you shine something in their eyes. They're hypnotized by light.

So we put out the surrogate wildlife and when the guy shoots we catch him and then he says he was only trying to scare it off the road.

Eighty yards off the road and he wants to scare it away. With a gun. And a bullet through the heart.

The treaty Indians come down here too. They can hunt anywhere on crown land at any season. But they have to follow the other laws.

You can tell when it's an old timer. The Natives always build a little fire near the body. And nearby there's a pile—guts in the centre and then, in the four directions, little pieces—esophagus here, heart . . .

Some poachers try to copy the Natives. They cut off the nose and tongue. They think I won't investigate if I think it was a treaty-kill.

12. The Dainty Hunter's Joke

Some guys take the heart and tongue first, say it's the best. Me, personally, I'd never eat anything from an animal's mouth.

But I eat eggs!

13. The Waitress

I have a soft spot for Americans. They're sort of innocent, you know. They come up here with their L. L. Bean clothes and their high-powered magnums with the telescopic sights. They think it's great up here. Wildlife and wilderness, they say. They envy us. They always say they'd live up here except for their wives. Their wives have to live near a mall, they say.

They always worry about the exchange. Think everything costs so much up here and we're trying to cheat them on the difference in the dollar. There's one guy brings his whole truck full of groceries, even toilet paper.

After all that, when they come in, even just for coffee, they leave a tip.

14. The Cook

What you have to do with moose is this: you have to take your meat hammer and just smash it. Put in garlic and seasoning. But who's going to do that with eight hundred pounds, a thousand pounds of meat? Best to take it to the butcher and tell him to grind it up, add fat, and make it into sausage. But who wants to know they're eating two hundred pounds of fat? And who wants a thousand pounds of sausage?

Better just to take a picture. Buy your food in little packages.

15. After Hunting Season

The animals—how do they know it's over?

They come back out of trees into the oats left standing by an early snowfall. They eat. The deer in groups led by the does—after the rut a matriarchy is established for the long winter. The mule deer bouncing across the field, the whitetailed deer—white flags on their haunches and tails. The moose come separately. The cows come with calves. The bulls come each one on his own.

The geese are gone, the swans, the sandhill cranes. The ducks—gone. In the sky and on branches, the snowy owls down from the north watch, hanging on.

The hunters clean their guns, oil them, put them in cabinets, behind fancy, glassed doors. The women presoak the hunting clothes, remove the dirt and the glory.

Snow settles out of the grey sky onto the great watershed.

The small rivers and creeks that snake through the bush to the concourse of the Peace seem to seize with ice, but in certain places there are still holes where you can see the dark water move.

The black highway disappears under the snow, then reappears temporarily in the wake of each passing vehicle.

Grey plumes from the chimneys in the small town rise straight and then suddenly dissipate in the falling snow.

GARY BANKAY • *EDMONTON, ALBERTA*

SID MARTY

Sid Marty was raised in Medicine Hat and Calgary. He studied English Literature at Sir George Williams University in Montreal, and at the University of Calgary. He financed his education in part by playing guitar and singing in coffee houses and bars. In 1990, he recorded an audiotape of his songs, Let the River Run. Starting in 1966, Mr Marty worked as a seasonal park warden in the mountain national parks, and he was a full-time warden from 1972 to 1978. He drew on his experiences in the mountains of Alberta and British Columbia in writing his 1978 best-seller, Men for the Mountains, which won both the Canadian Authors' Association Non-Fiction Prize and the Alberta Culture Non-Fiction Award. Published in seven countries, this title is cited by Borealis magazine as one of the 35 books most influential in the Canadian environment movement. Mr Marty has published two books of poetry: Nobody Danced with Miss Rodeo (McClelland and Stewart, 1981) and Headwaters (McClelland and Stewart, 1973). His poems have appeared in numerous anthologies and school texts. In 1968 he married Myrna Jamison of Calgary, and they have two sons, Paul and Nathan.

Bull-pine Courage

Part of the Northwest Quarter of Section 30, Township 9 West of the 5th Meridian. Comprising 20 acres more or less

A white house tucked into a hill
at the foot of the Livingstone Range
Eden glimpsed from a realtor's car
"They call it—Willow Valley"

Each square foot to be fiercely loved
on angles too steep and wind-blown
for anything but bull-pine courage
rooted in stone

"He's going to buy it,"
said the old woman as I sat dazed
in the kitchen, its floors
tilting uphill, like the land

I had been climbing all my life
to reach this dimple
on the Lewis Overthrust
to be, suddenly, home

All my failures whining at the gate
grew fearful and still behind me

So I shut my eyes to the poor foundation
the crumbling barn
the stable roof tacking like a sail
into endless wind

For nighthawks sang, chorus frogs trilled
the lark ruled the fence
and the whole eastern sky
gloried over that Blackfoot altar
the Porcupines
Where Oldman first shaped men
from a bit of clay

"What are we waiting for?"
asked my wife. It seemed too easy
All it took was every penny we had
to buy what we cannot own
Until our ashes are scattered on this hill
Until our voices join the wind

by Sid Marty

Hands of My Fathers

They should be soft and supple
these writer's hands
But writing poems all day
won't pay mechanic's wages

Today they are black with grease
bruised and punctured
groping under the manifold
of the Jeep 2–58

These hands can shape a chord
with calloused fingertips
bend dollars from a git-box string

Musician's fingers, nervous
of all roaring power tools
still play the handyman's tune

There is no shelter in a poem
for a family of four
No piped water, no power juice

I had to build so I could write
These hands have wasted half a life
to build a life for art

Poor fingers, stiff with work
you have touched death
on warden service duty
Held the drowned man's head
Delved the avalanche for souls
Gathered up the jigsaw puzzle
parts of reckless men
These fisherman's hands
These hunter's hands that
make meat from beasts, yet
love to gently rein
a horse's mouth, still tremble
on the satin of a woman's thigh

They have unlocked a mountain's secrets
stone by stone. Axeman's hands
poet's hands

Just now, they shaped a tool
to pull these lifters free of the cam
Ground it from an old steel tent peg
barely informed by the mind

I stare at these fingers, baffled
Whose hands are these?
All of my fathers, every man
who ever taught me

It would mean something
if one of those outliving me would say
"He was a good man"
And one older than the rest would add
"He was a hand"

Scruples

Don't let thoughts cloud your thinking
the day you say "I quit"
While there is desire
the will must follow

I tossed my badge on that clown's desk
with a satisfying ring of certainty

Now it's ten years later
One summer of passion
Ten Decembers of doubt

Sometimes we forget what we want most
repeating stories of a life before desire
The body's comfort makes the soul embarrassed

The will, it turns out
is not made of iron
More like Plaster of Paris

Steve

Steve is out in the raw wind
sawing boards from a pallet
salvaging hardwood to smoke some meat
wasting nothing

He built this ranch from a miner's wages
Hard work purchased more hard work

Good-natured, he forgives my trade
My life of words not real to him
for whom work means everything

He hays our little field, lends me his tractor
Helps us skin and split an elk each fall
Very little Steve and Rosy wouldn't do
to help a neighbour. They're the kind
that feed this nation

I give him a bottle, New Year's gift
"What for?" he wants to know
"Because you're such a nice guy"

He says there's work at Forestry
"Why doncha go cut them beetle-bug trees?"
I talk of deadlines, writing scripts
It makes him blush

I know he's thinking as I leave
"The poor bugger's got nothing to do"
In his torn parka with the ragged sleeves
does he pity me, my neighbour Steve?

Elk Jump Up All Around You

Often you tried to get this close
tracking them upwind, smelling their musk
in wet aspen woods, to catch them sleeping

Still you are not ready
when elk wake and jump up all around you

Long-necked giants among the trees
rise up with bristling manes. One barks
and the hair on your head goes up too

Feeling those eyes and ears
all trained on you, you cannot raise
the rifle. You are hungry
but not fast enough
to pick one fat bounty out of thirty

All you take home will be
two heartbeats worth of mercy
A blessing, when Earth leapt
into flesh and you counted coup
The whole doomed herd was yours
and you let it go

Drought

They plough the burnt crops under
Out there, between those hills
Up here a mountain sun
withers the garden all day
At night frost falls on the wounded

Steve comes to cut our hay
amazed by the green thickness
of a crop we do not need
Stares at the red peonies, the sprinkler
whirling over black potato vines

"What the hell you doin', Siddy?"

I can't say writing poems
to a man whose hay has failed
To a man whose hands are cracked
like the mud of the dried-up sloughs

An Arrowhead

It seemed too perfectly wrought
to be lost, or found by chance
That ivory coloured point
shaped for an ancient strife
gleamed, in my son's hand

I have felt the presence
of those old souls, hunting
every turn of these hills of home

Ancestors that I cannot claim
a history I can never own

Theirs were the children
our fathers brushed aside
Who find our guilt contemptible
and false. Yet this is a gift
of an artist's hand
notched by more than want

In the bend of a bow
it would sing true
centuries from now

Be a cruel elegance
Still sharp, the thought
—you never were alone
O Brain that conquered stars
O proud Heart, stoop
to the conquering stone

Going Up

I can't go back to the reserve
It's a long story
Besides my mother has another man
It's his home now

I go to see my dad:
Soon's I come in
he's reach in his pocket
to give me money

It's not his money I want

I told the judge
—send me to Drumheller
They got a program there,
you can go to school

You see I made up my mind
I got to go up
Sometimes I know I go sideways awhile
Okay. But I'm gonna go up
no matter how long it takes

I'm gonna find all the words I need
to figure it all out
That world is made of words
The one where I have to live

The Amulet
(found by an imaginary archeologist)

It might have been the child's
We found her broken skeleton buried
near that pile of bison bones

Back before the bow
they were buried sitting up
As if waiting
(we don't know for what)

A child already had survived so much
And then—swept over the piskun's edge
drowning in the buffalo . . . or so it seems

Was it for love they carved such things?
We can't know what love was like then
There was hunger, fear, and pain
All of the ugly surprises

Oh we could find those models still
but love's not my department
I'm just a kind of miner
chipping away the ages
with a grapefruit knife

No hope of finding gods this amulet might appease,
What need for gods, with the grass ploughed under?

Winter was real then, not a dream behind glass
Not much time to moon for love, or mourn

Yes, well maybe after the hides were softened
and the winter camp attained
down on the river bottom, where there was wood
After the stories had been told

Too dark to ply the needle
too bright by moonlight yet to sleep
—the prairie wolves gone hunting elsewhere
—the Great Plains Grizzly gone to den

Maybe then, over a lock of hair kept
in a skin bag, or a piece of willow
some hand had whittled hurriedly to a doll

Maybe then there was time
for tears of amazement, and maybe
—see what you've got me doing!

Maybe love began in bewilderment
with a shoulder suffered there to cling to
And a harsh voice saying
one soft word

If Love Was Enough

If love was enough
we could save worlds
Even this one

Nighthawk, rescue the night
from a mere darkness
Moths in the yard light cannot escape
the cat's quick claws

Out of nowhere
an armoured hand
If hate was enough

Our weak eyes crave
light. We speak of love
Where is it? There
it goes

Nighthawk, sing the cat to sleep

Let the Earth return
to itself, the gentle rain
make green these yellow hills

If death was enough
The grass would smile

As skulls look up
to greet the stars

Southern Alberta

Sometimes great uncles came up from Montana
The family tried to see itself entire
Ashamed to mention nationality

Divided by president and queen
the potency of beer
anthems, coloured rags, history

Almost puzzled to discover
we all spoke English
Related, alienated

Yet we drank from the same river
that crosses the border and ignores it

As few men ever do
except the Blackfoot
hating us all, impartially

The Wrench
(for the Webbers)

The kind of box wrench a rancher carries
half-inch one end, 9/16 the other
A common thing for simpler machines
Black with rust, found by a broken seed drill
on Terry's place,

My neighbour Terry is dead
and the ranch dies with him

In morning mist
His sons' voices echo up-valley
Their horses sound wild with grief
They drive steers down to a liner

Bent over an engine
Terry's wrench in hand
I hear hooves
thundering on a steel deck

The terrified bawl of the cattle
The bitter voices of Terry's sons
roll from hill to hill

I keep this piece of steel in memory of him
And one more thing that won't get buried
is his name. That ridge above his house,
unnamed before; now that he's gone
we call it Terry's

The Dam

Three years before the dam
they took our names from the district map
We're in the way; they want us to un-be

They took my bottom land
in a bumper year for hay
Our water goes to Lethbridge
60 miles away

I went into the town
and saw their faces slick with greed
They yap of progress as they steal
Two years of boom and to hell
with generations of a farmer's trade

I thought of violence, and the law
(It's never been our way)
I took my title out
and threw it to the fields

I know we stole this land before
Those teepee rings
will soon be under water
with the bare foundations of our kin

Before they drowned our memory
they stripped the soil away
I felt it coming off me
like a second skin

I'm raw and giddy
moving in such pain
I'm like a tumbleweed
Roots torn up
and waiting for the wind

Deathsong For the Oldman River

Down by the river, she bent to swim
where limestone dipped to lead us in
Raspberries roll down on the banks
and everything that lives, gives thanks

Our ponies wondered, as we stripped
I held some berries to her lips
Painted a turtle on her thigh
Our laughter echoed from cliff to cliff

Last summer, by the Oldman River
Gifts that were stolen
from the hands of the Giver

Because my mouth was drought so dry
that no water satisfied
she pressed the berries on my tongue
and on her lips I tasted them

Then we rolled in the water down to the sand
to the painted gravel where the rainbows spawn
The red paint melted in the flood
She held me there in another mood

Last summer by the Oldman River
Gifts that were stolen
from the hands of the Giver

Raspberry mouth in the river's lift
Rosehips pointing her lovely breasts
The blue river in her eyes
as the water laughed and cried

And our ponies stood listening
As a voice, in the Earth, began to sing

WILLIAM SARA • *BLAIRMORE, ALBERTA*

MYRNA KOSTASH

Myrna Kostash was born in Edmonton, Alberta. She is a full-time writer and has been for her entire professional career. She has published three nonfiction books: No Kidding: Inside the World of Teenage Girls *(McClelland and Stewart, 1987);* Long Way From Home: The Story of the Sixties Generation in Canada *(James Lorimer, 1980); and* All of Baba's Children *(Hurtig, 1977). It was the researching of the latter book, an examination of Ukrainian settlement in Canada, that brought Ms Kostash back to Alberta in 1975 in the midst of a successful freelance career in Toronto. Her grandparents were immigrants from western Ukraine and her parents, both schoolteachers, met in Hairy Hill, Alberta, in the area of the province known as the "Ukrainian Bloc." The researching and writing of* All of Baba's Children *reshaped Myrna Kostash's life. She would later purchase a small farm near Hairy Hill and name it "Tulova" after her paternal grandparents' Galician village, the village they left for Canada. Ms Kostash writes, "The fact that I am so firmly and deeply rooted in my childhood space (Edmonton and Tulova), and yet have spent so much time elsewhere, indulging my curiosity about other histories and cultures, proves, it seems to me, the old adage that if you would understand the world, you must first understand your home place."*

Round Trip

IN THE SUMMER OF 1984, WHEN TRAVELing in Ukraine, I visited my baba's village. She had left it in 1911 and never returned. When she died in Edmonton in 1980, I realized that she was the last of the "Europeans," that after her we are all North Americans. But the pull of my memories of her, of her speech, her stories, her music which had been laid down in me like a kind of inner scaffolding was so strong that, even though I had never been to Ukraine, I said, in 1984, that I was "going back."

And now I keep hearing it. Second, third, even fourth generation Canadians "going back" to a place they've never been. To the "Old Country." Fascinated by this play of genetic memory, I searched out some other Albertans who, like me, had grown up inside *two* homelands: the birthplace and that other, legendary realm of the ancestors known for so long as "the village" over there "behind the Iron Curtain." I wanted to hear from them what "over there" has to do with them *here*, especially now that the curtain has been hauled down and the light of ordinary day falls upon the legend.

Richard S. — born in 1956 in Mayerthorpe, Alberta, the son of post-war Polish immigrants; he is an artist in Edmonton who studied six years in the Fine Arts Academy in Cracow, Poland, from 1981 to 1987.

Irena B. — born in 1947 in Prague, Czechoslovakia; she left that country in 1968 and arrived in Canada in 1982 where she works as an administrative assistant at the University of Alberta in Edmonton. In 1990, she visited Czechoslovakia for the first time since her departure.

Cori S. — born in 1962 in Calgary of a Romanian-Canadian mother and a British/Irish-Canadian father; she lives in Calgary and works for a cultural agency. She has never been to Romania.

by Myrna Kostash

Bohdan S. and Natalka O. — married in 1988, they traveled to Kiev, Ukraine in 1989 on an academic exchange. Bohdan, born in Australia in 1954 of post-war immigrants from Ukraine, was raised in Burlington, Ontario; Natalka was born in 1965 in Edmonton, the daughter of a man who had immigrated to Canada from Ukraine as a baby and had grown up on a farm near Lamont, Alberta.

THE LEAVE-TAKING: RICHARD

It was the war that changed everything, wrecked people's lives and scattered them halfway around the world. Before the war, his father hadn't even *imagined* Western Canada, let alone the little town at the foot of the Alaska Highway known affectionately as "Mudthorpe." The Halifax pier, 1954: two kids underarm, a sackful of pots and pans, a train ticket to Alberta and Mayerthorpe.

THE LEAVE-TAKING: IRENA

The feeling of being suspended came later. In August 1968, she was on a study leave in Holland, never dreaming she wouldn't see home again for twenty-two years. She had packed only one small suitcase. But when the tanks rolled into Prague, she waited in anguish in the tiny foreign country on the North Sea for news from home. When it came, it was her father's note, saying, "Don't come back."

She had a rail ticket to London and this is where she went, still planning her life from day to day. She got a job as an au pair and enrolled in university in London. She began all over again, studying language and literature, English and Bengali. Much later would come the questions: "Where do I fit?" "Where do I stand?" "Who am I?"

Try to understand this: the world outside Czechoslovakia was like a dream. No one from her generation had seen it. It was a mythological, shining thing, tantalizingly just out of reach, beyond the cage of home, parental and political. To get out required the most extraordinary efforts—the money you had to have, the black market you had to negotiate, the levels of permission you were forced to scale—only to be denied the exit visa in the end. And then you started all over again. Try to imagine this: an unslakeable thirst to see the rest of the world.

And now, here she was, free. She had all the freedom in the world, living on her own, earning some money, having a foreign adventure in a new language—it was intoxicating. She remembers the swoon of stepping into Oxford Street and seeing nothing but shops. She remembers seeing a pile of bananas on a barrow—exotic fruit that back home in Prague you peeled meticulously and laid out on a dessert plate, eating it with a knife and fork, bit by tiny, succulent bit.

It was the invasion of her homeland that freed her.

STAYING IN TOUCH: IRENA

None of her friends was denied the right of correspondence, so she wrote to them for years as she made the move from studies in England to marriage and academic work and, finally, emigration to Canada in 1982. And sometimes they sent her clippings or even bulk mailings of old newspapers. Sometimes news of what was happening would get back to her by word of mouth. But it was the books that kept the lines open. She read Czech books. She had had to leave all her books behind, of course, but an aunt in Prague mailed them out to her, two or three at a time. In this way, she says, her homeland remained a real, immediate, and vital place.

STAYING IN TOUCH: RICHARD

His parents didn't hate Poland; they hated Communism. They knew that whenever their family back in Augustów received mail or packages from the West (called the "Capitalist West"), someone would be hauled into the local militia office and questioned. But they were all stubborn and spiteful enough to keep up the contact anyway, no matter what. And when Richard's father finally decided it was safe to go back for a visit, and knowing that everything was in short supply in the motherland (called "Kooky Communism"), he packed his bags full of large boxes of detergent.

STAYING IN TOUCH: CORI

It was Aunt Betty in Dysart, Saskatchewan, who was the activist in the family. Cori remembers her mother collecting old clothes, packing them into cardboard boxes and sending them off to Aunt Betty who would send them to the cousins in Romania. She had no idea what they looked like but she understood they were having a hard time—that the Canadian family had to send them the money for an electric range and then, later, money for the plug, when plugs became available. Their hardship, she understood, was a morality tale.

MY TRIP TO ROMANIA: CORI'S MUM

Sunday, August 5, 1984: Gelu took Nick, Elaine, Vivian, and me to the small town of Făgăraş—our mother's birthplace. The Vasile Nistor family still resides there—we were served a duck dinner—their furnishings as meagre as we had ever seen—one butcher knife was all they had—dishes sparse—homemade woven wool rugs covered dirt floors—walls were whitewashed and the only picture on the wall was one that our dad had sent them many years ago of family members. We visited the local church where Grandpa Nistor had donated a church bell many years before. It was still hanging out in the entrance to the church.

—Eva Stent's Journal

STAYING IN TOUCH: NATALKA

This is what she knew about her relatives "back there": they were poor. She knew they were poor because they lived in a village, which she imagined to be something like her *dido*'s (grandfather's) farm near Lamont, except with thatched roofs. She had no idea who they were individually (they never sent pictures) but she was fascinated by the knowledge that she had relations somewhere out there in the deep unknown cosmos called Ukraine.

THE OLD COUNTRY: BOHDAN

Ukraine? It looked, in his child's mind, like a mixture of the steppes, the Carpathian Mountains, and thatched-roof cottages alongside a bubbling brook—just like the one in the painting that hung in their house: his father's favourite picture, a scene from the Carpathian foothills. Ukraine? It was folk tales and fables (Canadians didn't seem to have any) and the priest coming to the house to bless it with holy water, and the backdrop on the stage in the national hall—an idyllic forest scene. Later, as he grew interested in—*curious* about—politics, he thought of Ukraine as the oppressed ethnic homeland where—as in the stories he heard from his father and his friends—if you had been lucky enough to survive murder at the hands of the Germans, you could count on being shipped out to Siberia by the Russians.

LOSING TOUCH: IRENA

She became utterly comfortable in the English language and among those who spoke it, and she felt at home and deeply privileged in her material success. But there was the unbidden pang to remind her she would never really belong emotionally, the realization which would suddenly blind-side her, that a certain kind of openness and self-expression were unavailable to her in a foreign language. Her emotional being had been formed by the sensations of childhood and these she could never recreate, not even among the most intimate and sympathetic companions. In that sense, she knew, she was alone. And when her son, Peter, was born, she spoke to him in Czech. Naturally. It was the first language.

KISS ME, I'M UKRAINIAN: NATALKA

The roots to her grandparents' farm near Lamont were very strong. She remembers family get-togethers of all the relatives, farm and city, at Christmas and Easter; the staggering amounts of food and conversation and hilarity. She remembers going out to pick blueberries and hearing the stampede of the buffalo at Elk Island Park. Her grandfather was a cantor in the Ukrainian-Catholic church. She was content to go along to that church too, for it had never occurred to her there was any point in going to another sort of church.

KISS ME, I'M ROMANIAN: CORI

It was in her grandmother's kitchen, on her grandmother's noodlemaker, that she learned to make noodles for the chicken soup. This was how they got to know and love each other: cooking up a storm in gram's kitchen. Strudel, *mamaliga*, and doughnuts. It took the place of not being able to talk to each other: neither had the other's language. She had had no lessons. Her mother's position on this was that she was a Canadian, they would speak English, period.

KISS ME, I'M UKRAINIAN: BOHDAN

Eventually he would rebel, argue that dinosaurs and astronomy were a lot more important and relevant to him than all this musty stuff about Ukrainian history and geography. Eventually, he would find ways to sneak out of Ukrainian dance classes and disappear with some buddies to the burger joint down the road. But for now, ten, eleven years old, he was made to sit down with his father every night with a pile of inky Ukrainian-language books and study, while his friends rode around on their bicycles in the warm summer evenings. By twelve he was an atheist, by way of Newtonian deism. If he was interested in Ukrainian politics, it wasn't because he wanted to participate. He was only *curious*.

KISS ME, I'M POLISH: RICHARD

You couldn't really flaunt any Polish patriotism in a place like Mayerthorpe where there were no other Polish families and where the priests at the Catholic Church had names like McDougall and Villeneuve. The only time he saw his father exhibit any kind of "Polish Pride" was when he put on his veteran's medal and went to Edmonton to a "do" at the Polish Combatants' Hall.

His mother tried, oh she tried. She spoke to her children in Polish and sat them down at the kitchen table after supper for Polish reading lessons, but Richard was a brat: twitched and whined and finally just ran outside to play baseball. Why should he speak Polish? There weren't any Poles around for hundreds of miles.

Nobody gave him any trouble at school about his last name (he taught them how to pronounce it correctly) or about his father's accent. *He* was the one who fretted about it, wishing his rather small and frail father, the town accountant with the heavy accent, could be more like the other fathers, the *Canadian* ones, the big, lumberjack types.

KISS, ME, I'M UKRAINIAN: NATALKA

She went to university and enrolled in Ukrainian 100 and, that summer, got a job at the Ukrainian Cultural Heritage Village role-playing a Ukrainian pioneer woman, Anna Pylypiw. She tied a babushka around her head, cooked up a pot of borsch, and stood stirring and chatting all day with the old-timers who came to see her in "her" house. It made her feel competent, it made her feel secure, it made her feel Ukrainian.

GOING BACK: RICHARD

When he went away to university, he enrolled in Polish 100, for "easy credits." Actually, it was kind of tough. Then he heard about Polish Culture summer courses for English-speakers in Warsaw. Well, why not? Poland just happened to be the most interesting place to be, that summer of 1981.

GOING BACK: IRENA

It took twenty-two years and a velvet revolution, but in 1990 she made it back, for a visit. Out of curiosity? Sentiment? The knowledge of still being bound to certain people, certain memories? She touched down in Prague and felt—her feet on the motherland—that the decades had miraculously contracted into days.

GOING BACK: NATALKA

It was her parents' generation that had started to travel to Ukraine, the ones who felt that it was finally safe to do so. This had been her father's dream—to retire and to go, not to Florida, but back home. He died before he could make the trip. Natalka made it for him, completing the circle of his longing by going "back" to a place she had never been.

CULTURE SHOCK: BOHDAN

He was told to "speak civilized," meaning Russian. He would not. He had been given a room at the student residence with a smashed window, demolished furniture, food rotting on the counter and cockroaches overrunning the entire space. He was given soap and a bucket and told to clean it up if he wanted to live there. He would not. He yelled in Ukrainian that he wanted a better place, they yelled back in Russian, and then, behold! a better room. This was his first lesson. To get what you want, be loud and offensive. It worked, but it made him feel dirty.

CULTURE SHOCK: NATALKA

Trying to get clean sheets. Trying to find a toilet seat. The toilet tank not filling; using a bucket of water. Doing the laundry in pails.

CULTURE SHOCK: BOHDAN

He would say "please" and "thank you." People were amazed. Such a cultured gentleman!

CULTURE SHOCK: RICHARD

He boarded the Polish train in Frankfurt and right away noticed how it was grungy and beat-up. Inside Poland he took surprised note of the horses working in the fields and the mega-line-ups for gas at the filling stations. Maybe there was a connection? He was all for Solidarity but he noticed that, thanks to the strikes, the stores were completely empty save for plastic bottles of vinegar. When he ascended from the underground railroad station, his first sight of Warsaw was of that Stalinist behemoth of architecture, the Palace of Culture: bulky, heroic, socialist-realist figures of the labouring proletariat. Meanwhile, past him in drab and shabby clothes strutted the real working class of People's Poland, on strike.

CULTURE SHOCK: IRENA

At first she was not shocked. At first she simply did not see how very dirty and dilapidated and "downhill" were the magnificent façades of Prague. At first all she was aware of was that she was with her friends again. Then she started seeing some reality—the neglected buildings, the rude and sullen service, the unrelievedly dreary neighbourhoods—and she became angry and depressed. Is it possible it had always looked like this?

WHAT A LIFE: RICHARD

Wow, all this history, all this art. He canceled his return flight to Canada and enrolled in a six-year program at the Academy of Fine Arts in Cracow. It was cheap like borsch to study art in Poland where, thanks to the exchange rates on the black market, he could buy a pair of shoes for a dollar, take friends out for dinner for a couple of bucks, rent a big flat furnished with antiques and paintings for twenty-five dollars a month. He felt the opposite of deprived. Compared to the suffering Poles, who earned pitiable sums at their jobs, then scrambled to make ends meet with endless wheelings and dealings, he was the man from El Dorado. His attitude wasn't the greatest. He liked to throw his money around, to be the guy who'd score the case of Czech pilsner for a party and have everyone give him a cheer. "Hey Canada!" That's what they called him at the Academy. "Hey, Canada, you're a really great guy! Lend me some money, okay?"

WHAT A LIFE: BOHDAN

Eventually, he found people who liked the fact he spoke Ukrainian—the bottle depot woman, the woman in the milk shop, the guy with the potatoes. They'd call him behind the counter and give him the choice bit of cheese, invite him over for supper. He had a whole list of working-class Kievans who wanted to meet him.

WHAT A LIFE: NATALKA

She had a project: to meet and interview members of unofficial rock groups. It wasn't so difficult to befriend them; they wanted to talk, and they wanted to give her experiences. Like the parties at hippy pads, the artsy slide shows, or—the best—the trip down a literal rabbit hole to an abandoned underground monastery. She knew she was a Ukrainian-Canadian when another visitor, a local boy, standing with her in the chapel, lit up a cigarette, an act that enraged her. This was the birthplace of their church, a holy site—but only she had any respect. She was the only one who *knew*.

WHAT A LIFE: IRENA

The intensity of public discussion about politics was stunning. Even in the pubs where people were drunk as skunks they still talk politics. And literature. Imagine long queues in front of bookstores! Imagine a playwright president! Culture has prestige, damn it, and not just among the elite. *Everybody* goes to the theatre and to concerts; culture isn't some class's private property. If the writers were to become private and all holed up with their muse, literature would simply dry up. Writers have become so intertwined with events that they are inseparable from public life. Imagine.

VISITING THE REVOLUTION: IRENA

Her friends were all enthusiastic—elated and even reborn—by Czechoslovakia's velvet revolution in the winter of 1989: the peaceful overthrow of an oppressive government by mass assemblies of citizens. They were thinking about starting a new life even though they weren't sure how this might happen. How do you suddenly change the morality of a nation that, for forty-some years, had cheated, thieved and made deals to survive? Where it was considered perfectly legitimate to steal "state property"—bricks for your summer cottage, say? Or to work only two, three hours and knock off and go to the pub? One thing about the old system: you had security. No one starved. Everyone had a job. Now you're expected to be "disciplined," but for what? For how long? For whom? Irena understands that it's the system that has made the people cautious and selfish—that attitude of, "I'm willing to make all kinds of sacrifices, of course, but I know my neighbour won't." Deep down, Irena guessed, her friends were ashamed of themselves and their compromises; so she never pried, never asked for details.

INVITED TO THE REVOLUTION: BOHDAN

Unlike the bad old days, pre-Gorbachev, there were now layers and layers of intellectual and political life in Kiev. The students on hunger strike, the rock bands in the parks, the Greens, the former dissidents, the liberal democrats in parliament, the pornographers and street photographers, the comedians . . . He went to hear a stand-up comic and didn't get a single joke; even when it was explained to him, he couldn't see what was so funny. He was invited to a rather clandestine political meeting by people terrified there were police under every bush; it was clear that to work with them required a certain political investment. In the end, some very interesting young people—students, computer engineers, young lawyers—sought him out (they'd heard a Ukrainian-Canadian was in town), looked him over, checked him out, and invited him to hang out with them. Good talk, good music, good times.

CAUGHT IN THE COUNTER-REVOLUTION: RICHARD

It got real exciting in People's Poland, the last summer of the strikes and riots. His dad told him for God's sake not to get involved in any of the political stuff, but he just had to go with some buddies in Solidarity and watch them take on the riot police, goons pumped up on drugs and alcohol flinging tear gas around and beating up little old ladies coming out of church. His friends would up-end park benches, heave paint at the Lenin statues, throw bricks at the police cars.

Then came Martial Law and militia in armoured vehicles on every street. He was on his way, in the middle of the day, to a party with some friends when they were stopped by cops with submachine guns and asked to show their papers. He clicked his heels together, saluted them and shouted, "Heil, Hitler!" They took him down to the cop shop and beat him up a bit—no sense of humour, these guys—then sent him to court where he said he was sorry and was fined a few thousand zlotys.

The thing was, he didn't want to be made to leave the country. He was having the time of his life. A whole bunch of people had seen him salute the police and word got around at the Academy. "Way to go, Canada!" It was different for them, of course. Curfew and harassment, people losing their jobs at the university, students being thrown out of school and into jail. For the first time in his life, he understood, really understood, what it meant to say Poland was oppressed.

WATCHING THE REVOLUTION: CORI

They were all in front of the television that Christmas season of 1989, watching the news of the overthrow and execution of the Romanian beast, President Ceauşescu. She suddenly had this portentous thought: that "people of my blood" were actually living through these terrible events. She was *related*.

THE TRIBE: BOHDAN

Your relatives arrive unannounced on your doorstep and give you five minutes to pack for a week's stay in the village. You protest you can't possibly stay that long. They pay no attention. They hustle you around, they feed you non-stop and make you drink until you're ready to burst. You are, in fact, at the mercy of their Slavic hospitality. It's lovely in some ways, maddening in others.

So off he went to his father's hometown, Koval. And walked right into the middle of a family drama: the meeting of the Communist uncle and the uncle who'd been sent to Siberia. The two hadn't spoken to each other for years. Reconciliation? Ha. They argued all night long. Then began the reminiscences—hearing his father's stories filled in about how his uncles had died and who had disappeared, seeing the spot where his grandfather had been shot, being shown the country of his father's life as a young man, and being overwhelmed by the thought, over and over again, "There but for the grace of God go I." Because, if his father hadn't left Ukraine, he, the son, would be just like his cousin Fedir, working as a welder in a factory and living in a small and shabby apartment, dreaming of invitations from the rich cousins in Canada, and of a Sony VCR on the sideboard.

THE TRIBE: NATALKA

The telegram came to her apartment in Kiev saying to expect a call from her aunties in the village at the telephone in the district post office. She got the call—screaming over the bad connection—and learned the aunties would be paying a visit that very weekend. Panic! She scrubbed the place down, got a hold of some meat and made a stew, then put on a skirt, bought a bunch of flowers, and went tearing down to the train station. Because she had no idea of what these aunties looked like, she had fashioned a large placard with her own name written on it. She flashed it at every old person getting off the train from Lviv.

Surprise! The aunties weren't old! They rolled out bedding on the floor and made themselves at home. Lifted up the cover on her stew pot, sniffed, and said they'd feed that to the pigs. Here, take these: coils of fresh kubassa, jars of pickles and marinated mushrooms, fresh bread and tortes, vodka. Ever after, they sent her packages of food from the village, including potatoes in the mail, in an ironic, fitting obverse to the cardboard boxes, the CARE packages, filled with second-hand clothing and wool babushkas, that her family had sent over for years to the Old Country. Now it was their turn to take care of her.

So, a visit to the village for Easter. A quarrel between sisters as to whose house she would be taken to for Easter dinner. The promenade around the village, eating and drinking in each one, being shown off in a way, and realizing she must be related to half the town.

Roots, with a vengeance.

THE TRIBE: CORI

She'd be folding laundry with her mother or sitting at the dinner table with her aunt and uncle, or looking at photo albums, and the stories would come tumbling out. A memory would be triggered and out would come the story. Family stories. Stories about people's husbands and children and triumphs and tragedies. The thing about these stories was that they were always and only about the family in Canada. It was as if: our story starts here.

MY TRIP TO ROMANIA: CORI'S MUM

Friday, July 27: Spent the night at Hotel Carpati in Baia Mare. During our travel next day, we visited a unique cemetery where all tombstones were painted a bright cobalt blue with pictures of the deceased resting there. We found many bearing the name "Stan." Visited a centenarian living in a squalid hovel who remembered Stan families emigrating to Canada in the early 1900s (40 men and 35 women).

—Eva Stent's Journal

WHAT IF? IRENA

If she had stayed in Czechoslovakia, if she had had to live through those twenty-one terrible years of occupation and repression, would she have been one of the courageous ones, the oppositionists with ideals and convictions who risked imprisonment and even death? It's the hardest question possible to answer. She thinks about it, but how can she know? How can any of us know how strong we would be? Instead, she sometimes feels guilty, guilty that she lived a comfortable life while her people were suffering. It's a useless feeling, a kind of self-punishment, but it's there. A kind of unfulfilled sense of responsibility that she no longer has to bear, now that they've made their revolution.

BECOMING UKRAINIAN: NATALKA

I could see myself wearing my hustka *(headscarf) just like Annie Pylypiw at the Ukrainian Cultural Heritage Village, and continuing her life.*

BECOMING POLISH: RICHARD

The student dorm where I was living had been the Gestapo HQ; there had been torture chambers in the basement where we went down to take showers. There's not so much as a bomb crater in Edmonton.

BECOMING UKRAINIAN: BOHDAN

I could see my beginnings in the village. Half the graves in the cemetery had the same last name as me.

BECOMING ROMANIAN: CORI

At the funeral of her beloved gram, the old woman she had never been able to speak to except with gestures of love, she was given a little bowl of cooked wheat imbedded with a cross of raisins. She held it as though it were a living thing, a kind of heart. It was, in fact, one of the most ancient rites of her people, inherited from a past dimmed even to them: pagans of the Mediterranean. And it had come all the way to her, in Dysart, Saskatchewan.

COMING HOME: CORI'S MUM

Monday, August 13: We have arrived home finally and I'm sure we all feel a sense of relief and certainly appreciation of our homes and Canadian lifestyle—the freedom of speech, the press, worship and the countless other freedoms we take for granted and which the people of Romania dare not think of enjoying. Among my thoughts when I saw peasants working in the fields, many of whom were women, was, "There but for the Grace of God and the foresight of my grandparents go I!"

—Eva Stent's Journal

COMING HOME: IRENA

She still hasn't figured out what "constitutes" being a Canadian. Something more than just creature comforts? Something about space and freedom? There are those Europeans who complain about the lack of a vibrant urban life in Edmonton, the inhabitants all locked away in their privacy, but, for her, the space *is* freedom, in which Canada slowly, generation-by-generation, builds itself.

COMING HOME: BOHDAN

He'd like another visit to Ukraine but he'd never live there. When he got off the plane in Canada, he felt profoundly, movingly *lucky*. And very Canadian. This is where he lives. This is where his sister and parents and wife and wife's family live. This is where they will be buried. *This* is the family homeland now. That was, after all, the reason for the great migration in the first place: to start again, to begin the legends anew.

GRACE POPIEL • *BLAIRMORE, ALBERTA*

KAREN CONNELLY

Karen Connelly was born in Calgary in 1969. In 1986, at the age of seventeen, she won the Air Canada Award as "the most promising writer in Canada under thirty-five." The prediction was not long in being fulfilled. In 1990, her first book of poetry, The Small Words in My Body, *was published by Kalamalka Press. The book earned Ms Connelly the Pat Lowther Award, given for the best book of poetry by a Canadian woman published in the previous year. Karen Connelly is involved in a process of world discovery and the conversion of that discovery into literature. Her one year voyage into rural Thailand (1986–87) is the basis for the essay that follows and for her non-fiction book* Touch the Dragon *(Turnstone Press, 1992). From 1988 to 1990, she taught English in Spain, and traveled from that base throughout Europe. Her second book of poetry,* This Brighter Prison, *is based on these travels and will be published by Brick Books in 1993. At the time of this writing, more travels are planned, more books are in the works. There is no predicting where Ms Connelly might be at the time of this anthology's publication; no predicting either how much longer her list of accomplishments might have become.*

To Open the World

*W*HEN I WAS SEVENTEEN, I LEFT CALGARY. *"I'M going away," I told people, deliberately edging my voice with mystery. I read certain entries in encyclopedias and books about foreign lands; Karen Blixen's* Out of Africa *literally quickened my heartbeat. I went to a doctor to stock up on malaria pills and receive shots for diphtheria and hepatitis. My departure date was at the end of August: all that summer I felt breathless, hopeful, and terrified. While walking along the Bow River on certain warm evenings, I watched the reflections of trees and rocks dance over the black water. The sound of the river made me think of Asia.*

I knew the country of my destination, Thailand, could be a very wet place. I'd seen photographs of the monsoons in Bangkok. Old Siam, known in eighteenth-century Europe as "the Venice of the Orient," endures its rainy season every year; the flooding in the lowlands floats up whole villages. I knew I would be living on fairly high ground in a small northern town called Denchai, where I would become part of a Thai family; they would treat me as one of their own. I would go to a Thai school, eat Thai food, wear Thai clothes; learn to speak, read, dance, cook Thai. Genuinely kind gentlemen in expensive business suits explained all of this to me. They were Rotarians and I was a Rotary Exchange Student. In Canada, my mission seemed very clear: I was to become as completely Thai as possible. Through this transformation, I was to learn what it meant to live not simply in my own country but in my own world.

When I left Canada I was crying, fitful and sad, thinking about plane crashes and fatal accidents in foreign lands. I was in love and I didn't want to leave him. Yet I did want to leave, needed to leave, because I'd grown up restlessly, flipping the pages of the *National Geographic*, continually telling myself that I'd—go away someday—escape. Even before I arrived there, Thailand became the world to me, came to symbolize the beginning of my real life, my new life, my own. Rising over the Rockies, those great giants of stone with their blue-green veins and aquamarine sockets of ice

by Karen Connelly

water, I vowed that never again would I be shackled by polynomial equations and certain pig-headed teachers. I said to myself, "This is the beginning, because I'm leaving it behind, I'm going." Then I blew my nose furiously and bid the mountains goodbye.

My life in Denchai began in the middle of the night. Like everywhere else in the north, it had, apparently, just stopped raining. When we drove through the puddles in the street, I had the impression that we might never completely surface. I was afraid the water would come into the car. We eventually pulled up in front of the building which was my new home. It was a liquor store. The top floors were for the family: my two small Thai brothers, my Thai mother and father, my Thai aunt, and my Thai grandparents. An enormous German shepherd was kept on a thick chain in the back of the house, which was also the kitchen and the garage. That first night, everyone was asleep except the dog, who obviously didn't like foreigners. All hackles and vicious teeth, she lunged at me again and again while my new Thai father smiled jovially and pulled up a vestige of his long-forgotten English, "Velly nice dog!" I was led up to a room on the top floor. My Thai father left me. I sat down on my very hard bed and howled, as quietly as possible, into my hands.

I was the only foreigner in town, and I was a girl. This combination fascinated the towns-people. Initially, I was treated as a spectacle, the only attraction in a small zoo. Those first days, when "aunt" Pee-Moi showed me how to wash clothes by hand and eat with chopsticks, the children of Denchai came on their ramshackle bicycles and leaned over the handlebars, staring at me from the street and giggling when I greeted them with "*Sawatdee kaa.*" The only way I could entice them to come close to me was by tempting them with photographs. My sister, who has long blonde hair, especially delighted them. They thought my younger brother looked like James Dean. The candy I brought for them—licorice Goodies—caused a stir. They liked the bright colours but thought the dark brown filling looked exactly like lizard shit. I met Lin, Deh, Boh, and Sak those first days, all of them between the ages of fifteen and seventeen. They later became some of my closest friends.

Within two days, still afflicted by jet lag and just noticing the effects of the new food on my stomach, I was at Nareerat School in the small city of Prae, twenty-five kilometres from Denchai. Over three thousand students, almost all of them girls, came from many of the small towns and villages in the province to attend Nareerat. When I first walked into the compound of those apple-green buildings, hundreds of pretty girls with gleaming black hair leaned over the second- and third-floor balconies to watch my passage. They giggled behind their hands. Some threw roses. I was the only white student in the school.

I began my life in Thailand wearing a Thai school girl's starched white blouse, pleated blue skirt, and patent leather Mary Janes with bobby socks. At first, this uniform mortified me, but eventually I became reconciled to everything but the Mary Janes. I hated those toe-cramming black shoes every time I put them on. (Fortunately, we always took our shoes off before entering a room, so I spent most of the day in stocking or bare feet.) The uniform helped by camouflaging me a little. I needed to become a Thai girl, and was obliged to accept many rigid traditions, even if I didn't agree with them. I came to appreciate the Canadian confusion over culture. I'm glad Canada has no specific, defined culture, because I've experienced the restrictions of living in a society which does.

But I also experienced the benefits of those old traditions. I became a real part of a real community—something I'd never experienced in Calgary. Within a couple of months, I knew hundreds of people in Denchai and Prae, waved to them in the street, chatted, smiled. The Thai smile—*yim siam*—is a Thai characteristic. In Thailand, I learned how much people really do communicate through facial expression and laughter was my first Thai sound.

I studied voraciously. Thai is a tonal language of over seventy alphabetical characters which resemble spermatozoa in motion: all twirls, loops, and squiggles. A beautiful script, but very difficult to write. I concentrated on the five different tones and all the words which comprised daily living and communicating. I carried a notebook of phonetic lists around and pestered people with the constant question, "*Cheuh allai nee, na ka?*" "What is this called?" I practised with my friends at the badminton court where we met every day after school (and where, for an entire year, I lost every game I played). I worked hard at my Thai, sometimes even desperately. The need to communicate became one of my primary drives because I was deeply lonely. Though I'd performed the operation myself, I'd been amputated from Canada, from my friends, and especially from my language, which I'd always used to define myself. As I struggled to remember the words "hand" and "face" and "sky," I realized that losing English was easily comparable to losing a limb. One of my dozen Thai fathers (all members of the Denchai Rotary Club) spoke English but I only saw him once a week. To everyone else in Denchai, English was gibberish. Until I could rename the world in Thai, I was handicapped.

Even after plunging deep into that beautiful singing language, learning hundreds, thousands of new words, I knew English was still my real voice, and Alberta was the place where that voice had first grown and learned something of itself. I dreamed of snow in Thailand; I dreamed of hiking in the Kananaskis, of canoeing the Sheep River. In the morning, driving to Prae in the back of an open truck, careening through the green glimmer and silver sheen of rice paddies, I looked to the northern mountains and thought: those are hills. I know what real mountains look like and they are nothing like those stubby things.

Yet I never tired of my adopted country's landscape. It was wild, tropical, constantly growing, changing, forever new. A four-inch long, lime-green praying mantis lived in my bedroom. A large striped lizard lived in Pee-Moi's rose garden. The butterflies were bigger than my hands and I followed them from flower to flower with unhinged jaws. Their wings were bright red, green, purple, blue. As a child I'd painted such fanciful butterflies, imagining they might exist on some brighter planet. In the mornings, I was often greeted by red-shelled beetles scrambling around the sink; they came up the drains. Under my desk, I once found a tiny baby lizard, a mere wisp of dark green, so delicate and small that I wanted to close it in a book and press it like a flower.

I loved living in Denchai and exploring the surrounding countryside because it always gifted me with surprises. Once Deh and Boh and I flew over the narrow field roads on noisy motorcycles, passing through miniature jungles and hamlets of waving children and flapping chickens. We almost killed ourselves several times by swerving into deep wagon ruts; we were trying to avoid running over sunning snakes. Domesticated water buffalo watched us flash by their deep pools of mud. After roaring through groves of coconut, teak, and bamboo, we arrived at a whitewashed temple in the middle of nowhere. Not a village anywhere nearby, not a soul to be seen in all the blue-green world, but there was a deep clay basin of water and a high-ceilinged temple. Its walls were painted with colourful depictions of Buddha's life, its floor was cool beneath our feet. We padded up to the image of the Enlightened One, knelt, and bowed three times in respect. We drank some water, then sat in the shadows and marveled at the painted ceiling. After a while, we left the temple and traveled north, clattered over a narrow swinging bridge, then stopped to swim in the river below. By the time I arrived home late in the afternoon, I felt I'd traveled half the circumference of the Earth.

In many ways, I had. Denchai, whose name no one would know if the Bangkok train didn't pass through twice a day, taught me that countries are constellations connected by invisible lines. Those connections create a greater picture of who and what we are as human beings. I learned about history in Southeast Asia; I learned how the lens of the past clouds and deepens our vision of the future. Talking with old people in an old country teaches these things. Canada became young to me when I discovered how ancient Thailand was. One of my older teachers once said, "I hope you will be patient. Thailand is like an old man, hard to reason with, tough as a sun-dried shoe. You come from a country that still has the skin of a child."

There it is, in my mind, my old man country, and the town of Denchai just a dot in the north. Its long main road, Yantrakitkosol, is still lined with noodle stands and jewelry stores, with tailor shops and dark, cramped pharmacies. I rode down that street on Pee-Moi's rattling bicycle, the one without fenders; when Boh and I raced, the wet, red mud from the road streaked our legs, our backs, our hair. For the first months, the rain still came every day, often at night, and the sky roiled, rolled out close to us, its castle-high clouds muscled with wind and sunlight.

I spent hours in the market places of Denchai and Prae, wandering the rows of dried fish, wet fish, still-flapping fish, the endless pyramids of chickens, vegetables, exotic fruits which resembled red sea urchins with green spikes. I came to love the markets because they were so alive with human voices, the dance of so many shining eyes. The variety and quantity of food never failed to stun me. Thai people, especially the more traditional northern people, eat fish and cow intestines, certain water beetles, bee pupae, cicadas, black frogs, tiny birds, pigeons, pickled chicken feet . . . More typically, they eat spicy chicken or pork and a wide variety of fresh vegetables. Once my stomach learned how to digest garlic, curries, and red and green peppers, I loved Thai food.

I loved the country itself. As in any passion-based relationship, I also could be furious with it. At times living there almost drove me mad. I couldn't wear shorts (it was not nice for girls to wear revealing clothes) or stay out past nine o'clock or take any trips alone (girls don't travel alone, it's too dangerous) or spend any time alone with men (lest the cultural exchange go too far). In Canada, I'd grown up very independently, left home at sixteen, lived as I wanted, taken responsibility for my actions. All of this changed when I went to Thailand. I could not act like a liberated young woman if I wanted to learn about traditional Thai life. I had to change myself, adapt myself, refrain from passing judgements, and generally keep my mouth shut.

Unfortunately, I rarely succeeded in the last category. I did not rant and rave, but I was an insidious, quiet troublemaker. Once I learned to speak Thai, I couldn't keep myself from using my new words. I asked about embarrassing things, like the child prostitution in Bangkok, the mistreatment of women, the political corruption. Some people were annoyed by my questions; a few were equally concerned, even searching for solutions; but most people were impressed, not with my humanitarian interests, but with the level of my Thai. I knew I was not supposed to be a social activist or a raving feminist, and most of the time I wasn't, but occasionally I couldn't help myself. Women who knew my opinions often confided in me, and I offered them genuine sympathy, but being a Canadian-Thai girl in a school uniform left me powerless to change anything. I was never so naive as to think I *could* change the millennia-old structure of an Asian culture, but the problems which existed all around me—the poverty, the abuse of women's and children's rights—were endless sources of frustration. As often as not, my friends said, "*Mai pen lai,*" the famous Thai saying which means "never mind."

I minded, but not constantly. My year in Thailand was an exercise in *jai yen yen*, another oft-used Thai phrase meaning "cool your heart." My heart cooled in Thailand. I learned patience with myself, with others. I learned to walk Thai, to walk slowly, to hurry as seldom as possible, to be late without worrying about it (for everything but school where late students received a few swipes with a bamboo switch). I learned the art of lounging around, drinking iced orange pulp and taking long aimless walks to the train station where traveling acrobats sometimes set up ragged puppet shows and built themselves into human pyramids and breathed fire. My friends and I discussed the very likely existence of vampires, the absolute existence of ghosts, the unquestionable logic of reincarnation. I found out where the ghosts of Denchai lived, and though I later haunted each of these sites, I was never privileged enough to see one of their spirit inhabitants. In the hot season, I lay in front of my fan for hours, feeling the hot air undulate over my body instead of settling on my skin like a smouldering quilt. I longed for winter days then, and fantasized about snowfalls and frozen lakes. I still studied my Thai, but less desperately now because it wasn't hard any more. I could speak another language, not completely, not perfectly, but well enough to understand and to make jokes.

June rolled into July, and I stood on the top floor of the shop looking out at the busy streets of my town, the pedlars bobbing along under their loads of grapes and pineapples, the people on bicycles, entire families packed onto motorcycles. I pressed my fingers against the tattered screen on the window, thinking, "Next month is August. A year. I'm going back to Canada." I shivered despite the heat. Thinking about Canada occasionally made me happy but I was not looking forward to returning. My love of the previous year had dissolved during the course of my stay; he was now living with a librarian. I had to go back to Calgary and make some decisions about the future. I knew I wanted to write a book about living in Thailand; I knew I wanted to be a writer, felt I was a writer already, but I needed to learn the discipline of my craft. The Thais laughed when they saw me scribbling in my notebook, laughed even harder when I explained that I was writing about them. They thought I was ridiculous, and though I often agreed with them, I continued writing everything down.

Yes, I was leaving. I packed. I had delicious dinners. A party was thrown in my honour. I made a speech to the students and teachers of Nareerat, all those black heads in the assembly field, those faces watching me curiously, affectionately, as they had all year. So many people had befriended me, participated in educating my Western barbarism. The smallest children had taught me the national anthem, a song I'd loved even the first time I'd heard it. I packed my clothes, my treasure of Thai silver, my silk dress, my lapis lazuli necklace, my notebooks. People gave me orchids, roses, lilies. I wept. Some of my friends cried, too. I was going away, and Canada seemed like the most distant country on Earth.

I left Asia just as I left North America: sobbing, searching for Kleenex while my green country was yanked out from under me. I slept for a few hours while flying over the Pacific. While transferring planes in Seattle, I started crying again because all the people were big, white, and looked alike; they all had pale hair, bony faces, big bodies. I missed Thailand and I deeply missed the Thais. Every time I opened my mouth, Thai came out of it. "Thank you" was "*Cop koon kaa*" and "Pardon me?" turned into "*Allai na ka?*"

Calgary was no better. I was happy to see my family and friends again but I missed Thailand more than I'd missed Canada, perhaps because I'd worked so hard to love it. In Calgary, people didn't greet me and smile on the street; people weren't interested in me. After all, I was part of a white majority; I wasn't interesting any more. The neighbourhood I lived in seemed to just be row on row of ugly condos full of people who worked in offices all day and didn't want to make any new friends. I thought, how cold these people are, how dull; they wear gray and black clothes and no one carries around a guitar. I longed for the easy familiarity I had had with so many people in Denchai and Prae.

I began to stop unsuspecting Asian people on the street, the buses, in shopping markets, in malls. "Excuse me," I would say, "are you Thai?" I inquired matter-of-factly, as if asking for the time. They always laughed and said, no, I'm Filipino, or Cambodian, or Vietnamese, or Indonesian. I started tutoring Asian students at a local high school. We traded stories about living in an adopted country; they experienced many of the things I'd experienced in Thailand. Newspapers were mysterious. The television was peopled by voices which might have been transmitted from Mars. Using public transportation became a matter of blind luck. The world suddenly became strange. One young Vietnamese girl was shocked when she saw her first turkey. "I never knew chickens, even Canadian chickens, could get that big." I spent hours teaching the pronunciation and meanings of words like beach and bitch, wild and while, steel and still, and many of the frustrating homonyms of English. "Why can we say `to sweeten' but not `to colden' and `to heaten'? And why does `marked' turn back into `mark' but `naked' never turns into `nake'? English is much harder than Vietnamese." I started studying Vietnamese with some of my students. I listened to Thai music every day and read books about China.

When an acquaintance of mine told me about a Thai woman she knew, I was overjoyed. I called Ling immediately and spoke Thai for an hour, grinning the entire time. Through Ling I discovered a small Thai community in Calgary and managed to keep speaking Thai. It wasn't the same as being in Denchai but it eased the transition for me. These Thais had become Canadian, and all of them preferred Canada to Thailand, enjoyed living in Alberta, being close to the mountains and the prairies. One Thai-Canadian said, "The sky is higher here. I like that. And I come from Bangkok, big dirty city. It's clean here. I like Thailand, but I live here now, and if I leave, I know I'll return. It's my home."

I slowly discovered the same is true for me. Though I've since left and lived in another foreign country, and though I'll leave again, I know that something here will always call me back. This place, too, is a point in the constellation, part of the painting of an extraordinary, open world.

PETER MALOFF and RHODA JANE MALOFF • *COWLEY, ALBERTA*

ROBERT KROETSCH

Robert Kroetsch was born in Heisler, a small town in the Battle River region of east-central Alberta. His was a farming family and he left the family farm in the late forties to seek adventure in the Canadian North. For three seasons he worked on Mackenzie riverboats and for two-and-a-half more years he worked as a civilian information and education specialist for the United States Air Force at Goose Bay, Labrador. From that time to this, Mr Kroetsch has been a writer and a professor, gaining national and international recognition as both.

His many published works include the novels The Studhorse Man *(Simon and Schuster, 1969); and* Badlands *(New Press, 1975); the poetry collection* Completed Field Notes *(McClelland and Stewart, 1989); and the collection of essays* The Lovely Treachery of Words *(Oxford Press, 1989).* The Studhorse Man *won the Governor General's Award for Fiction in 1969.*

Mr Kroetsch has lived in many places and traveled to many more: China, Iraq, Italy, Greece and, recently, Russia. He says, "My boyhood on an Alberta farm turned me into a gardener. Travel and gardening are hard acts to put together."

Dancing with the Time Machine, or, Where Are You From?

(1)

"WHERE ARE YOU FROM?" PEOPLE ASK ME, IN THE way we have, on this continent, in this ever new world, of trying to map our very selves into a position on the blank map.

"Alberta," I answer.

Or at least, when I was a boy the map seemed blank. Now our map is a beehive. We live in a living map, a map that swells and changes while we try to locate ourselves and others. Alberta is a story of constant transformation. Boom and bust and boom become a rhythm, a kind of dance.

"Where are you from?" the woman asked in the bar in a town north of Ottawa, watching the guy with the grey hair try to jitterbug.

"Alberta," I said.

What do I mean by that answer? Why do I give that answer, having lived in a dozen places since growing up in Alberta, since leaving there when I was twenty, since leaving again when I was twenty-seven?

In a province where so many people are from somewhere else, I am, when somewhere else, always from Alberta.

(2)

When my father was in his prime and I was a boy of eight, I decided one morning to take his pocket watch apart—without his noticing. He had left his pocket watch on the dresser in my parents' bedroom.

by Robert Kroetsch

(3)

Alberta is, as it often claims to be, next-year country. It is, like the conventional portrait of the sun, a face that radiates many beams of light. It is plurality, abundance, excess, an overdoing. It is its own extravagance. It is the face of my father's watch become a portrait of the sun.

(4)

Why did my mother let me take the watch from my parents' bedroom and out onto the veranda on the east side of the house? The sun, of course, was hot, that summer morning, on the veranda. There was a table on the veranda that my mother used in spring to place her house plants on. Or her seedlings. I sat at that table to work on the watch that I was going to dismantle and reassemble.

We lived on a farm 100 miles south and east of Edmonton, near the Battle River. Rivers too are maps of Alberta, maps that shift, change, alter the landscape itself. It was the Battle River, with its deep, post-glacial valley, dancing the landscape into form, that defined our parklands location. My father was gone all the way to Edmonton. It was a full day's journey, going to Edmonton and returning. I had a whole day in which to work on the watch. But why did I want to take apart and reassemble my father's watch without his ever knowing?

I think I expected to find in that watch the future itself.

(5)

Aritha van Herk, in one of the epigraphs to *Judith*, quotes in a passage from a folk song the line, "When pigs they do fly like swallows in the sky . . . ," then begins the novel with the sentence, "Pig shit and wet greasy straw were piled high in the wheelbarrow."

Albertans inhabit the space between those two possibilities. We live a zany life, refusing to make a choice between the impossible dream and the (sometimes unpleasant) real. It is in that allowing of contradictions that we find our future, that we make our future.

(6)

When my novel *The Studhorse Man* came out, back in 1969, my New York editor said to me over a lunch of salmon and strawberries in Manhattan, "Now tell me—this Alberta that you write about. Is it a real place, or did you make it up?"

His question plunged me into mind-boggling doubt. How does one speak of the reality of a place that exists in minds as well as on a huge patch of the North American interior? What is the connection for someone who lives away from that patch? And why do I, living away from Alberta, write obsessively about it?

(7)

Perhaps I write from voluntary exile. I wrote most of my novels while living in Binghamton, New York. I write now from Winnipeg, Manitoba.

Where are you from? people ask, and perhaps the word "from" is the word that hurts me into existence.

The journey to Alberta—is it a return to a geography fashioned by nature? Or is it a search for a landscape always being shaped, refashioned, by perceptions and actions that are almost tribal?

Albertans are, supremely, storytellers. I have lived in a number of places—Iowa, New York State, Sussex, Rome, to name some of them—and yet I have not ever, anywhere, met people who so ground themselves in stories as do Albertans. Gossip. The tall tale. Two cars stopped on a street or road, their drivers telling stories.

If home is stories, then we will go on talking ourselves home until the cows come home.

(8)

The journey home is not the past, it is the future. The journey home is the journey into the future.

(9)

We have a rich and elaborate culture on the prairies, something that people from elsewhere—from Ontario and Quebec, for whatever lugubrious reasons—often don't understand. That culture speaks most humorously and seriously of itself in Alberta.

(10)

Like sandhill cranes, we Albertans like to dance our story.

I was turning the handle of the cream separator—it was after milking time, in the evening—it was harvest time. We had a lot of hired men at that time of year. I was down in the basement, turning the handle of the cream separator. The men were in a hurry. It was Saturday night, they were going into town to a dance. I was, I would guess, thirteen years old at the time. My father came down the stairs into the cool of the basement. He stopped halfway down the stairs, his head hardly showing, in the cool and semi-dark basement.

And then he spoke. He said, to me, "You can go with the men to the dance tonight." And then in a gruffer tone he added, "I want you home by midnight." It was the first time, ever, I had been permitted to go to a dance. I remember nothing about the dance itself. I remember midnight sweeping down on me like the hand of a clock.

(11)

Our culture is precious to us. We wear it in the luminosity of our laughter.

(12)

One spring when I was teaching at the State University of New York in Binghamton I felt exhausted and decided to take a break. I jumped into my car on a Thursday afternoon and drove to Ottawa.

When I got to Ottawa, I found that the friend I had gone to see was busy beyond words, and in love on top of that. On the Friday morning I drove north again, into bush country, forest, pulp and paper country.

At noon I stopped in a mill town for lunch. I went into a beer parlor, out of nostalgia for my Alberta youth. I sat down at a table on the edge of a dance floor and ordered two beers and a cheeseburger and fries.

There were three other people in the beer parlor, besides the waiter—an old Indian man playing a fiddle where he sat having a beer, an Indian woman who played the spoons and sang to herself while she listened to the fiddle, a white woman dancing by herself, going back once in a while to the table to pick up her glass and take a sip of beer.

We are story-makers. I made up a story, guessed a story, while I watched. The bored, well-dressed dancer, I thought to myself, is a hooker, waiting for the Friday afternoon crowd. Then I gave myself a rap on the knuckles for not letting the dancer make her own story. I should explain that I was wearing a red plaid shirt and jeans, a pair of boots, a beard. I was on vacation from myself. That's why I was surprised by what happened next.

After a while the dancer came over to me and said, "Hey, professor. You wanna dance?"

I was astonished, and even hurt, I suppose. My attempt at announcing my true self had once again failed me. I couldn't resist. I got up and joined the woman. We had hardly started to dance when I asked her, "Where are you from?"

"Ottawa," she said. "Just in for two nights."

We were waltzing. "A weekend off?" I said.

"No," she said. "I'm a hooker."

(13)

Sometimes we Albertans disguise ourselves as ourselves, sometimes we disguise ourselves as others. It fools a lot of people. The Calgary Stampede. Klondike Days. Winter Festivals. Rodeos and sports days and wedding dances and ski weekends. This elaborate dressing up, in Calgary, in Edmonton, in the smaller towns of Alberta, in the mountains and out on the prairie and up in the bush, is part of our being who we are. Transformations. We live in the carnival spirit. By our disguises we free ourselves, we speak to each other of hidden selves, we reenact our history, adapting it, reshaping it. The horse allowing the rider, the rider allowing the horse.

The ability to transform oneself is at the heart of the Alberta experience. It makes for generosity of many kinds.

(14)

Perhaps I am always that small boy, out on the veranda, trying to get my father's watch back together before he returns from the city. I see the sun rising toward noon, I see it moving to the far side of the house and feel the shade cooling the sweat on the back of my neck. I touch the small machines of time together as if they must, out of my longing, out of the larger need to love a father and to resist him, let me learn to live my own life. That too is a version of the future.

My mother brought me milk, oatmeal cookies. She lured me into the house for lunch, then, in her quiet way, in her way of pretending not to see, let me go back to my impossible task. And taking the watch apart had been easy.

(15)

What stories do we tell ourselves in Alberta, and how do those stories read us forward, into the continuing world?

We like stories of animals. Bear stories. Moose stories. Pig stories. Fish stories. We like stories of astonishing encounters and fearful escapes. We like watch stories. The graduation watch. The watch you wore in swimming that still works like a charm.

In the middle of the continent, we live on the edge of the world.

(16)

Headline in the *Red Deer Advocate*, Monday, November 26, 1990: "Tranquilizer Fails to Slow Pig." And under a photograph of Francis, the famous pig that escaped from an abattoir and lived in the wild for weeks on end, the heading: "Famed Fugitive Pig Faces Photographer."

We like stories of escape.

(17)

And my father—did he leave his pocket watch behind by accident or by design?

I was having difficulties. My eyes were tired. My fingers behaved like thumbs. The chair was getting harder and harder. It was a lot like writing a novel, sitting there trying to get all the parts together into the rhythmic ticking of a watch. It was a version of expatriation too—I had left something behind and I would never get back to it and I would always be trying to get back to it.

(18)

Sometimes I dream of writing a novel of Alberta that will explain everything, the obsession with roads, the politics of future pleasure, the hockey games, the pride in sudden weather, the grace of sky and horizon.

I am going to start on it first thing next year.

(19)

My father looked at me where I was sitting on the veranda, trying to get his watch back together. My mother had gone out and met the car in the yard. She'd been watching the lane, listening, for a long time.

My father looked at the table as if it might be bare. I thought for a moment that by some miracle the watch was all back together, I'd been mistaken in thinking I'd failed in my attempt to reassemble it.

I was watching my father's face.

"Too bad about the watch," he said. He glanced at the parts of his watch, there on the table—the cogwheels, the screws, the hands. I thought I saw the flicker of a smile. "Oh well," he said. He reached to the pocket where he usually carried his watch. "I was planning to give it to you," he added.

(20)

My father had made it back, just in the nick of time, for supper.